THE ANTI-WARRIOR

SINGULAR LIVES

THE IOWA SERIES

IN NORTH AMERICAN

AUTOBIOGRAPHY

Albert E. Stone, Series Editor

THE ANTI-WARRIOR

A MEMOIR BY

MILT FELSEN

Introduction by Albert E. Stone

University of Iowa Press   Iowa City

University of Iowa Press,
Iowa City 52242
Copyright © 1989 by
Milt Felsen
All rights reserved
Printed in the
United States of America
First edition, 1989

Design by Richard Hendel
Typesetting by
G & S Typesetters,
Austin, Texas
Printing and binding by
Edwards Brothers,
Ann Arbor, Michigan

Library of Congress
Cataloging-in-Publication Data

Felsen, Milt, 1912–
    The anti-warrior: a memoir/by Milt Felsen;
introduction by Albert E. Stone.—1st ed.
        p.   cm.—(Singular lives)
    ISBN 0-87745-222-9; ISBN 0-87745-241-5 (pbk.)
        1. Spain—History—Civil War, 1936–
1939—Personal narratives, American.
2. World War, 1939–1945—Personal
narratives, American.   3. Felsen, Milt,
1912–   .   4. United States—Biography.
I. Title.   II. Series.
DP269.9.F36   1989   88-30301
940.54'81'73—dc19   CIP

On July 18, 1941,

Roberta and I were married.

We still are.

This book is for her.

CONTENTS

Acknowledgments

My good friend and erstwhile colleague on the national board of directors of the Directors Guild of America, Franklin M. Heller, is directly responsible for this book being written. It is too late for him to deny that, once having suggested it, he rode shotgun until I finished it, and I thank him.

My fellow veterans of the Abraham Lincoln Brigade and the OSS will understand if I limit myself to singling out Irv Goff, Saul Wellman, Fred Keller, and Joe Brandt. The enthusiasm of my longtime partner, Mike Todd, Jr., and his gifted wife, Susan, came invariably at just the right times. And Victor Burch, curator emeritus of the Lincoln Brigade archives at Brandeis University, managed in a very short time to be of great help.

INTRODUCTION

By Albert E. Stone

The Anti-Warrior: A Memoir is a vivid manifestation of a distinctive feature of contemporary culture, in which the reading, writing, and critical discussion of autobiographies are widely shared activities. Experiencing others' lives in life stories and learning thereby about others' activities, valued ideas, and characteristic emotional states have become popular parts of the communication network which, in a vital sense, makes us Americans. With this social process—at once democratic and inclusive as well as the elite preoccupation of artists and scholars—the University of Iowa Press is now identified through Singular Lives: The Iowa Series in North American Autobiography. As the inaugural volume in the series, Milt Felsen's memoir is, as the reader will speedily discover, very much a singular life, yet in important respects it speaks to other twentieth-century American lives. What is singular is this author's way of seeing, thinking, expressing himself, exemplifying what Margaret Mead describes as the creative deviant—the individual with "an extra intensity of response." More representative are the experiences and events that Felsen recreates with so much verve and bite: growing up in Brooklyn and the Catskills, hitchhiking across America in the Great Depression, earning an education at the University of Iowa, fighting fascism with the famous Lincoln Brigade in the Spanish Civil War and then with the equally famous, more clandestine OSS in World War II. Felsen's memoir climaxes in a searing account of his months in a German prisoner-of-war camp, from which this tough, compassionate, witty Jew emerges with his skin and his anti-war ideals intact. In rich, convincing detail, *The Anti-Warrior* records an individual version of public history during two decisive decades. It therefore illustrates the dual nature of all autobiographies by expressing a unique vision and version of common social experiences.

With this book Felsen joins the corps of writers who, by turning private experience into sharable story, carry on the native tradition in autobiography. The corpus of life stories by Americans is now estimated to exceed ten thousand volumes. Among recent additions to this ever-growing literature are two works also published by the University of Iowa Press: *Tales of an Old Horsetrader: The First Hundred Years* and *"A Secret to Be Burried": The Diary and Life of Emily Hawley Gillespie.*

In distinctively different ways these three works reconstruct strikingly ordinary American lives. Yet each shares qualities and aspirations with more famous autobiographies recognized as American prose classics. Among the revealing titles in this select company are *The Autobiography of Benjamin Franklin, Personal Memoirs of U. S. Grant, The Education of Henry Adams, The Autobiography of Alice B. Toklas, Memories of a Catholic Girlhood, The Autobiography of Malcolm X,* and *The Narrative of the Life of Frederick Douglass, An American Slave, Written by Himself.* Imagining *The Anti-Warrior* on the same shelf with Grant's *Personal Memoirs* may not be an act of hubris. A Union army commander and an ambulance driver in Spain are indeed peers by virtue of the awful, leveling experience of war; each veteran places his version of a major historical event on record and in the process forges a self distinct from other survivors.

As William Dean Howells declared at the beginning of this century, autobiography is "the most democratic province in the republic of letters." Unlike war novels such as e. e. cummings' *The Enormous Room* or Norman Mailer's *The Naked and the Dead*, an autobiography does not necessarily demand an accomplished writer with a distinguished style and artistic imagination. It is a different kind of story, at once historical record, artful (or artless) narrative, and psychological self-analysis. These aims and functions make autobiography a *content* as well as a *form*. Yet both descriptions are ultimately subordinated to the author's revelation of a unique identity. This characteristic mixture of motives and modes of discourse has been succinctly defined by Erik Erikson: "Autobiographies are written at certain later stages of life for the purpose of re-creating oneself in the image of one's own method; and they are written to make that image convincing." Enlisted in pursuit of this goal is a growing army of volunteers who, in recent decades, have made themselves part of American history and consciousness. The lure of putting oneself on the stage of history, often with concomitant rewards of praise and profit, has attracted a remarkable cross section of the population. *The Anti-Warrior* adds its author's unmistakably individual voice to the chorus of storytellers relating their experiences and achievements, expressing past beliefs, current feelings, and hopes for the future, arguing political or religious convictions, recording dreams and sins and mystic visions, defining and stroking their egos.

Who, we may reasonably ask, is this new recruit? Within the text itself we cannot find all the biographical data we may crave. Attempting to flesh out the laconic entries in other biographical sources, I wrote the author, asking for more details on what has clearly been a long, busy, and varied career. Following World War II, he reported, Felsen worked for a series of labor unions. In 1958 he became head of Motion Picture Assistant Directors and Script Supervisors Local 161 in New York. When that union merged in 1963 with the Directors Guild of America, he ended up in charge of East Coast operations. Though he continued active in DGA affairs, Felsen also formed his own independent film-packaging company, coproducing a series of "critically well received and financially disastrous films." He coproduced *Saturday Night Fever* and with Mike Todd, Jr., coproduced *The Bell Jar.* Retiring to Sarasota about a decade ago, he was encouraged to start this memoir by a longtime friend, Franklin Heller, director of the TV series "What's My Line?" Felsen confesses: "To me it seemed the height of presumption at the age then of 68, and never having written anything more than a union plant gate leaflet in my life, to seriously attempt to write a book."

One prime motive for shedding his reticence was historical. "After reading (or skimming) thru stories and books about the Spanish war, and OSS, by famous authors, historians and fellow vets I did not feel I recognized my Spain in their Spain (and for sure not my OSS in anyone else's). I don't pretend that my version of events is revealed scripture, only one more witness that may help to add detail to the canvas and to demythologise the idea of anyone's 'history' being the official one." With this clue, one can consult the subject index of Louis Kaplan's A *Bibliography of American Autobiographies* in search of other versions to set alongside Felsen's Spain. Kaplan confirms the fact that although libraries contain many memoirs dealing with World War II, the number of autobiographies recording Americans' involvement in the Spanish Civil War is not large. Besides chapters or passages in the autobiographies of Ernest Hemingway, Lillian Hellman, Ely Culbertson, and a few other well-known figures, there are but a handful of firsthand accounts. All are very contemporary accounts with the values of fresh memories and current relevance. Felsen, on the other hand, has waited four decades, thus fitting Erikson's model and gaining other advantages from the perspective of age and experience. *The Anti-Warrior* is atypically valuable, too, for linking Spain and World War II as parts of a single historical process experienced by this young man and recreated by the older writer in Sarasota.

This retrospective act of trying to order and make sense of one's wartime memories has been going on for at least two centuries. Occasions like the American Revolution and the American Civil War, together with the states of mind of combatants and observers, have constituted the *content* of many American life stories. For most readers, what actually happened to an individual, how that person later looks back and reevaluates the past by means of a chronological prose narrative— *this* is what defines an autobiography. The *forms* of autobiography are likewise traditional and readers can usually distinguish among them: *memoir,* the story of an actor in or observer of significant public events; *confession,* the revelation of inner states of consciousness and conscience; *testament,* the narrativized beliefs by which one has come to live; *apology,* setting the record straight and defending one's life and reputation. Milt Felsen's subtitle signals his awareness of these conventions. He invites the reader to experience a chronological account which is more or less trustworthy despite and because of its built-in bias. A memoir recaptures the self as the onetime occupant of specific historical moments within a recognized web of relationships. Its historicity—and consequently its claims to verifiability—is usually announced by real names, dates, events, and settings. We cannot read far in Felsen's personal history, however, without recognizing that this author, while meeting our expectations of a memoirist, has also written a testament to deep-seated (and occasionally contradictory) convictions about the futility of war, the venality of institutions like capitalism and organized religion, and the propensity of individuals and groups to practice violence and brutality on a mammoth scale.

As if memoir and testament were not sufficiently rich modes of communication, *The Anti-Warrior* also demonstrates that its author is a literary artist adept at dramatizing scenes and evoking others' characters as well as his own. Perhaps Hemingway, whom Felsen encounters in Madrid, had something to do with the spare force of this typical description:

> We climbed past the timberline and reached snow. Feet and hands were near to freezing. Heads hanging down, we kept our eyes only on the feet ahead of us. Sometimes it felt as if we must be nearing the crest, but another, higher peak would loom inexorably above us. We had to surmount a jumble of snow-covered, huge rocks. The Hollander lost his footing, fell, and slid to the bottom of a rock. His knee was painfully wrenched and he couldn't move. The climbing stopped, and the old man hurried back to see what was wrong. After a glance, he said, "We must leave him. Come. There is no time to lose. We must cross the border before the dawn."
>
> No one moved. "He will be found very soon. The police. We are near the border," the old man continued. "Shall we all fail?"
>
> The group got up to follow. "I will stay with him," said one of the Austrians. And that is how it was. Just before the dawn broke, we crossed the crest of the Pyrenees and the border. We had come to Spain.

As with other autobiographies—including Hemingway's A *Moveable Feast* with its preface warning readers against taking his story as fiction—this passage could readily be mistaken for fiction. What makes it autobiographical is the context. The brief episode of struggle and suffering is embedded not in a plot with a climax or some other satisfying ending but in an ongoing historical experience presided over by the author/narrator, who explicitly identifies himself with the actor who once clambered over these rocks. To be sure, the narrator's vocabulary and effective sequence of short sentences are marks of an artistry which, other characteristics aside, might be mistaken for that of the author of *For Whom the Bell Tolls*. Felsen is not a particularly bookish writer, however, and elsewhere in his story we encounter few if any literary allusions or references to other books about war, hospitals, or prison camps. (He does, to be sure, excoriate television's exploitation of Stalag Seventeen.) We are free—indeed, enjoined by the nature of the contract linking autobiographers and their audiences—to test this narrative as an accurate version of history. We may wish to check *The Anti-Warrior* not only for internal inconsistencies and ambiguities but also against external evidence in newspapers, history books, biographies, other autobiographies, even photographs in *Life* or newsreels. We can thereby assess Felsen's (to me) evident aim of trying to relate a trustworthy story of a survivor's memories.

Despite Felsen's apt description, terse dialogue, and the symbolic overtones of this episode of international idealism in early action—all features of "literature"—we may decide that *The Anti-Warrior* is equally "history." If so, we commit ourselves to a certain position in the current discussion about the nature of autobiography. Alfred Kazin, himself a practicing autobiographer, argues that if one uses fictional devices like dramatic scenes, dialogue, and metaphoric language then one has written fiction, not history. To this claim—with which I believe Felsen would disagree with a grin—Barrett J. Mandel, another wise critic of autobiography, has replied, "Of course, it is true that autobiographers use techniques of fiction, but such usage does not turn an autobiography into a fiction any more than Dvorak's use of folk motifs turns the *New World Symphony* into a folk song. At every moment of any true autobiography (I do not speak here of autobiographical novels) the author's intention is to convey the sense that 'this happened to me,' and it is this intention that is always carried through in a way which, I believe, makes the result different from fiction."

Though I think most readers of *The Anti-Warrior* will be persuaded that it is "true autobiography," there are formal questions to be raised. What, for instance, are we to say about Felsen's liberal doses of dialogue? How is it possible for a septuagenarian historian, no matter how powerful his memory, to reconstruct accurately all the verbal give-and-take of campus, battlefield, or bordello recorded in this action-packed account? To be sure, some exchanges are so graphically evoked as to suggest that the author *couldn't* have made them up—they were un-

forgettable. One passage of this sort describes the radical undergradu-
ate busily organizing the Iowa campus to oppose war. He and his
friends are caught illegally placarding the Pentacrest; they take refuge
in a tree, only to be caught by the police:

> "What's the charge?" I demanded. I prided myself on my knowl-
> edge of constitutional rights.
> There was a short, intense conference down below, then
> agreement.
> "For COMMITTING COMMUNISM!" the sheriff shouted, waving his
> long-barreled pistol.
> "Yeah," added the American Legion, inspired. "AT NIGHT."

Other conversations are even more arresting, and certain extended
scenes are so vividly re-presented that we are powerfully aware of the
authorial presence at work. Indeed, historians and literary critics can
agree that it is simply realistic to place more confidence in autobiographical utterance as reflecting the writer's present consciousness (at
the moments, that is, of composition and publication) than as the
record of actual past behavior. What we read in this text, then, is the
fruit of transactions between two Milt Felsens. Only from this perspective can we grasp the complex temporal status of a dramatic description
like that of the death of Renaldo, the Cuban ammo carrier:

> "I don't need the exercise," said Renaldo, "especially in this 95-
> degree heat. Could you spare a shot of water before I go? I'm fresh
> out."
> "Sure," I said, "just save me a drop."
> Renaldo lifted the canteen that I held out to him to his lips,
> threw his head back, and swallowed. As he did I watched a small,
> perfectly round hole open in the center of his throat. A stray bullet
> had fired at random, perhaps even accidentally, and Renaldo's life
> spilled out red on the ground. It was over in seconds.
> Inured as I had become—as all volunteers had become—to sud-
> den endings, I stared at the lifeless body and was sick to the pit of
> my being. The waste, the pointless, random, insane waste. The
> man who fired the shot had no idea what had happened to his bul-

let, what an easy, soft, vulnerable spot it had found. What would he have thought if he could have known? Certainly not that he had killed a decent, caring, admirable young man, perhaps much like himself. More likely he would have celebrated the death of another Red and asked for the military commendation due him. What ancestral, manipulating genius had first discovered man's fear and hatred of what he perceives to be different as well as the boundless profitability to which such knowledge could be put? For a long while I lay flat behind the olive tree. Some bullets came whistling by low overhead with the distinctive whine that close ones make, and they brought me back to the world of the briefly living.

There is no clear way to distinguish the thoughts and perceptions of the young machine gunner from those of the reminiscing writer. It may be that the latter made up the words of Renaldo's ironic request for "a shot of water before I go." We have no way of knowing. But Felsen's reflections on death and war emanate from "the pit of my being" and so plausibly connect the two selves here and elsewhere in the text. This conclusion is further underscored by Felsen's indifference to the rhetorical game of contrasting his past innocence or ignorance with present enlightenment. Continuities are often more prominent than dramatic changes in this self's history and developing identity.

What is more representative as narrative strategy is the interplay between description, dramatization, and reflection. Felsen the actor is given much less to philosophizing than to activity. "Not much time was spent in thought. Maybe the American educational system is long on information and short on the thinking process," he remarks of his fellow American prisoners at one juncture, and this offhand comment applies in part to his own youthful character. Though the story is dotted with statements about war and fascism and the tension between them which explains the book's title, these reflections almost always emerge from specific situations. Felsen spends little space developing ideas and ideology.

If Felsen is American to the core by virtue of his preference for activity over reflection and his deep distaste for militarism, he diverges from many of his countrymen both in his refusal to take life simply as a daily routine and in his rejection of any concept of an afterlife. "Religion and soldiers. Why were they so linked together in my mind?" This combination of typicality and marginality is epitomized by— because grounded in—his Jewishness. On this subject Felsen is often silent though never evasive. As an atheist, being a Jew isn't a religious identification. By his radical college friends and fellow brigade members he is joyfully greeted as their "Eastern Jew commie bastard." But in the stalag it becomes clear that Felsen identifies himself as a Jew only in his mind. In barracks bull sessions, he recalls:

> The Jewish question came up early. Our camp committee discovered that when work details were sent to farms, suspected Jews would be taken alone by a guard to an isolated field and be shot "trying to escape." Countermeasures included discarding or altering dog tags stamped with an H that identified the bearer as Hebrew.
>
> Deprived of H tags, the Germans relied on their own test, the facial characteristics labeled *Juden* that appeared almost daily in their press—dark-eyed, hook-nosed, beetle-browed caricatures. Here and there in the camp, a Bible-pounding anti-Semitic, fundamentalist American discovered that if a Nazi thinks you *look* like a Jew, then perforce you damn well *are* a Jew.
>
> I was not as shocked or surprised as many of my fellow prisoners. Jews have never agreed on a self-definition, leaving an age-old vacuum most often filled by the enemies of Jews. "If anti-Semitism were to disappear, most likely the Jews would too, there being no further use for them," I argued.

In passages like this Felsen makes clear that his ego identity is different from his social identity. He does not describe specific situations involving hiding or revealing his Jewishness. Nor does *The Anti-Warrior* raise retrospective (or contemporaneous) questions about the Holocaust or the author's later feelings about the German people.

The fact that present-day readers are understandably curious about what is said and not said in this autobiography underlines the fact that

The Anti-Warrior, like all personal histories, is a particular kind of imaginative and emotional transaction between author and audience. Although essentially a history, Felsen's story is not a biography. Hence it does not demand the detached, even skeptical response which such histories commonly evoke. On the other hand, this narrative isn't a novel with its author's life as its plot; hence uncritical immersion or acceptance—that familiar "willing suspension of disbelief"—is equally inappropriate. Some dynamic combination of both reactions is, I believe, called for. Reading autobiographies is an individual act of strenuous, skeptical sympathy.

In my experience of the pleasures of this text, the abrupt and dramatic ending of *The Anti-Warrior* left a skein of tantalizing questions about Felsen's future self. Striding through his apartment door into his wife's arms with "Hi, baby, . . . I'm back. So how's things?" is a convincing image of the Milt Felsen of 1945. Nevertheless, I was curious about those four intervening decades. Of course, no sensible reader of autobiography expects—or desires—coverage of a lifetime. Far more revealing is the selection made from experience, in light of chosen ends and artistic means. Yet I could not help wondering about subsequent events and the Anti-Warrior's responses to them. To my inquiry, then, about the McCarthy era of Cold War repressions and persecutions, the Vietnam protests of the sixties, and other recurrences, Milt Felsen wrote characteristically revealing replies. He said that his wife, "an organizer for the R. H. Macy union, was called before the anti-union Mundt-Nixon committee and I was summoned to Senator Roman Hruska's equally discredited cold war circus." His comments on other challenges to official policies often reflect his proud loyalty to and continuing involvement with fellow veterans of the Lincoln Brigade. "There was Peekskill in 1949, fierce opposition to McCarthyism and the Korean War, civil rights marches and anti-Vietnam demonstrations in the sixties and seventies, El Salvador and Nicaragua. To date the Lincoln Brigade has sent seventeen ambulances to Nicaragua."

Surely these are the addenda we should expect of the author of *The Anti-Warrior.* They are of a piece with the utterances and the identity, public and private, in the present text. Equally consistent, too, are some reflections in this same letter about his deepest motives for writing his autobiography. Milt Felsen compressed his credo into three simple, eloquent testamentary statements. He has written this life story, he declares:

1. To urge against the continued bland acceptance of the inevitability of future wars when it is so clear that either war is obsolete or humankind is.
2. Concern for the aimless self-absorption of the young in America, because for one thing they seem so unhappy. I wanted to describe the intense inner joy of participation in the central issues of one's time, not as a bystander but as a voluntary, passionate participant.
3. To counteract, in a small way, the prevalent anti-radical caricature that portrays people of the Left as unthinking humorless automatons created by a mindless cookie cutter and controlled by bewhiskered aliens from an evil empire where they don't even speak English.

Sustained partisanship of Left ideals, the passionate pleasures of active participation in history making, and an unquenchable sense of humor—these qualities in the youth, the ambulance driver, and the prisoner of war are indeed reflected everywhere in the narrative created forty years later by the Anti-Warrior. What Milt Felsen has selected as significant portions of his life composes a convincing image of the man he once was and clearly still remains. Like all autobiographies, *The Anti-Warrior: A Memoir* is an open-ended story. Its protagonist is depicted sustaining his unique personality within a constantly changing, often threateningly inhumane society. The delicate balance of continuity amid change is carried through this absorbing narrative to the conclusion, which, one realizes, is neither the actual end of the youthful veteran nor, one hopes, the last words of the first-time older writer.

CHAPTER 1

1918

1930

Earliest memories are not neatly dated and filed. They lie in the dusty debris of the mind, stubbornly resistant to orderly recall and just out of reach, except for tantalizingly brief images of exceptional clarity. Mine go back to the corner of Nostrand Avenue and Monroe Street in Brooklyn, New York, then a decaying, white, middle-class area, now the heart of the black ghetto called Bed-Stuy.

We lived one flight up over a German butcher shop in a "railroad flat." It had a tiny parlor and just behind it an even smaller, windowless bedroom with enough room for one bed, in which I slept with my two brothers, eight-year-old Sid and baby Hank. Then came my parents' bedroom, a small kitchen, and a bath.

My father's family had been modestly landed gentry in Russia. They had packed their newly married son off to America to avoid his being drafted into the czar's army. They also wanted him to escape the pogroms that were sweeping eastern Europe in the early 1900s.

At Ellis Island, America welcomed the huddled masses yearning to work for very low wages, sending my mother's four younger sisters at once to the notorious, sweating textile mills of New Bedford, Massachusetts. At the same time, America renamed the hapless immigrants. My father, Heschel, became Harry; my mother, Sheva, blossomed into Sabina; and from somewhere in his muddy subconscious, a minor bureaucrat changed the family name of Peltzmann to the rather odd family name of Felsen.

It was 1918, and I was six years old. World War I, the Victorian Age, czarist Russia, and horse-drawn trolley cars were coming to an end, but there was no lack of excitement. I was madly in love with a dark-eyed Spanish beauty, whose attention I tried to catch by hanging head-down by the heels from storefront awnings on the way to Public School 3 on Bedford Avenue. Sometimes, very deliberately, she introduced me to ecstasy by letting me carry her books. The next day, just as deliberately, she taught me agony by letting a hated rival carry them instead.

1

The socks show my readiness
to ride off to a holy war. The
pony looks wise and sad.

Once there was a big explosion, perhaps a bomb, at Broad and Wall streets in front of the statue of George Washington. When we looked at the papers on the stand in front of the green-painted Reeve's Grocery Store on the corner, they had pictures of a wagon and horses dying and scary cartoons of bewhiskered BOLSHEVIKS. We smelled and felt the panicky fear of the grown-ups, but it vanished quickly.

New excitement: THE WAR IS OVER. THE BOYS ARE COMING HOME! But the boys looked like old, old men, marching up Bedford Avenue rank on endless rank, wearing wide-brimmed hats and knee-high leggings, surrounded by flags and bands and all of us, cheering and waving our tiny American flags that had suddenly appeared from somewhere.

We played our games in the streets and dodged the cars, though not always—forever I'll have the memory of a friend's limp, bloody body lifted off the huge bumper of a Pierce-Arrow. In those days it never occurred to us that toys could be more complicated than a rubber ball and a broomstick, or that after the street-watering truck turned the dry gutters into rushing rivers we needed anything more than small sticks for our very own speedboats to race toward the gulping sewers.

The open trolley-cars ran past us down toward Coney Island. The women sat on the side-to-side benches and the men stood on the wide board platforms, while the conductor swung around them like a giant ape collecting the nickel fare and pulling the cord that recorded the total number of passengers on a giant clock at the front of the car. We put pennies on the tracks hoping to derail a car, but failing that we were delighted with the flattened, misshapen, and suddenly more valuable coins.

We were city kids and we learned the tough city language—WOP, POLACK, KIKE, SHEENY, MICK, NIGGER, DIRTY JEW BASTARD. And we learned that behind the verbal litany of the unmelted pot was the physical reality of cuts and bruises if one wandered a step or two onto the wrong turf. Just crossing an innocent-looking street to the wrong side was an invitation to a fight.

Day after day, we learned the tough city ways. The trick of retrieving dropped coins by lowering a piece of chewed gum on a string through a subway grating. The danger of getting too close to drunks fighting in the street, especially if the swinging, swearing contestants were man and wife. The way to steal and run from street vendors, to sneak into movie-theater exits as people left, and to get seltzer the cheap way— "two cents plain."

The city entered my bloodstream, teaching its daily survival lessons, but I was dimly aware that somewhere far away it was different. I could see that in picture books at school and on the sides of milk wagons, with their painted scenes of blood-red barns, little white houses, bilious green fields, and enormous brown cows with bulging udders. There was no hint of it, though, in our home, where so few words were ever spoken. And yet, my father had never ceased to pressure my mother privately to leave the city "for the sake of the children." He too must have fantasized about red barns, brown cows, and himself as a country squire overseeing an estate of fertile green fields, just like his own father in the Old Country. It was quixotic, even ridiculous, but this was not a time when European-born women defied the whims of their European-born husbands.

Not that I thought of my parents as foreign-born. They fell over themselves in the effort to exceed one hundred percent in their Americanism. My mother came from that part of the old Austro-Hungarian empire that collided with Poland, Russia, and Slovakia. She spoke five languages fluently but only English in front of the children. In fact, my parents robbed us and themselves of a precious and rich cultural heritage, including music. My father played the violin beautifully, but one day he heard Mischa Elman. "He plays," lamented my father, "I fiddle." Then he placed his violin in its case and never played again.

I still have mixed feelings about my father. In today's terms it would be hard to defend him against the charge of being a self-centered, politically witless, male-supremacist son of a bitch who starved his wife of affection and mistreated her shamelessly. Yet he insisted on adhering to a code of honesty so unbending as to bar him from advancement and finally from employment in the normal business world. He could be witty and irresistibly charming, and I think in his own way he loved his wife and his children too.

In a neighborhood where most everyone was—as my friend Roger Hargrave would say many years later—"sucking hind economic tit," our own extreme penury was hardly noticeable. I assumed that all mothers darned socks, mended kneeholes, and knit sweaters and scarves and that all shoes were resoled and reheeled until the uppers disintegrated. If there was chicken on the table it had to be Sunday. Brooklyn was my turf and I liked it.

And then it was gone. With the sudden, insane incoherence of a scene change in a nightmare or a lap dissolve in a film, city became country. One moment we were a family of devoted city-dwellers, the next we were in a big farmhouse in a tiny farm community in the foothills of the Catskill Mountains. Everything about that journey and the reasons for it is a blank.

I remember only one thing—the night we arrived. There had been nights in Brooklyn when it was cold, but not cold like this. Nostrils glued together with each intake of breath as we ran up and down the stairs trying to find out what had happened to the heating system in this enormous barn of a house in a strange country in the middle of nowhere. When my father started a fire in the cellar furnace, nothing happened. Water had to be added to the pipes and radiators. After a frantic search, we found a place at the top of the house where water could indeed be poured into the system. Out in back of the kitchen there was a deep well, the kind that contained, naturally, an old oaken bucket. Somehow we found pails. Somehow we avoided the instant onset of pneumonia. My mother cried bitterly at our bleak introduction to what she already knew was to be her life of exile.

We soon learned how our father had achieved his dream of living on the land. After saving enough for a tiny down payment, he had accepted an agreement with terms so onerous as to mortgage his family for the rest of their lives and to chain him to the city in a hopeless battle to meet the payments. When we moved, he stayed only three days. Then he had to go back to his job with the Singer Sewing Machine Company, managing several of their stores.

That company, Singer, was to be his nemesis. One week after the Wall Street crash of October 1929, he was fired without pay or notice despite eighteen years of loyal and abject service. He was thrown away like a used tissue, and he never recovered. In spite of our repeated attempts to cheer him—telling him that he wasn't alone, that the whole country was under water—he blamed himself. He went to his pre-

Dad in a rare moment of
repose. Even he could not
resist the old-fashioned
hammock, which I share
with him while Hank stands
guard at the rear.

maturely senile death in 1943 still loving the Singer Company. Early
in his life he had come to hate religion, seeing it as a cause of endless
strife and bloodshed. But nothing could shake his belief in and devotion to his own idea of the great savior, the giant American corpora-
tion. After all, it had given him the means to "own" his country estate.

By any standard, our farmhouse was big, and to my brothers and me
it became the Taj Mahal. It had a huge lawn and in its center a Greek
Revival fountain, now rusting in greenish, faded splendor. The house
was circled by a row of giant maple trees, which we later learned could
be tapped for sap that rendered the purest of syrup. Out back was a
garage, barn, chicken coops, woodshed, truck garden, berry patches,
apple orchard, grape arbors, fields, and a brook. To our city-bred eyes,
here was a wonderland—mysterious, exciting, and in many ways
fearsome.

Even today the socioeconomic distance between Brooklyn, New York, and Wawarsing, New York, is vast. In 1919 Wawarsing was another planet, seemingly full of unfriendly natives and loaded with booby traps for Jew-boys from the city. But it turned out that since we were the only Jewish family in the village—an oddity, not a threat— we were adopted, much like a litter of puppies found on a doorstep.

A few years later, this strange, proprietary tolerance took an absurd twist during a mainly anti-Catholic renaissance of the Ku Klux Klan. There were no blacks in Wawarsing and very few Catholics either, so Klan members did the best they could with what they had, burning crosses in the fields at night, ranting, hating, and threatening at the tops of their voices. It was about the cheapest kind of entertainment we kids had ever known. The Klan had only a brief fling in the Northeast before it died from a shortage of hate objects. In Wawarsing there was a piquant moment before it did.

Answering a midafternoon knock at the door, my mother faced the head Kleagle.

"Afternoon, Ma'am," said John Cartwright, "I'll only be a minute. We'd like for you to join us in the KKK."

Taken aback, alarmed but also amused, my mother could only stammer, "That's mighty kind of you, John, and we are honored to be thought of, but finances just now make it awkward to take advantage of your offer."

But he had his instructions and would not be put off. "Everyone in town is a member," he persisted, "and it's been decided that you are not to be left out. I'm offering you a family membership for just one dollar down." Before my mother could answer he rushed on, "And if you ain't got the buck just now we'll let it hang for a while." So at the age of nine, I became a non-dues-paying member of the Ku Klux Klan.

Our first days in the Wawarsing classroom brought shameful, ego-destroying evidence of our vast ignorance. We knew nothing, and our schoolmates moved in for the kill with that special cruelty that kids reserve for the alien. Our quest for learning, however, was speeded up enormously by the price we paid in snickering ridicule for every lesson.

The school itself was one room, with a pot-bellied stove and one teacher for the eight grades. Out back were crude, two-holer johns,

Wawarsing, New York.
Mother standing left, brother
Sid on right. Note the others'
seriousness, my sensing the
cosmic joke. And
anticipating Calvin Klein.
Our henhouse in the rear.

"Boys" and "Girls" abutting each other, the intervening wall scarred by the boys' attempts to carve peepholes with jackknives. Behind the outhouse were the river and the woods.

We city kids didn't know a bean plant from a tomato, a maple tree from an elm, a heifer from a cow, corn from wheat. We didn't know what a whiffle tree was, or a peavey, or a hayrick, or a butter churn. Initiation, however, came fast. We learned about hunting, fishing, trapping, the myriad skills of farming—and sex.

I sat behind Jessie in school and used to idly dip her golden, eight-year-old curls in my inkwell. This may have been a subliminal erotic signal, because she often asked if I wanted to play doctor. One memorable day she invited me to her house. I could not understand why she wanted to crawl under the couch where it was cramped and hot and where there were no toys. Or so I thought.

After directing me to rub her in various places, she guided my hand to a particular place and said, "Pinch me." Dutifully, albeit tentatively, I obeyed. "Harder," she commanded. A certain note of disdain had entered her voice, and she obviously realized that she had chosen a prize dummy as a playmate. I can only remember thinking that perhaps I shouldn't dip her curls in my inkwell anymore.

Attendance at District 18 School averaged sixteen to twenty students for all eight grades. Until my brother Sid and I passed the New York State Regents Exam and went on to high school, no one had ever graduated. The boys lasted until they got their working papers and the girls until they got pregnant. The timing worked out quite well.

Years later when I got to the University of Iowa, I basked in the sympathy extended to me for having surmounted such early educational privation. Current theory, however, holds the opposite view, citing the actual advantage of having different age groups and class levels freely interacting. The learning process is still a mystery and occurs in many guises, in those days some very attractive ones, as I remember.

For me, lessons in school and lessons in life were inseparably linked. I never understood why cows insisted on being milked at such an ungodly early hour, but I can still hear my mother shouting, "What do you kids want to do, sleep till six o'clock in the morning?" After that chore was the mile walk past Anna Dowling's post office, across the bridge over the Roundout River, and down the dirt road toward Port Ben and school. In spring, thick mud forced us to go on horseback, and in midwinter, snowdrifts made us use skis. Introduced to me as plebeian transportation, those activities could never be considered sports.

Muskrat traps, laid carefully in nearby, icy mountain streams, had to be checked before the school bell rang. If there was a catch, the wet, bloody carcass was laid in the outer hall where we hung our coats. By noon, of course, the odor was pungent, and the girls said, "How disgusting!" My friend Jim Smith taught me how to skin the animals and pack them off to the I. J. Fox Fur Company in New York City. Money was hard to come by, and we got seventy-five cents a pelt.

Our bucolic valley ran north and south from Wurtsboro to Kingston, with the Shawangunk Range on the east and the foothills of the Catskills running up past Woodstock on the west. Topping the Shawangunk were Lake Minnewaska and Lake Mohonk, and for miles along the mountains' almost inaccessible upper ridges wild huckleberries grew.

Each summer when we were between eleven and thirteen years old, Jim and I would pitch a tent at the 4-Mile Post. It was the favored spot for a collection of tar-paper shacks and tents put up by the berry pickers, mostly Tobacco Road-type families, single drifters, and kids like us. We wore brief denim shorts and nothing else. By the end of the summer, the callouses on our feet were an inch thick and we looked like Indians.

During the day we roamed the wild, craggy mountain top, five-quart pails tied to our middles, watching for rattlesnakes and copperheads, trying and failing to find a little shade among the stunted pine trees, and reaching carefully into rock crevices where the juiciest berries hid with the snakes. We didn't mind the rattlers so much since they had the decency to sound a warning. Copperheads, though, lay hidden in the path among dead leaves. Word had spread about the man who had stepped over one and was bitten on the upper thigh. All summer we guarded our testicles.

In the evening, entrepreneurs came up the mountain with burros.

They brought canned goods and coffee, which they sold at very high prices, and bought our berries at very low prices, a penny or two a quart.

There was no law at the 4-Mile Post—the campers made their own. There was, however, plenty of drinking, arguing, stabbing, and shooting, and every night there was a poker game, usually in the shack occupied by a family named Quick. There were a father, Sam, a mother, a little boy, and four girls from thirteen to nineteen. All the cardplayers wore knives and guns. To get into the game all you needed was money, and mine was accepted like any one else's.

One night Sam Quick was losing heavily. The pot was being raised and he had what he thought was the winning hand, but he couldn't match the ante. He was desperate. "Boys," he said, "I'm putting up LaurieMae." (LaurieMae was his seventeen-year-old daughter, vaguely pretty but a little dumpy.) While the details are now dim in my memory, the fierceness of the battle that ensued remains clear. Not only the players but the whole camp took sides. Among the males, I was among a decided minority in opposition to the deal. As a twelve-year-old kid, I couldn't think of much use in acquiring LaurieMae. The issue became moot when along about 2 A.M. a torrential thunderstorm hit the camp, bouncing lightning off the lignite rocks, scarring the bark off the pines, and knocking over the tents.

During the big contest, one of Sam Quick's other daughters had wandered off, and in the storm's intermittent light she was seen lying in water at the edge of a big rock. She was very still, and we all stood in the rain and had guilty thoughts while her mother wailed and screamed awful words at us. About twenty minutes later, the child began to stir and then to recover. Lightning had traveled through the water and shocked her senseless without doing lasting harm. We couldn't start the game again because while we were all out there someone had sneaked in and stolen all the money off the table.

The money I made those summers picking berries was not much, but it was enough to buy a few school clothes and I liked it better than washing glasses and mountains of pots in the hotels. In some ways, I think my working days were a great deal more educational than my school days. When things got tough, Jason and Medea also used their children, but it didn't occur to me until many years later to make the connection with Sam Quick and LaurieMae.

Some connections were easier to make. In the pasture and in the barnyard, the animals taught all of us biology. Conception followed mating—no country girl was unaware of that. Realization that only the human male was always in heat came soon after, inspiring countless stratagems to deal with that most troublesome phenomenon.

There was no television, of course, and in our valley not even a radio set. In the Shawangunk Mountains the winter evenings are very long, and young people spent them together. We went bobsledding and had ice-skating parties on Honk Lake with roasted hot dogs around a midnight fire. We played pinochle and whist in each other's houses and then paired off and walked home, sharing each other. Because we couldn't buy entertainment, in some deep sense we entertained each other. Perhaps something quite wonderful has been lost by exchanging that social participation for the isolated passivity of the living-room couch.

While we learned much from each other, we also learned occasionally from outsiders. A truth of some magnitude—the essential difference between reality and illusion—forced its way into my consciousness in an unsubtle way at Yama Farms in Napanoch, some two miles from Wawarsing. It was a naughty, super-luxurious hideaway with a clientele that included Henry Ford, Sr., Harvey Firestone, and John D. Rockefeller, Sr. Its dining room featured nubile French waitresses, and the locals had all they could do to stifle a natural tendency to refer to it as a high-class whorehouse.

Attached to Yama Farms, almost hidden in a primeval pine forest, was a trout hatchery managed by Frank Townsend, the father of my school friend Fats. Deep in sun-dappled shadow, it was a magical place, sure to invite childhood fantasy. After the fish were hatched, we watched the careful way they were put into a series of cold, clear pools and separated as they grew. The largest trout, speckled and rainbow, were kept together in the largest pool at the very end. To keep them active they were kept hungry, and we delighted in holding a stick out over them and watching their flashing, iridescent bodies as they leaped at it, hoping it was food.

Mr. Townsend shooed us away one day to make room for a long, black limousine. It stopped close to our favorite, the end pool. A gray-gloved, uniformed chauffeur stepped out, went to the rear, and from the large outside trunk removed a fishing pole in two sections. He assembled it, checked its flexibility, and then opened the back door.

After a moment, rear end first, a very large man emerged. He reached in and put on an African safari hat, and when he turned we saw that he was dressed like the great white hunters we knew from the movies. Except for a protruding potbelly, he looked the part too. He took the fishing rod in his gloved hand, walked a few steps toward our pool, seething with large trout, and heaved the line in the general direction of the fish. Half a dozen leaped at it and one hooked itself. In moments several trout lay flopping on the bank.

The chauffeur took the rod from the sportsman and returned it to the trunk. Then he strung the fish through the gills onto a short line. Carefully handing the "catch" to the sportsman, the chauffeur brought out a camera, stepped back, and clicked off half a dozen poses as instructed by his employer. Mr. Townsend stepped forward then, took the fish, and as the limo rolled away, threw them back in the pool. Fats and I almost died laughing, and for days, with Fats as the rich man and me as the chauffeur, we were a big hit in school. But that wasn't the end.

About two weeks later we were down at the post office (our reading room and hangout) going through the Sunday papers, and there, in the middle of the sepia rotogravure section, was a photo layout of our very own rich man. The captions described the skill with which his accurate fly casting had overcome the rushing waters of the famed Roundout. And by God there were the pictures of his catch to prove it.

The rich man and his dangling fish are right there in front of me still. I wish I could remember the name of that anonymous contributor to my maturity—he was a better instructor than many I knew in academia.

As the years passed, my father, whose $14 a week from Singer kept us going, drove up less and less often in his Locomobile touring car and later in his secondhand Chandler Eight. When he did, he brought presents and played the visiting benefactor, which must have driven

The family. Back row:
Mother, Hank (if you look
real close), and Dad; front
row: Sid and me. Behind us
the still white lilies on a
fading relic of a fountain.

my harried mother to distraction. There were veiled hints that back in the city he was not always alone, but in front of us boys there was never even a whisper of disharmony. And my mother did love him truly, and alone among men. He failed her and himself, but it never occurred to her to do anything but bear it, as she did her mountain of other burdens. If she ever felt that life had dealt her a losing hand, she never showed it.

She raised, fed, and clothed three unruly boys until we graduated from high school. She did it by ruining her eyes foot-pumping an old Singer sewing machine, turning out piecework for New York City sweatshop owners at worse than sweatshop pittances. She also took in summer boarders and ran our farm, baking, canning, pickling, and preserving. If we thought about it at all we thought that's what mothers were for.

Years later in June of 1945, a week or two after I returned from a German prisoner-of-war camp, my mother ran a party for me in Brooklyn. She invited all her friends and served all the wrong food (I weighed less than a hundred pounds and couldn't handle Flatbush Avenue deli). She had a marvelous time relaxing from years of tension and worry. A few days later, the OSS told my wife and me to get out of town because we were being deluged with inquiries from relatives of other U.S. prisoners. We were sent to Virginia Beach but got only to Washington when a phone call told us my mother had died alone in a hospital where she had gone for a checkup. They said she had had a heart attack, but I think she just wore out.

Only now when I think of her do I wonder what her dreams, her fantasies, could have been. In the jazzy twenties of my youth I didn't think of her at all. I thought of myself, exclusively, almost all the time.

My God, did I give her anxiety attacks. I had a certain genius for self-imposed disaster, a quality I've never completely lost. Having learned how to impress my first love in Brooklyn, I had tried again with Jessie of the inkwell. The boys would jump off the church shed's roof, but realizing that leadership requires innovation, I did it backwards, landed on my head, and broke my arm. Dr. Munson did me the exquisite honor of putting me in a cast. I rushed home, banged in the door, and yelled "Hey, Mom, look! I broke my arm!" The only cast in the Shawangunk Mountains, and she couldn't see its value or why, weeks later, I fought so hard against having it removed.

There was also my falling through the clear, transparent ice on the river and almost drowning, because I alone thought of pushing a large rock in front of me with a hockey stick to see if the ice was thick enough to hold the gang that followed. And later, when the ice broke up in the spring, I was the one who jumped onto a floating iceberg. The whole town turned out and ran along the banks, throwing ropes and screaming advice and getting thrills of horror as the sound of the falls got louder, until at the last moment a bend in the river threw me close enough for the fire department's rope to reach.

My mother, though, must have been used to anxiety. She was the eldest of five sisters, three of whom became teachers and died in middle age of cancer. The other, Jenny, ran off in an uncontrollable fit of romanticism with a musician who worshiped two things, his oboe and Leon Trotsky. Before abandoning her in Chicago, he presented her with a gallant token of his affection, a son named Sascha Leon Lenin Bedrick.

Jenny returned to New York, found a job deep in the catacombs of the Columbia University library, and devoted the rest of her life to her son and her dream of one day visiting the state of Israel. For thirty years she saved penny by penny, finally made the trip, and then wrote each member of her family long, detailed letters bitterly critical of everything she saw.

When her sister Fanny died, Jenny married, according to a centuries-old Jewish tradition, her surviving brother-in-law, Jack. It was a marriage that threatened that custom with extinction. They detested each other. All his life Jack had gone to work as a master tinsmith in overalls, smoking a big black cigar. Jenny aspired to the "intelligentsia"— the arts, books, ballet—to CULTURE. Both in their sixties, they at last had something purposeful to live for, the determination to bury the other. Jenny won out, and then, her work done, she too soon died.

All my mother's sisters hated my father. When they came up to the farm one by one during the summer, they nagged my mother about it when they thought they were out of earshot of the children. But

New York City, circa 1919.
Grandma, left rear, and four
of her five daughters: Fanny,
left front, my mother
Sabina, Jenny, and Dora.
Fanny's two sons became
scientists, Dora's two
daughters a teacher and a
photographer, and Jenny's
son a fine dancer.

we knew and were hurt and resentful, allies in our feelings, at least
temporarily.

My brother Sid was two years older than I. We were friendly but
not close. From the very beginning he was a loner, much more at
ease with one person than with many. He had one girlfriend, Evelyn
VanWynen, all through high school. She owned an air-cooled Franklin automobile, the only one in Ulster County. It had high seats and a
very high top, and when they rode in it, sitting very straight, they
looked like the British royal couple come to review the troops. I think
he had three girlfriends in his life, and he married two of them.

Wawarsing is midway between Ellenville and Kerhonkson, and in 1926 when they opened a high school in Kerhonkson, most of us chose to walk there. It would be the first class and it would belong to us. I became an athlete and a drunk.

Everybody drank. It was the time of prohibition, so we drank. Without discriminating, we imbibed speakeasy rotgut and local applejack. The twenties were roaring, and though ours was more of a squeak we tried to roar along. Besides drinking, we took to necking in the rumble seat, according to our own strange rules.

The custom may not have been a national one, but it was our way that the girl would keep one item of clothing, however sheer, between her and her panting partner. All positions, probings and pumpings were permitted. Climaxes were reached, ecstasy attained, and only penetration was tacitly out of bounds. On Monday mornings you could tell which of the boys had been most active over the weekend by the careful way they walked, favoring as much as possible their angrily irritated members.

In school, I was one of those students who found it easy to pass and boring to study, especially since I couldn't think of anything I really wanted to be when I grew up. The present was good enough, and though we were all dirt-poor, the *Saturday Evening Post* atmosphere of American capitalism on a roll permeated our dreams of the fortunes we'd make as soon as we graduated. How could we know that the bull-market freshmen of 1926 were to become the Great Depression seniors of 1930?

It must have been 1928 when I met Joseph Freeman, editor of *New Masses*. A real-life Communist in the flesh, he spoke everyday English with us locals but strange, arcane words as mysterious as Sanskrit with his friends. He had bought a country house, and he shopped in the general store in Accord owned by the Friedman family. Jack Friedman, like me, was sixteen and my friend, and sometimes when he had to deliver things to the Freeman house I went along. Freeman's wife was the former Charmion Von Wiegand, the daughter of W. R. Hearst's top reporter, Karl Von Wiegand, the one who gave the world the false report of an armistice at the end of World War I. Their weekend houseguests were the leading leftist writers of the day—Maurice Hindus, Max

Eastman, Floyd Dell—all the panjandrums of Greenwich Village Bohemia. How they could talk.

World revolution, all agreed, was on the agenda of history. The intense disagreement was over the timing. Would it be 1927 or 1928? And what would their own role as intellectuals be when it happened? What would happen to the subjective role of the ego, the soul, the introspective mysteries of love, the worship of art for art's sake? Some participants, like Scott Nearing and Mike Gold, were impatient with such fears. "Bourgeois intellectual baggage" they called them, and then they led the discussion into whether Odysseus was the first real imperialist.

Jack and I would listen for hours, and it was more the style of their lives than the content of their polemics that fired our wonder. They didn't just drop names, they dropped countries: "Last month in Leningrad when I was having dinner with Emma Goldman . . ."; "Lady Astor is very interested and said to be sure next time you're in London . . ."; "Paris is very excited about this young painter, Picasso."

Perhaps through some kind of intellectual osmosis, their discussions about the nature of the capitalist crisis, the inevitability of class conflict, the rising threat of fascism in Italy, and the certainty of bigger, more devastating wars to come did rub off on us to some degree. Less than ten years later, three thousand Americans volunteered to fight Franco and fascism in Spain. Two of them were graduates of tiny Kerhonkson High School, Jack Friedman and me. One night in 1929, the KHS girls' and boys' basketball teams got on a bus and rode over the mountain to play New Paltz Normal. A more even match would be Vassar against Notre Dame, but we won both games. Frank Grey and I were nominated to find a speakeasy. We used everybody's money and got enough liquor for a celebration. It was a cold night, and there was hugging and kissing and singing. Our principal was along as official chaperon, but that did not prevent a scandal from erupting about our bacchanalian orgy. Pulpit sermons and general outrage poured out of the bluenoses. A propitiating sacrifice had to be made, and Frank and I were suspended from school indefinitely.

Forced to consider seriously our entire future, we spent a good ten minutes and decided the hell with school. We would go to Florida, find jobs, and make our way in the real world. It was one month after the stock market crash, and ripples were already being felt. We bought a Chevy two-door for $5, threw in our possessions (rifles and hunting gear), and headed south.

We took turns at nonstop driving, and I was at the wheel when we lost our way barreling down a remote Pennsylvania road at 4 A.M. At the bottom of a hill, the road made a ninety-degree turn but we didn't. Our headlights met each other on the other side of a large oak tree. I woke from unconsciousness sitting on the hood holding two pieces of steering wheel. No sign of Frank Grey.

It was a moment of desolation and panic. The car was empty, except that where we had been, the motor now was. Bleeding and scared, I kept calling his name till from directly beneath me came a faint answer. The doors of that Chevy opened forward, and on impact Frank had been thrown out. He had hit the tree and rolled under the car, where now a leaking battery was slowly rearranging and eroding his face.

Dazed and disoriented, we began walking through the heavy fog but were driven away from farmhouses by angry dogs. We were near Kennet Square, Mushroom Capital of the World. At daybreak a farmer, obviously terrified at the sight of two bloody strangers with rifles, made the mistake of opening his door. At least ten of his kids came down the stairs one at a time to stare at us silently while we made arrangements to sell our wreck for $7, realizing a handsome $2 profit. We decided to continue on to Florida—on foot.

Drivers were skittish about offering a ride when they noticed that these otherwise appealing young hitchhikers were each carrying a well-oiled rifle in the crook of the right arm. An occasional local truck-driver did let curiosity overcome better judgment, but the rides were short and the walking very, very long, all the heel-blistered way to Washington, D.C.

"What do we do now?" asked Frank as we walked past Union Station and into the scrungy section of the city. "We're broke, we'll never make it to Florida, and nobody will offer two bums like us a job."

"I'm a little short of ideas just now," I stalled. "Let's sleep on it."

"Where?"

We slept cold in a park near the White House. In the morning we spent a dime each for doughnuts and coffee and went to a pawn shop to sell our dearly beloved rifles for $1.75 each. When we left, we passed a recruiting poster for the United States Marines.

"What the hell," said Frank. "If you don't die it's a living."

"Maybe we should check out the navy before we rush into this," I said, expressing vague misgivings. "Perhaps we shouldn't make a decision like this on an empty stomach."

"It's my empty stomach that's already decided," said Frank, "and that blue uniform goes good with my eyes."

By nightfall we were on a bus headed for Quantico, Virginia. Papers were put in front of us, and we signed them without looking. We were given fatigues and assigned to a barracks. Physical exams began at 9 A.M. and were over by noon. Frank returned to the barracks first, and when I came in he was already there and was putting on his old clothes.

"What the hell are you up to, Frank?"

Frank looked up at me and his face wore an expression I had never seen—old, defeated, shaken. "I've got a bad ticker. They threw me out."

I couldn't believe it. Frank Grey? The greatest natural athlete any of us had ever seen? The strong-muscled, graceful guy who could outrun, outjump, outperform anyone he had ever come up against? It couldn't be true.

"They're crazy," I said. "It's a stupid mistake."

"They explained it to me. There's a fault in the rhythm, not serious, but enough to keep me out." Frank stuck out his hand. "Be a good soldier."

"Balls," I said, "if you ain't good enough, I ain't good enough. We came together, we leave together."

It wasn't that easy. Officers with loud, mean voices told me my signature was irrevocable. I was a marine now, they said, and marines followed orders, goddammit, not whims. What in hell did I think this was, a tea party? I was near panic and must have made a first-class pest of myself because right around 10 P.M. they loaded Frank and me onto a bus, dropped us off in a lonely spot on U.S. Route 1 just south of Richmond, Virginia, and drove off in ill-concealed disgust.

"Well, Frank," I said, "how does it feel to be a civilian again?"

He was not in a good mood. "YOU can say about that," he said bitterly. "At least you got in, so you can joke about getting out."

"Are we about to have a real serious conversation?" I asked. "Because if we are, we should get off this damn road."

Our belongings were down to what we could put in two small laundry bags. We found a clearing in the woods and used the bags as pillows. Our country Loden coats served as blankets.

"Listen, Frank," I said, "maybe it's not so bad. I wasn't that excited about spending three years with those guys. Did you see their haircuts? And maybe they really did make a mistake about your heart. No doctors ever mentioned this before, did they?"

Frank sat a while looking at the ground. Then, quite deliberately, he spoke. "You're right. I'm glad in a way that we didn't get in. We did it for a bad reason, for three meals a day. Maybe that's why they put recruiting stations so close to skid row. It bothers me about my heart, but I'll handle it. What I want to say is that I've had it. I want to go back home, and it's not just the marines or my health. I've felt this way ever since we cracked up in Pennsylvania. We'll never make it to Florida. We'll never make it. We made a mistake."

He stopped talking but I could tell he wasn't finished. Waiting, I became aware of discomfort. It had rained some earlier, and everything felt damp and cold and lumpy to lie on.

Then he began again. "The whole town will laugh at us, especially at school. It will be real shitty, I know that. But it's better than walking to nowhere, and that's what we're doing—walking straight into a big, dumb, blank wall."

It was the longest speech he'd ever made, and I figured he'd been hit real hard by that marine doc. If it had been up to me I probably would have continued on, too ashamed to think of going back. But his decision gave me an out I was not too displeased with, since it gave me the chance to play the generous, understanding, self-sacrificing friend.

"Hey, take it easy, Frank. It's OK with me. The main thing is we stick together. Maybe we'll go to Florida when we're old farts."

None the worse for wear.
Frank Grey, right, and I
happily back in Wawarsing,
a few weeks after being
mustered (or thrown) out of
the marines in Virginia.

In the morning a filthy cattle-truck filled with dung got us back to Richmond, where we called Frank's schoolteacher-sister, Ruby, collect. She wired us railroad fare home. There, instead of running a gauntlet of derision, we were met with cheers, the basketball team having lost all its games while we were gone. Frank and I quickly put out of our minds our preview of the grim reality that awaited the high school graduates of 1930. Our world became again a warm collie to play with, and we enjoyed ourselves with the heightened intensity of those who knew how brief the good times would be and how cold it was outside.

CHAPTER 2

1930

1937

I graduated in June, and in July our farm was sold for the mortgage. The family was broke. We moved to Brooklyn and got a cheap apartment on Sterling Street, across Bedford Avenue from Ebbets Field. We couldn't afford to go to the games, but it was enough for us to hear the cheers of the fans. The Dodgers belonged as much to us as to them anyway, maybe more. We lived on a little welfare and menial, low-paid, temporary, nothing jobs.

For me the ugly facts of the Depression had come like an unexpected blow on the head from behind. I looked at the high school yearbook I had kept and at the pictures with predictions underneath of rich futures, big jobs, cars, and homes. I stood on the street and was ashamed and angry, sensing that the unemployed selling apples to the unemployed was an obscene economic joke.

I worked as a shipping clerk, roofer's helper, pretzel baker, batik colorist, hod carrier, chauffeur for a traveling salesman, and sheet-metal riveter. For a while I worked six nights a week on machines that knitted fringes on men's scarves, and my salary was $8 a week. The jobs didn't last, though. The foremen demanded payoffs—payoff or layoff. Women workers paid a higher price.

Our very distant cousins, Benjamin and Samuel Goodman, owned a business, the Goody Manufacturing Company. They had an eight-story factory building at 17 West Seventeenth Street, just off Union Square in an area of ugly, decaying lofts inhabited even then by depressed and defeated people. They manufactured five-and-ten-cent-store junk. They gave me a job as a shipping clerk.

Next to the building, huge trucks lined the curbs. During the noon hour their drivers, in dirty undershirts, pendulous bellies hanging over their belts, harassed passing factory girls with the obligatory promises of bedroom performance, which both they and the girls knew could not be kept. Overall hung the stench of moldering uncollected garbage, factory rags discarded in greasy piles, and dried sweat from the bodies of the machine operators as they sat with the *Daily News* on their laps, picking the numbers they would play that would bring them a great fortune and whisk them out of the slums forever.

Goody shipping clerks worked in a row of tiny stalls on the street level of the factory, desperately trying to stay ahead of the huge numbers of orders that grew inexorably into menacing piles beside them.

I was convinced that the chief foreman, Ted Crain, had been chosen for this job from a graduating class of Georgia chain-gang bosses. He bullied the $12-a-week clerks mercilessly, pushing, shoving, slapping, and cursing, sure that the dread of losing even this lousy job would keep us silent and in line. He concentrated on me because he suspected that I was trying to organize the clerks into a union. He was right, except that I had very little idea of how to do it, and the other clerks were dubious of success and terrified of failure.

So it was out of frustration as much as anger that I hit him one day with the butt end of my curved shipping knife. I had been trying to pack, wrap, tie, and address a particularly awkward lot, and Ted Crain was behind me, pushing, jabbing, and goading until something inside me said the hell with it. I turned and aimed a knee at his groin, which so surprised him that he seemed for a second to be more startled than hurt. Then he reddened from his bull neck up and with an angry roar let fly at my head with a hammy fist. It must have been pure instinct for survival that helped me duck the swing and come up full force against his face with the back end of my heavy twine knife.

"Fuck you, Simon Legree!" I could not help exulting, as I heard the sharp crack and felt the impact. He went down in a heap and there was a lot of confusion. Bosses poured in from upstairs. The cops came. Ted Crain's jaw was fractured, and I was arrested for assault.

In jail awaiting a hearing, I had time to think about things. Some of the other shipping clerks came to visit and expressed their admiration and delight with my bravery while explaining that of course they could not testify on my behalf since they needed their jobs. They knew—me being the kind of person I was—that I would understand.

I mulled it over. Without money, they could not afford the luxury of free speech. I could see that. More money, more freedom; no money, no freedom. What about all that other stuff—a good education, travel, the alluring commodities in the magazine ads that defined "the good life"? All yours only if you possessed the magic ingredient. I was in prison, but so was everyone else I knew. We were all chained somewhere along the wheel of economic necessity. The "free-society" rhetoric was baloney without the money key to get in.

The justice system was a bit sloppy in the thirties. When they got around to standing me in front of a judge, he was amused by the sight of burly Ted Crain accusing a 160-pounder of aggravated assault. I got thirty days' probation and what I imagined was an approving little smile from the judge.

When I returned to the streets, things were the same. When people could not pay their rent, their furniture was thrown out into the street. But then other people came with signs and leaflets of protest and fought to put it back. I began to meet these people, the Communists, socialists, and anarchists. They knew so much and had so much to say: the capitalist system was breaking down; it could no longer pretend to meet the needs of the people; it must be replaced by a more humane and equitable system that would erase the immoral exploitation of the oppressed masses for the benefit of a privileged few.

I went to Union Square and was amazed that there were speakers scattered throughout who stood on little boxes and could speak for hours about what was happening the world over without even pausing for breath. Everyone was reading like mad. Marx, Engels, Lenin, the *Daily Worker*, and books, tracts, and periodicals. Over a five-cent cup of coffee and the financial section of the *New York Times*, they would sit for hours tracing and analyzing the economic plunder being carried on by Wall Street's "malefactors of great wealth."

I experienced, read a lot, observed the colossal suffering, and was radicalized. I was not much of a theorist, though. I went to countless meetings and found myself soon bored, even when I agreed with what was being said. I had reached the basic conclusion that it was high time mankind moved forward to a system that would eliminate war, poverty, racism, and chauvinistic nationalism in an atmosphere of freedom and cultural creativity. After that, much of the talk seemed superfluous.

Most of the time I was unemployed and felt the devastating loss of self-worth that comes each day, watching the rest of the world get up and go someplace where they felt needed and useful. It was infinitely more shattering than just not having money. I felt I was a burden to myself and my family at home, so I went down to the railroad yards and hopped on an empty freight-car and headed west to find a job and a future. I was gone for a year and a half.

More than half a million youths my age and younger were drifting around the land chasing the rumors of jobs. There were the occasional short-term stints of harvesting wheat in Kansas, stoop labor in the burning fields of Texas, and stacking malodorous cut corn in the silos of Iowa. But mostly we left our railroad-siding "jungles" to beg for food at the kitchen doors of small-town, middle-class homes, paying heavily with lawns mowed, furnaces stoked, and firewood chopped and stacked in high piles. We rode the rods under the trains, and when we were lucky we crossed whole states inside freight-cars loaded with foodstuffs. Almost everywhere we were chased and clubbed by burly railroad dicks. There were young girls as well as boys, and we paired off, loved, fought, betrayed, deserted, and behaved generally like respectable people in their country clubs.

We would knock on a door that a grimly suspicious matron would open just a crack. "Yes, what do you want?" she'd say, gazing with distaste at the young, unkempt bum at her door.

"I'd like some food, Ma'am. Be glad to work it out if you have some chores to do."

"Well," she'd reply suspiciously, "we could use some wood cut," pointing to a mountainous pile of logs. "Can you use an axe?"

"Sure."

Two hours later, muscles sore and aching, I would receive a sandwich, a glass of milk, and advice: "A healthy young man like you, it's shameful. You should go get a decent job instead of becoming a lazy beggar."

In the late summer of 1933, I was working as a busboy in an all-night diner in Columbia, Missouri. I called my mother in Brooklyn and my younger brother, Hank, answered the phone. He had recently graduated from high school, and he made a proposition: "How about meeting me in Iowa City in a couple of weeks and enrolling in the

University of Iowa? I've checked it out, and we don't need money. We can get jobs and a student loan from the Strong Foundation."

I thought it over carefully for a second or two. Why not? "OK. Meet you there."

Between us, Hank and I had $25. We sat in Dean Reinow's office fully prepared to be told that he admired our aspirations but not our sense of reality. But that remarkable man fooled us. "We are most interested in students motivated enough to make sacrifices to get an education," he told us. "Eighty percent of the students are working their way either wholly or partially. We accept hogs or cattle for in-state students, but we'll have to come up with the $67-a-semester tuition for you two. We'll do it two ways. We'll arrange a student loan, and we'll get some jobs lined up for you two—the heavy jobs for Milt."

We found cheap rooms at the Kimmels' on Dubuque Street. The house and those nearby were rabbit warrens of poor students from all over the country, drawn by Iowa's enlightened work-learn formula. Hank got lucky with a cushy job in the university library, where he met Penny Vincent, the lovely, blond daughter of an unemployed Iowa railwayman. Impatient for love and life, they left school in their junior year to get married and become, they were sure, famous writers.

There was a slight hitch. Iowa law required the posting of banns for three days before the ceremony. Hank and Penny shacked up in a motel to enjoy the wait. Penny's parents, hard-bitten, ultraconservative Methodists, had been furiously opposed to the marriage, but at the last moment they relented and decided to visit the newlyweds bearing forgiveness and gifts. They arrived a day too soon, forcing Hank and Penny to pretend her parents had missed the wedding by a day. They never did get married until ten years later when they had two children. Hank was then a marine in World War II and ineligible for dependents' coverage without a marriage certificate, so the romantic option became an economic necessity.

For me the university—in spite of the hard work stoking furnaces, waiting on tables and being a waiter-bouncer by night—was, after three years of scraping for jobs and living on the road, a luxury cruise on a faraway sea in the company of wonderful companions. I knew it wouldn't last, though. Being a student was a temporary haven from a harsher world, and these bright, energetic, idealistic friends of mine would get their heads knocked together soon enough by a tough, cynical system that would concentrate all their energy into a mind-crushing struggle for personal survival.

Meanwhile, I couldn't help feeling that I had drawn a lucky ticket—books, music, art, athletics, politics, and girls. A secret I had learned early on, which I did not share with my male friends, was that women were by any reasonable measure far superior to men. And Iowa college girls—smart, and beautiful as ripe red apples—were even more so. My studies were almost incidental. I took a smorgasbord of courses because fundamentally I was much more interested in what the world would be than in what I would be.

That world was becoming more and more worrisome, with the deepening depression at home and the rise of Mussolini's fascism and Hitler's nazism abroad. In my senior year I became chairman of the Iowa chapter of the American Student Union. More than four hundred students became active members.

In September of 1936 we decided to hold an anti-war rally. Dick Gates, a gifted young artist, had drawn a graphic poster, a grinning skeleton wearing an American-style helmet against a background of bristling guns. We took copies to be routinely stamped "approved by the President's office" before putting them up around campus. The president's office was artistically and politically shocked to its shoelaces and refused to apply its little stamp.

I called a meeting of the ASU executive committee, and we decided to defy the ban and put up the posters late that night. The Iowa campus is graced by some of the oldest, leafiest, and most beautiful trees to be found on the green earth, and my brother Hank and I and Merle Miller were well up in one of them when a powerful beam of light was aimed at us.

Standing below was the entire Iowa City police force of eight men, the Johnson County sheriff, and the head of the American Legion.

"Come down out of there!" the shout came from the sheriff. He was weaving a bit. He and the American Legion had been drinking, quite heavily.

"Sorry," I said, "we're busy. Got some work to do up here."

"You're under arrest, goddammit. Come down!"

"What's the charge?" I demanded. I prided myself on my knowledge of constitutional rights.

There was a short, intense conference down below, then agreement.

"For COMMITTING COMMUNISM!" the sheriff shouted, waving his long-barreled pistol.

"Yeah," added the American Legion, inspired. "AT NIGHT."

I consulted with Hank and Merle. "It sounds to me," I said, "like a real conceptual breakthrough. I think it would be best to go down."

We were thrown into the police cars and taken to the station house. We sat while one of the cops twirled the barrel of his pistol menacingly, pointing it at us just as he had seen it done in the movies. I demanded our right to make a phone call. The chief came in.

"And just whom is it you wish to call?" he asked sardonically.

"Mayor Tom Martin," I said. Merle and I had headed up a student political action committee that had helped Martin win.

Some of the air went visibly out of the chief's balloon. Martin came on the phone, half-asleep. It was after 1 A.M. I explained.

"Let me talk to the dumb bastard," said the mayor.

We sat and enjoyed the chief's discomfiture and listened to his "Yes, Mr. Mayor. OK, Tom, right away, Tom."

Finally he hung up, turned to us, and snapped, "All right, you can go home now."

"We need our posters," said Merle.

"No way," said the chief.

"Gimme the phone again," I said.

The chief glared but he gave up the posters.

We still hadn't won, though. Not quite yet. There was a vagrancy law in Iowa—after 11 P.M. it was illegal to stop moving. Wherever we went, the cops followed us, so we finally went home.

Some of the most politically active ASU members were in the so-rorities, and we called around and explained the emergency. A dozen young women, among them the Hickenlooper sisters, eagerly accepted such an exciting and challenging assignment. By 4 A.M. posters had sprouted like night-blooming flowers all over the campus.

Bourke B. Hickenlooper, owning a name that sounded like it belonged in the first line of an off-color limerick, was president of the
Iowa state senate and would soon become one of the more atrocious
U.S. senators. He made a phone call to the university's President
Gilmore. According to the Hickenlooper sisters, who were mightily
amused, the conversation went something like this. Hickenloooper:
"Gilmore? I hear there's a whole bunch of goddamn Reds running
your goddamn school down there. If you don't see to it that my daughters stop being molested by Commie New York Jews, you can kiss any
of those appropriations you asked for good-bye. You've seen your last
goddamn state dollar. Understand?" Gilmore: "Yes, Sir. I understand."

Shortly thereafter there was a meeting in President Gilmore's office.
He hinted that he had had a message from Senator Hickenlooper,
chairman of the committee that appropriated, or withheld, funds for
land-grant institutions, of which the university was one.

Clearly uncomfortable, he addressed his remarks to me. "If this university has any validity, it lies in the encouragement of free inquiry,
free expression, the pursuit of truth in an open marketplace of ideas.
I believe your group has expressed similar objectives." He paused.
"The freedom of students is not to be inhibited but the university must
deal with the real world, with practical problems." He went on to talk
about appropriations and budgets and to ask of what use were ideals if
they couldn't keep the doors open.

I smiled to myself, thinking, He who pays the piper calls the tune.
All of us on the committee had gotten the point, and I sensed it was
time to make a deal. We held a strong hand.

"OK, President Gilmore, we see the problem and we have no wish
to embarrass the school. We will have a talk with the Hickenlooper
sisters. We cannot, of course, censure them, but we will try to get their
cooperation, and we are sure we can. We expect in return that there
will be no more nonsense about stamps on our posted material. One
more thing. We are planning a public debate entitled 'What is Americanism?' We would like you to be one of the participants."

President Gilmore knew when to fold the cards. "I predict for you,"
he remarked to me, "a brilliant future in the field of extortion."

In 1936 there were thirteen thousand students at the U of I, the vast

majority of whom concentrated their normally brief span of attention
on their chances for material advancement, football, and casual sex.
Yet almost eight hundred of them attended the anti-war rally we had
undergone such trauma to advertise, and almost all signed a form of
the Oxford Pledge, in essence "I refuse to bear arms in any war." (The
train of history takes many turns. Only five years later they would forget they'd ever made such a pledge.)

All during that fall of 1936 things had not been going well in Spain.
By November Hitler's air force, under the command of Hermann
Goering, was bombing Madrid. Franco's forces, abetted by Moors and
Mussolini's divisions, were surrounding the city. Fighting raged building by building in the university, and the front could be reached by
trolley car. And for the first time, we in the States heard that International Brigade volunteers were helping to defend the Republic.

In Iowa City, discussion raged. Deep anti-war convictions clashed
head-on with anti-Fascist convictions. After centuries of poverty, exploitation, and military, clerical, and monarchic dictatorships, the
Spanish people had voted overwhelmingly for a democratic republic.
In less than a year they'd set land reforms in motion, built schools,
hospitals, and nurseries, and provided support for artists, writers, and
intellectuals in an outburst of constructive energy that thrilled their
own people and progressives throughout the world. But on the eigh-
teenth of July, the old ruling triumvirate had struck. The army, the
landowners, and the church hierarchy wanted their fiefdoms back.
As chief of their crusade, they'd appointed Generalíssimo Francisco
Franco, second to none in his admiration and friendship for Adolf
Hitler.

The great democracies, the U.S.A., France, and Great Britain,
watched these events with an astounding detachment. The League of
Nations meeting in Geneva heard heartbreaking appeals from the rep-
resentatives of the legitimate government of Spain. They asked for the
right not to be given but to *buy* arms with which to defend themselves
from invasion by the armed forces of Nazi Germany and Fascist Italy.
The gentlemen of the "freedom-loving democracies" coughed into
their handkerchiefs and came up with the nonintervention policy. The
indecent fiction they chose to invent was that the war was an internal

affair. Moreover, they would place an export embargo on any assistance to the government in Madrid. Germany and Italy were left free
to pour in the guns to Franco.

I didn't know it then, but I was to be troubled and intrigued for the
rest of my life by the questions of how exactly this policy was arrived at,
who exactly made these decisions, and why exactly they were made.
They are questions that have never been asked, let alone answered.
The answers could very well explain much of the history of the last half
of the twentieth century.

Having been denied official help, the Spanish republic sent a delegation of three to visit college campuses. It included Isabel de Palencia,
the Spanish ambassador to Sweden, a Catholic priest, Father Sarasola,
and a member of the Madrid city council. They spoke movingly to two
hundred students and professors about what was happening in their
country. They described the volunteers, including Americans, who
were forming the International Brigade to fight side by side with them.

That night my roommate, Roger Hargrave, and I had a long talk
about war, fascism, the meaning of life, and the nature of commitment. Then I said, "Enough bullshit. Let's go to Spain."

"Of course," said Roger.

Roger and I had been roommates for two years. Roger's family were
original Iowa homesteaders, and when we first met in Iowa City, Roger
was a state amateur-boxing champion and a staunchly conservative
Republican. He was appalled by the talk that swirled around him
about building a new and better society. He was also confused that I, a
fellow wrestler he liked personally, participated and often led it.

Although conservative, Roger was far from slavish, and he had a
sharp, inquiring mind. He challenged angrily much that he heard.
Then he would read thoroughly everything he could find on the subject. His interest was sharpened by the crisis on the farms. Mortgages
were being foreclosed and farms taken over by large eastern insurance
companies. His own family was in trouble, and his uncle had lost a
farm that had been in the family for eighty-five years. By the time of
our momentous decision, Roger had moved considerably to the left
of me.

We discussed who else would go. Roger said what about Merle

Miller, cochairman of the ASU, so we had a chat with Merle. He was all for the idea but pointed out that he was a gifted writer and could do much more for the cause with a pen than with a gun. Certainly got a point there, we agreed. Others had equally cogent reasons, so it got down to the two of us.

We had to raise money for the busfare to New York, and we had to say our good-byes. Roger had one steady girlfriend, but I was more eclectic so it took me a little longer. There was Laura Saldi, the first violinist in the university's symphony orchestra. She was a slender, highly emotional girl with long black hair, who dealt exclusively in superlatives—things were the best, the worst, the finest, etc. When I told her, she wanted us just to listen quietly to César Franck's Symphony in D Minor. Then she arose and went three steps up the stairs, motioning me to follow. She put a hand on my shoulder and said, "This is a most difficult moment. I will always, always, always remember you dark and intense on the stair." Then she threw her head back dramatically and ran to her room. It made me a little relieved that we were parting.

Beautiful and popular Fran Gustafson was easy. I told her over the phone. "Oh yeah? Groovy. Have fun now, will ya, Honey?"

"Sure," I said, "you bet."

Leah Newman was a different problem. She was quite pretty, with enormous dark eyes. Her father owned a large department store in Omaha, and she had grown up bored stiff with the monotonous repetition of small talk and the suffocating, middle-class rules of morality in which she was forever being instructed. She was curious and intelligent and had fallen in love with the whole anti-war movement. She hero-worshiped romantic student radicals, so it was natural for her to be infatuated with me. When she found out what I was about to do, she almost fainted with admiration.

She had a car and decided we must drive out in the country and wile the night away deciding the ultimate fate of the world. When we got to the country, she had another idea. She kissed me very warmly and said, "Let's make love. When you leave, I want you to be part of me."

We went through the usual manual-of-arms maneuvers and were finally panting and ready. An impenetrable barrier, however, barred the way. Good God, she was a virgin, and I could certainly understand why. I made heroic, increasingly painful efforts. I was afraid I might sustain some awful damage.

"It's no use," I said, "you have a hymen made of reinforced steel."

It hadn't been such a good time for her either, but she didn't want to give up. "Maybe we can go to your house and find a sharp instrument or something," she said. "It has to be done sometime."

But discomfort had cooled my ardor. "I'm truly sorry," I said, putting an arm around her shoulder more in the manner of a friend than a lover. "I am very fond of you, and I will always think of you with feelings of very great, ah, tenderness. There will be other times when everything will be natural and right. Let's not force it."

She accepted gracefully. "You are really a special person," she said.

We had fund-raising parties to raise the busfare to New York and made our departure. The Communist Party had a committee that was organizing the task of getting the volunteers to France, so Roger and I reported at the headquarters that had been set up in a big loft on Second Avenue and Twelfth Street. We applied for passports, stating as the purpose of our trip our intention to become exchange students at the Sorbonne in Paris.

During the wait for the passports, we were all outfitted with identical, ill-fitting cheap blue suits, berets, and, again identical, imitation-leather black valises. When thirty-six of us had gathered, mostly college students but also seamen and young workers from various trades, we were given tickets for an American Export Lines ship, the *President Harding*, leaving the next day. We were also given a short lecture: "Conduct yourselves as ordinary tourists. There are many enemies who do not want you to reach your destination. Be inconspicuous."

Be inconspicuous? Thirty-six young men dressed in similar suits, wearing berets, and carrying identical luggage? Disciplined, however, we were; no one even thought of laughing.

I was put in charge of half of the group and Dick Cloke, a student from Berkeley, of the other half. We went aboard on the fourth of March, 1937. I had an address. If we made it, my group was to rendezvous at 22, Place du Combat, Paris, the headquarters of the Parisian Central Trade Union Congress.

As the ship slid past the Statue of Liberty and out of the New York harbor, Roger and I leaned on the rail next to each other and shivered in the cold. We were silent and thoughtful. We were on our way to war, and in war, people die.

"So," I said, "got any second thoughts?"

"About going? Nope. You?"

"Not really. Not about whether it's the right thing to do. What would it be like for us if we didn't go? More meetings? More blah, blah, blah, blah about how somebody ought to do something about those nasty Nazis? No matter how it comes out, we would spend the rest of our lives making excuses, like Merle, or despising ourselves for being dilettantes, cheering the action on the field while sitting safely in the grandstand. Actually, if I were asked what in the world I would most like to be doing and where in the world I would most like to go, the answer would be just what we're doing and just where we're going. That doesn't mean I don't get nervous. Last night I couldn't sleep because I worried about the possibility of getting hit by a stray bullet. I thought I wouldn't mind if I were shooting at an enemy and he were shooting at me and I went down like in a Henry Fonda movie—that's OK, the luck of the draw. But if I were back of the lines eating breakfast during a quiet lull and some stray bullet not going anywhere in particular, not actually aimed at anyone, went through my brain and did me in purely by stupid accident, I would be very upset!"

Roger smiled. "You half-assed intellectuals are all alike. Things have to be tidy, delivered to you with a fancy, metaphysical bow on top. Now me, I was thinking there might be bullfights, dark-eyed señoritas, wine, and peasants singing *Carmen* in the village square."

"Roger, you remain, under that veneer of revolutionary dedication, a true son of the sexually repressed Methodists who replaced all the old worn-out chastity belts in Iowa with one big Bible belt."

"You used to come up with better stuff than that," said Roger. "Come on. Let's get some rest."

That turned out to be not so easy. The volunteers had been provided with the cheapest accommodations on the ship, barely above the water line. We were out of the harbor less than three hours when a violent, late-winter North Atlantic storm hit with overwhelming ferocity, almost tumbling us from our narrow beds. The gale was to follow us clear across the Atlantic, delaying our arrival in Le Havre by two full days. The passengers were in a panic, sure that the ship would founder and sink. We were beset by what the captain called a "quartering sea." Such a sea slams into the ship from the rear, midway between midship and stern. The wind from that direction whipped the waves into heaving mountains, lifted the stern clear out of the water, and drove the prow deep down into the next wave. Each time the stern came clear, the giant spinning propeller, freed of resistance, shook the ship with a sickening shudder. I was reminded of a long-haired dog shaking after a swim.

Down in the hold, the cargo began to shift after three days of battering. Two railroad-car wheels we were carrying broke loose and began to roll back and forth, slamming with each roll into the side of the ship with a terrifying bang. The passengers were sure it was a tolling of our watery doom, for one wheel or both, we were convinced, would break through the side and send the ship to the bottom.

Seasickness had hit the passengers by the second day, and all of the crew, including the captain, by the fourth day. There were only two exceptions—Roger Hargrave, who had never in his life seen a body of water larger than Spirit Lake, Iowa, and a German prostitute, who was being deported. Having the entire ship virtually abandoned to them alone, they roamed the heaving decks, clinging to each other, becoming friends and then lovers. Their only complaint was food. In the deserted dining rooms they would bang their dishes futilely, since the cooks and waiters were just as sick as everyone else. They made their own sandwiches, and Roger brought one to me. I looked at it with disgust and accused him of selling out to the German agent he was running around the ship with.

Neither passengers nor crew had any doubt about who the young "tourists" wearing berets were or about where we were going. Two hours before the ship docked in Le Havre, we were called into the ship's salon and given a speech by a State Department representative, who had come on board with the pilot boat.

"The government knows where you intend to go," he began, "and it is my duty to inform you that you are making a very serious and costly mistake. If you enlist in the armed forces of another country, you will

forfeit your American citizenship, and you may very well be prose-
cuted for violating the nonintervention policies of the U.S." He continued, threatening and cajoling, and then concluded, "The U.S. government has very generously arranged to pay for your return passage to
New York. If you will just sign these releases . . ." Dead silence. Then
a voice said, "Let's get the hell out of here. I just can't wait to see the
Eiffel Tower."

CHAPTER 3

1937

Thirty-six berets got on the boat train from Le Havre to Paris. When we reached the train station, La Gare Saint-Lazare, we smelled trouble. It was common knowledge that the Popular Front government was torn internally and vacillated from day to day about whether to cheer or jail the volunteers threading through France from fifty countries on their way to Madrid. From the heavy concentration of gendarmes visible at the end of the station platform, all of whom were eyeing the detraining passengers in a most unfriendly and suspicious manner, it was a good bet that this was one of the jail days.

Roger, Dick Cloke, and I held a quick conference. We would split into three groups and walk casually to the end of the platform. Just before reaching the gendarmes we would make a run, Roger's group straight ahead, Dick Cloke's to the left, and mine to the right. We all had the rendezvous address, about $20 in francs, and instructions to get there any way we could.

It went fine at first. Roger and another beret walked up to the stiff-backed cops with a smile. But when the smile was not returned and papers were demanded, Roger delivered a quite good left-right combination to one surprised man and headed for the exit, pursued by shouting, club-wielding police.

What had been a calm and normal depot turned into a French version of the Marx brothers' *A Day at the Races*. Clearly the majority of the crowd were not in love with the police, and while they had no idea what was going on, they threw themselves into the fray with enthusiasm, seeing it as their civic duty to impede the pursuing gendarmes, shouting, pushing, and cleverly getting in the way. It was everyone for himself, and I made it out the door. As we all scattered, I got to the front cab alone.

My French was rusty. "Quick," I said, "Vite, vite! Place du Combat!" The driver caught only the "combat" part. He could see there was a combat. What was it about, the driver wanted to know. There wasn't much time. I took all my money out of my pocket, waved it under the driver's nose, and shouted at him to get going, "Allez, allez!" The driver paid no attention to my garbled attempt at French but he spoke money very well, and my head almost came off when he jammed the Renault into gear and left on two wheels.

All afternoon the midwestern-looking berets kept straggling in to the Central Trade Union Hall with pleased tales of our ingenuity in avoiding the *flics*. We drank in the sights of an early Parisian spring, eyeing appreciatively the pretty young women and admiring their Continental flair. But where was Roger Hargrave?

Half a dozen others were also missing and we assumed they had been arrested. I knew that Roger, even if he was not in physical danger, would be embarrassed and frustrated and would blame himself for not having been skillful enough to reach our rendezvous address safely. I had grown very close to him over time and had come to rely on his solid good sense. When, later that evening, three members of the committee in charge of getting us down through France and into Spain addressed us and there was still no sign of Roger, I began to imagine dire scenarios and paid little attention.

The police action we had just witnessed was a reflection, they said, of the worsening political climate in "socialist" Leon Blum's France. While the people were overwhelmingly anti-Franco, the government was being pushed to the right by British and American pressure. Pope Pius XI had mobilized the church hierarchy to vilify and oppose the Spanish Loyalist government. I remembered then that there had been much speculation in Washington that Roosevelt had paid for Catholic church support in the 1936 election with a pledge to participate in the guillotining of the Spanish republic by supporting nonintervention.

Blum, nervous about his own position in a heavily Catholic country, was capitulating more each day. It would be more and more difficult to get the volunteers through. We might have to stay in Paris many days, perhaps weeks, until the underground could organize safe passage. Relatively safe, that is.

Meanwhile we would be called upon to exercise the most inordinate self-discipline. We were young men in Paris in the spring, but that was to be forgotten. We were vanguard members of the world's first anti-

Fascist volunteer army, and everything we did would reflect well or ill on the heroic Spanish people. We would be housed in cheap nearby hotels, would be fed in working-class cafes, and would spend our days at the Union Hall playing chess, reading inspiring literature, and discussing the finer points of the theory of surplus value. As a leader of my group, or what was left of it, I was asked to add a few words along the same lines, so I did.

For the next three weeks, most of the volunteers did not play much chess. Discreetly, we had a fine time poking around Montparnasse, the Left Bank, and Les Deux Magots. Most of us did, but not all. Two years later in a bombed-out olive grove I came across an emaciated, grimy, unshaven soldier whom I recognized with some difficulty as Dick Cloke.

"You misbegotten son of a bitch," said Dick with real feeling. "The last time I saw your ugly face was in Paris. You made a big speech about self-discipline and went right out and got laid and had yourself a ball for three weeks."

"What did you do?" I asked.

"I played fuckin' chess," said Dick.

"You have perhaps learned," I said, "that there is a certain gap between theory and practice."

During our wait in Paris, other volunteers joined us. One was David McKelvy White, son of the former governor of Ohio. He had left a post teaching English at the City College of New York. He was tall, very thin, balding, and wore enormous horn-rimmed glasses. At all times he carried with him, like a security blanket, a heavy, one-volume *Collected Works of Shakespeare*. He and I became friends at once.

Our liaison, Marcel, came in one morning finally and grabbed the first twenty men in sight, among them David and me. "Gather your things, we're leaving," he said. "Quickly! Quickly!" Sit on your ass for three weeks, and then quickly, quickly, I thought, but I was glad to go.

At La Gare de Lyon, it was still early morning. We boarded the third-class car, carrying paper bags with pâté on fresh rolls, cheese, and fruit. Marcel gave us each a ticket for Alès, shook hands, looked deeply into our eyes, said good luck, and was gone. After we boarded, another man from the underground entered our car and sat unobtrusively by himself in a rear seat.

David and I sat together. We talked about how the war was going in Spain, especially about the massacre in the bullring at Badajoz, where Franco had gathered and machine-gunned thousands. David was a student of Spain's history of blood and violence—its colonial expansion, its defeat and occupation for eight hundred years by the Moors, its degeneration under a corrupt and dissolute monarchy content to mire the mass of the population in poverty for the benefit of a few landowners, bishops, and generals.

But as we looked out the window, Spain seemed unreal and far away. The heartland of France rolled past, beautiful, fecund, and sleepily peaceful in the sunny spring day. David had a small Michelin map, and we could follow our progress through Loire-et-Cher, Haute Vienne, Dordogne, and into the Aude past Carcassonne. We had American tourist reactions to glimpses of châteaux and black-clad peasants working in the fields. We ate our delicious sandwiches and washed them down with local wine in pop bottles, which we'd purchased during long pauses at stations where freights and expresses would zoom by going in the opposite direction.

Late in the afternoon, relaxation ended with a snap. The underground man, silent and unnoticed during the trip, stood up suddenly and said, "We will get off at the next stop."

The next stop was Tameris, not even a town, not even a village. Just a few houses and a tiny depot. No one else got off. The train gave its distinctive French whistle, then added a few tootles like a salute. The underground man raised an arm and waved, the engineer waved back, and the train left.

Across from the depot, a slender red- and white-painted road barrier lifted its arm as the train rattled away. The underground man gathered the volunteers in a circle around him in the middle of the narrow dirt road. It was late afternoon.

"The rest of the way to Alès we will walk," he said in heavily accented but understandable English. "It is about two kilometers. The town is friendly and the chief of police also, who lived many years in

Chicago [I was not surprised]. But still we must be careful. There are everywhere enemies. As we approach the town it is necessary to look like normal tourists. Go in pairs. Stay at least seventy-five meters apart."

The volunteers, adrenalin rising to the thrill of clandestine adventure, followed his instructions to the letter. David and I walked together. As we neared the main square, the pair in front of us motioned somewhat frantically for us to fall back a few paces to maintain the prescribed distance. Dave and I began to giggle and then dissolved into helpless laughter. It was indeed a sight to delight a Daumier.

Picture twenty young men wearing identical berets, dressed in identical suits, and carrying identical suitcases, walking in pairs exactly seventy-five meters apart, pretending to be oblivious of each other, pretending even harder to behave as they imagined ordinary American tourists might behave, and succeeding only in looking like exactly what they really were. To Dave and me, and pretty soon to some of the others, it was irresistibly hilarious. The few onlookers who happened by must also have been carefully instructed because they too pretended that what they were seeing was not what they were seeing.

The underground man led us across the town square to the municipal *crèche*, the town nursery. It was housed in a large building one flight above street level, and we were to stay there for the next two weeks. The street level of the huge building had dozens of narrow doorways hung with brightly colored bead curtains, and lounging in front of each one, outlining themselves in the most provocative poses, were the officially recognized prostitutes of the province, who called out cheerful suggestions for group bargain rates for the nice American "tourists" as we made our way upstairs to the nursery.

We found ourselves in a very large room with walls decorated with children's crayon drawings, bright stick figures of people, animals, and buildings done with children's characteristic, direct honesty. The floor was almost entirely covered with a foot and a half of new straw. Blankets were issued. Dave and I staked out a spot and Dave said, "How long do you think it will be before we have a meeting?"

"I'd give it forty-five minutes at the outside," I said.

"Thirty," Dave guessed. He was right.

Hugh Slater, a British ex–foreign correspondent, chaired the meeting. A tall, handsome young man, he had already been in Spain with a group of English volunteers and had returned to help organize the larger groups that were now in formation. I felt that he dressed just a shade too nattily. Slater introduced a leathery-faced young-to-middle-aged man who wore a cap and had a bandanna around his neck.

"Comrades, you must stay here some days," he began. "It cannot be helped. To cross the border, many arrangements must be made. Government policy is each day worse. Yesterday, fourteen comrades were arrested on the Pyrenees, and they remain now in jail in Toulouse. Even here in Alès there is danger. It is much better if you go quickly. In the night, be ready to leave at each moment. In the day, as you wish, but *en garde*, eh?"

He left, and Slater began the obligatory declamation stating that we were symbols of all that was noble, good, and true in the anti-Fascist cause and that the comportment of Caesar's wife would be that of a slattern compared to the shining example we were constrained to provide. Many of the volunteers translated this to mean that we should avoid contracting syphilis.

No meeting was ever allowed to pass without an in-depth analysis of how that day's events affected the social, economic, and political balance of power in the world. My attention wandered. But at the end of the meeting, someone picked up a guitar and we began to sing the songs of Woody Guthrie and Joe Hill, and even some Gilbert and Sullivan. We sounded happy when we sang. We liked each other, we liked what we were doing, we liked ourselves.

Before we went to sleep that night, Dave said to me, "Someday I would like to teach a course on the dynamics of meetings. First session—things to be avoided: the Beating of Dead Horses, or the Repetition of the Obvious. We have volunteered to die for our beliefs, but not by being bored to death." I agreed. He continued, "Notify us in advance: 'This here meeting is to formulate policy; all theorists welcome. Next meeting is for carrying out policy; all convinced activists please attend.'"

Before long more volunteers arrived, older and more seasoned than the Americans—farmers and fishermen from the Scandinavian countries, miners from the Balkans, factory workers from France and Belgium, building-trades laborers from England and Canada. They came from many countries and all walks of life, and the babel of tongues drew us to sympathetic reconsideraton of George Bernard Shaw's dream of one international language. There were more than eighty of us jammed into the second-floor *crèche*, struggling to be nice to each other and to avoid the irritation of too many bodies too close to each other and too foreign to each other.

The leadership committee, chosen by vote and added to by volunteers, organized serious, uplifting activities for us. Dave gave hour-and-a-half-long classes both in aesthetics and on the politics of Julius Caesar. Hugh Slater taught philosophy and dialectics. A heavily bearded Yugoslav who spoke three languages, all badly, tried to teach the underlying economic objectives of World War I, but it came out as an unintelligible linguistic goulash.

There were also card games, a chess tournament, and in the evening more speeches and folk songs. Whether performed well or badly, the songs, from Belgium, Greece, Romania, Finland, Sweden, Croatia, France, and several other countries, were warmly applauded. At the end of one evening, someone in the audience remarked, rather tartly, that there had been no songs from Spain.

Ten days dragged by pleasantly enough but slowly. Having come so far, some were actually fearful that the war would end before they could be part of it. Much of that feeling came from a sense of a direct connection with history, but there was also the excitement and challenge of testing oneself under fire, a deep-rooted, ancient rite of male passage. Very handy for general staffs.

Dave and I often strolled around the bustling marketplace together, wondering what had happened to Roger Hargrave and whether he would make it to Alès in time to join the climb we knew we had to make over the snow-capped Pyrenees. This trek loomed constantly in our vision and in our thoughts. Meanwhile we shopped in the Bon Marché for toilet articles and listened to Edith Piaf songs over the loudspeaker. One time we came face to face with the local chief of police.

"Bonjour," said Dave, with what he imagined was a Continental bow.

The chief considered us for a moment. "Where are you from?" His tone was noncommittal, neither friendly nor unfriendly.

"Ohio."

"Iowa."

"Ah, yes," he beamed. "Perhaps you know Chicago? I was for two years living in Chicago."

"Sure," I said, "we know Chicago quite well."

"Then, maybe, you know my brother? Claude Letellier? He is *sous-chef* in the Palmer House."

The chief waited expectantly while we seemed to search our memories. No, the name was not familiar. The chief's manner then turned very cold. We must be charlatans, claiming to be from Chicago and not knowing Claude.

Dave jumped into the breech. "Next time I'm in Chicago, I'll certainly look Claude up, Sir."

Somewhat mollified, the chief shrugged his shoulders and walked away.

"As ridiculous and absurd as it may seem," I mused, "do you realize that if we had merely, by some wild chance, had the slightest contact with this Claude, the chief would have presented us with his favorite daughter in gratitude?"

"Sure," said Dave, "we humans are lonely molecules in limitless space. Show us in the slightest way that we are connected, and we fall on our faces in seizures of reassurance and thankfulness."

That night our liaison came wearing his cap and bandanna. "Make yourselves into groups of five and come quickly. Go downstairs and wait inside the door. When a car stops outside, five will get in, two in front, three in back. Go." Dave and I were assigned the second car.

We went very fast on back roads. Twice we stopped in villages where the driver used a pay telephone. After the second one, he said, "The border is closed. You cannot climb the mountain tonight. I will take you to a house in Port-la-Nouvelle where you can stay till the way is clear. I think not long."

He dropped us off in two houses, three in one, Dave and I in the other. Our hosts, a middle-aged couple, apologized for the plainness of their accommodations, a small working-class cottage. They spoke a bit of English, and Dave and I said it was just fine, and how very good it was of them to take the risks that must be involved in defying government policy.

"*Merde* on the government," snorted our host, who we learned was a fisherman. "They talk *antifascisme* while Spain burns. One day France will pay a dear price if Spain falls to the Bosche."

They could not do enough for the Americans who had come so far. They brought in their close, trusted friends and showed off Dave and me like rare artifacts. Food and wine were pressed on us. We tried very hard not to feel that we deserved all this, but we admitted a little corruption was setting in. We were beginning to enjoy it. Fortunately, as dusk was becoming night three days later, a car came for us and our self-respect was preserved—for the time being.

The car was a Citroen taxicab, black and old. The driver told us to scrunch down out of sight, so we piled on top of each other on the floor as the car bumped and raced along. Then it swerved off the road with a sickening lurch, the door opened, and we tumbled out.

We were under a huge tree, and we saw that others were there. We were about thirty in all, not all Americans, maybe a little more than half. There were Austrians, British, a Belgian, and a Hollander, mostly older than the Americans, but there wasn't time to get acquainted.

A very old man who carried what looked like a shepherd's staff stepped forward. Around his shoulders he wore what looked like an old-fashioned black opera-cloak, and on his feet were rope-soled *alpargatas*, the peasant footwear of Spain. He knew enough English for his task. "I will lead you to Spain," he said, "but you must do *exactamente* what I tell to you. From this moment no talking—not a sound. Closely, very close, you must follow me. It is far. You must be brave."

As he spoke, some had whispered to each other. "Shame. To send such an old man. Let's be careful not to push him too hard. Doesn't even have a decent pair of shoes. OK, OK." Before we could react the old man had turned and loped off at a deceptively fast pace. We crossed a road, and almost immediately we were climbing, at first gently and then more steeply.

Within twenty minutes we were panting and gasping for breath. The old man pushed on relentlessly.

Suddenly, we didn't know why, he stopped and motioned for us to lie flat and still. A minute or two later we heard the voices of French border guards. Arrests had become more frequent, we knew, and we tried to melt into the ground, hardly breathing. The voices seemed nearer but actually they were receding. When there was complete silence, the old man got up and resumed the climb. We were thankful that we had not been discovered, but we were almost as thankful for the opportunity to catch our breath.

The mountain got steeper, the terrain rougher. The old man followed a faint trail through heavy forest. There were rocks to climb, wet and slippery. Most of the volunteers wore ordinary shoes though some, like me, had modified walking boots. We slipped and stumbled and fell and learned respect for the humble *alpargatas*.

Always a trifle too proud of my physical condition, I was getting a cram course in humility. I had been a pretty good college wrestler and had a clavicle that had been detached from my sternum to prove it. I had jogged mile after mile in training with my friend Glenn Cunningham (who had come very close to the four-minute mile), and I could do fifty push-ups just to get started on a warm-up.

On that trek my chest felt like it was on fire. My legs were useless lead weights, and I was ready to beg for mercy. Most of the time I had carried Dave's *Shakespeare*, which really weighed a couple of pounds but seemed to weigh at least a hundred. I began to hate the bard and to think of him as a wordy old bastard. Bad as I felt, the others were in much worse shape. Soon we were climbing into the cold, and our wet leather shoes became stiff. We developed enormous blisters. We hated to, and fought against it, but we had to plead for rest.

As I sat next to Dave, who by this time was hardly conscious and going on pure nerve, I pointed ahead. "That," I gasped, "is not a man. It's a goddamn mountain goat or an ancient satyr sent by Nazi-minded Valkyries to destroy us." We were told later that our guide, like others, was one of the professional Basque smugglers who spent their lives roaming the Pyrenees along trails known only to them. And that he was seventy-four years old.

We climbed past the timberline and reached snow. Feet and hands were near to freezing. Heads hanging down, we kept our eyes only on the feet ahead of us. Sometimes it felt as if we must be nearing the crest, but another, higher peak would loom inexorably above us. We had to surmount a jumble of snow-covered, huge rocks. The Hollander lost his footing, fell, and slid to the bottom of a rock. His knee was painfully wrenched and he couldn't move. The climbing stopped, and the old man hurried back to see what was wrong. After a glance, he said, "We must leave him. Come. There is no time to lose. We must cross the border before the dawn."

No one moved. "He will be found very soon. The police. We are near the border," the old man continued. "Shall we all fail?"

The group got up to follow. "I will stay with him," said one of the Austrians. And that is how it was. Just before the dawn broke, we crossed the crest of the Pyrenees and the border. We had come to Spain.

CHAPTER 4

1937

In the *crèche* at Alès we had learned the anthem of the Spanish republic, and after crossing the border we sang it. We sang it self-consciously, because it is not easy to sing and sounds like music appropriate to performers marching in at the opening of the circus. An hour later we came to a plateau and saw what appeared to be all of Spain laid out at our feet, shining in the rising sun, dotted with villages and farms, as far as the eye could see. Nothing on earth could have looked more beautiful to us, or more peaceful.

Near the bottom, flatbed trucks picked us up. We were so near total exhaustion that the driver and his assistant, both soldiers, had to help us in. We were anxious to drink in the look of the country we had come to defend, but we could barely hold our heads up—until from about a mile away we could see, rising like a mirage from the plain, what it was we were headed for.

"It's a fuckin' castle in Spain," someone, probably a Britisher, said. "Too bloody much."

It was indeed a storybook castle. It even had a drawbridge and a moat. It was the property of the Duke of Alba, a strong supporter of Franco, financially and ideologically. It was one of his hunting lodges, the most northern one. It stood in the center of an area the size of two counties that he used as a preserve for an occasional hunting party. Around it for many miles peasants went hungry for lack of land to grow food.

The Republic had claimed the castle, at least temporarily, as its own. Spanish army soldiers lounged about and cheered us when we came in. They offered us terrible coffee in large mugs along with delicious hot bread.

Next morning we were taken to Figueras to the ancient Moorish fort, two-thirds of it underground. There was one room so immense that a hundred cots looked lost in it. Down from a seventy-foot-high ceiling hung black iron fixtures with what looked like gigantic meat hooks. Medieval knights, we were told, hung their spears and lances from those very hooks. Arches, Moorish naturally, led off everywhere to other spaces, other rooms.

A feeling of history pressed in on us. My cot was next to Dave's, and as we lay looking up at the massive lance-hangers I remarked, "One cannot say that civilization has not advanced. Those crude things must have left great, gaping holes in the foe, whilst today we have those neat round little bullets. I for one say hoorah for progress."

"Not so fast," said Dave. "I hear that on the Madrid front the Moors are using the newest in explosive bullets that leave great gaping holes."

"Sometimes," I sighed, "conversation with you certified college-teacher intellectuals can be very depressing. Particularly after a very depressing nightmare I had last night."

"I lie here atingle with anticipation," said Dave, "so what was the nightmare?"

"I dreamed that we were the victims of a giant hoax, that all the winners of all the battles from the beginning of time had really been the losers, and that the losers had really won."

"So why were you depressed?"

"Because no one could tell the difference."

"I do not find it easy to be friends with you," said Dave. "Please go to sleep, and for God's sake don't dream."

The fort was almost full, and volunteers were coming in from forty or fifty countries. While we waited for transportation to Albacete de la Mancha, the International Brigade headquarters city, some of the more zealous types felt no time should be wasted. Military training should begin at once. The Swedes, Danes, Serbs, Dutch, Palestinians, Germans, French, and most other volunteers had seen army service. The Germans, asserting an unchallengeable military birthright, took the lead, mobilizing everyone onto the parade ground.

"Have we officers here?" they asked in German. Translators volunteered and the question was laboriously sifted through a stew of languages. Two Frenchmen, a Pole, and a Serb stepped forward. With the dubious aid of volunteer translators who had the merest smattering of linguistic facility, the new, self-appointed officer corps discussed how the training should proceed.

There were disagreements, misunderstandings, misinterpretations. This was going to take some time. Everyone sat down and began to grumble.

"Who needs this shit," summed up, basically, the American position. The French muttered unkind words about the mechanical inflexibility of the Hun. The English got a fire going and made tea.

A compromise was worked out. We would form up in squads, march up and down in step, and sing "revolutionary" songs from each country. It didn't work out too badly, except when we tried to turn or do an about-face. By the time the translations were called out on those commands, the marching singers tangled in a hopeless mess. Training was silently abandoned.

We still had to wait, so on Sunday Dave and I went to a movie in the town of Figueras. All we knew was that it began at noon, and we were mystified when at the box office we were given tickets eight inches long. We asked for an explanation.

"For the first film," we were told, "we take the top part here and tear it off. From 2 P.M. until 3, you may take lunch, very light, eh? You come here at 3, we take this next part of your ticket, and you will enjoy the big movie. At 5:30 you will go to a nice cafe—there are many on this street—for an aperitif, a vermouth-cassis, or if you prefer, a fine *jerez*. And you will have olives and almonds, and you may watch the *chicas* as they make the *paseo*. You return here at 7, and we remove this part. At 9:30 there are in Figueras fine restaurants where you may take dinner. May I suggest the sea food of the Basques? This final part of your ticket we will remove when you come at 11 for the last *pelicula*, very nice. At 1 A.M. it is over, *finito*."

"*Finito*, indeed, and so will we be," I remarked to Dave. "When these people go to the movies they don't screw around."

All the films were American, dubbed into Spanish. It took time to adjust to Clark Gable gazing into a starlet's eyes and murmuring *Te quiero* in a voice one had always associated with villainous Mexicans in cowboy movies. When we returned at 3 after lunch, moviegoers were lined up around the block to see the big hit, Charlie Chaplin (Charlot) in *Tiempos Modernas*. I found it curious that a film satirizing the enslavement of modern workers by the very machinery that was supposed to free them was so popular in a country that had practically no machinery at all.

But Dave seemed absorbed in other thoughts. We were sitting at a sidewalk table. It was aperitif time and we were following the ticket-seller's instructions, eating olives and almonds from small dishes on the marble table and drinking dry sherry from tall glasses.

"What did you think of that training fiasco yesterday?" asked Dave.

"You hinting that if the workers of the world are to unite they will need to master Esperanto long before they get to Karl Marx?"

"Not exactly," Dave paused to light his pipe. "The problem is more fundamental than the funny sounds that come out of our mouths— more like the funny ideas that come out of our heads. Consider. We gather here from the four corners of the world with a shared political outlook, and the first stab we make at moving together shoves us apart. In the course of an hour we were transformed from warm, anti-Fascist brothers into Germans, Americans, Dutchmen, and what have you, irritated, annoyed, and exasperated with one another over nothing. Something deep in our psyches marches to our own national anthems. There is a long long way to go."

I chewed a delicious toasted almond. "So what do you want? A homogeneous glob? Wherever you look is Cleveland? Remove differences, underneath is sameness. Sameness is dullness."

"*Touché*," said Dave. "Same is tame. But on the other hand, differences can kill. Or hadn't you noticed?"

"What I did notice is how easy it is to tell a German from a Frenchman and a Frenchman from an Englishman. So what do they think of when they see an American?"

"Money," said Dave. "You may personally be a pauper but you represent a society that makes them into tenant farmers on an American plantation. Do not expect to be loved."

"Yeah," I said, "you have a point. Yesterday I was trying to explain to some of the Spanish soldiers at the fort that there was a big depression in America, that people were unemployed and starving. They wouldn't believe it, so I showed them a picture of an unemployment demonstration in Union Square. Instead of sympathy, they fell to laughing like mad. I got a little upset. 'Those people suffer from dire poverty,' I said. They burst out laughing again and pointed at the picture. 'But they all have shoes!'"

The day after our movie marathon we boarded a train for Barcelona. For days we had sensed a vague uneasiness in the air, more pronounced now as the train crawled hesitatingly toward the city. And just outside the city, we were handed rifles.

"No need for alarm," said a Spanish lieutenant, "the gun is only a precaution. There is some trouble in the city. It will soon be over. You will not be involved. Remain calm. *Viva la república. ¡Salud!"*

I looked over at Dave who was holding his rifle at arm's length and examining it gingerly through his heavy glasses as though it were some rare museum artifact. "You couldn't hit a bull in the ass with a steam shovel, Dave. Why don't you put the damn thing some place where it won't hurt anybody, and let's go and try to find out what the hell is going on."

The train pulled into the station. We heard shots and saw people running in the streets. It was the first of May, 1937; the Trotskyists and the Anarcho-Syndicalists were having themselves a revolution against the Madrid government. On the train, however, we did not know this. Then the train jerked convulsively and we were off at a clip no one had dreamed possible. An officer came through with several soldiers. They smiled warmly all around and collected the rifles.

At Tarragona a major came aboard to brief us. "The fighting is contained to a few areas. In a day or so it will be over."

"Are they underground Fascists? The fifth column?" asked a volunteer.

"No," the major grimaced. "They believe they are more anti-Fascist than you. The anarchists oppose the government because it is a government. When authority in any manner is given, that authority will be abused. It is their belief that all decisions, including military decisions, should be made by a democratic vote of all who will be affected by the decision. To give power to politicians or generals is to invite corruption. The Trotskyists oppose the Republic because they believe it to be a bourgeois capitalist state that also oppresses the workers."

"That is the kind of anti-fascism sure to warm the cockles of Francisco Franco's heart," murmured Dave to me.

"The timing does seem a mite suspect," I agreed. "Wonder what was holding back their revolt against the monarchy all those years."

Among the volunteers, discussion was heated, intense, troubled, and angry. Ideological, like theological, differences arouse the deepest passions. Catholics, Baptists, Methodists, Mormons, professed believers in one Bible and one Christ, someone observed, were pretty rough on each other, witness Ireland for one.

"It's the interpreters that bother me," came another voice, "the priests who tell you what Marx really meant, or God, or Muhammad. Those bastards always seem to live so well."

The major listened and said he thought the anarchists had the worst problem. They hated the idea, he explained, of an army structure, but many of them did want to fight for the Republic. So for months, early in the morning in Barcelona's Plaza de Cataluña, trucks would load up with men and women in overalls carrying a weird assortment of guns, suitcases packed with personal necessities, guitars, lunches, and bottles of wine. They would then conduct a vote as to which front they would attend that day. Precisely at 8:30 A.M. they would zoom off, singing anarchist songs and waving rifles with little flags tied to the barrel. At the selected front they fought fiercely till noon, the time for lunch, siesta, and more singing. At 2:30 fighting resumed till 6 P.M., the time to load up the trucks and go home. The Fascists caught on and inflicted great casualties both on the anarchists and on the regular troops at their exposed flanks. Fighting according to union rules soon ended. "Recently," the major went on, "the majority chose a leader, Durruti, formed a division, put on uniforms, and offered their support to the Madrid government."

David White, who had resumed reading, looked up from his big book and remarked, "Pure theory always seems to put up a losing fight in an impure world."

"Your man Shakespeare was pretty smart," I said, "sticking to murderous uncles, ungrateful daughters, scheming rivals, and backstabbing friends. He knew better than to speculate about what movers and shakers were behind all those kings, queens, and soldiers."

In Albacete we went to the big bullring and exchanged our civilian clothes for "uniforms" considerably richer in diversity than the black

suits we had been wearing for ten weeks since New York. We did keep
the berets. Mechanical skills were in short supply, and we were all
asked whether anyone had them. Two brothers from Cleveland, who
all the way from Paris had boasted of their fighting prowess, stepped
forward and volunteered—to drive trucks. The rest said we came here
to do it at the front.

The training village, twenty dusty miles away, was Tarazona de la
Mancha. We jounced along the dry, potholed road on the back of a
Russian truck.

"Cervantes country," observed Dave. "Don Quixote slept here."

"That," I noted, "sounds like an allusion to his well-known habit of
tilting at windmills. Are you suggesting in that elliptical way you have
that that is an analogy to what we have come to this place to do?"

"No," said Dave, "if it only were."

We were quartered all over the village in the homes of peasants.
They had been tenant farmers for generations, and the Republic's land
reform had given them a plot of their own and a share in the village
collective. They looked on the volunteers much as the embattled farmers of Massachusetts, beset by British redcoats, must have looked at
Lafayette. The house Dave and I were in had a dirt floor and a large
fireplace, with a hole in the thatched roof above it for a chimney. The
peasant's wife used an enormous, black iron frying pan to make potatoes and eggs fried in olive oil. She basted the eggs with spoonfuls of
the hot oil, and they were delicious. We decided the secret ingredient
was the smoke.

We were formed into a battalion of four companies commanded by
a six-foot-four ex–economics professor from Zagreb, Yugoslavia, by
the name of Mirko Markevitch, who greeted us each morning on the
parade ground by shouting NORRRT AHMARYCAN BATTALYOWN ATTEN-
TION! Then the four company commanders took their groups off for a
day of "training"—running, darting, falling, and fruitless attempts to
dig foxholes in the rock-hard clay soil. We had rifles, but we couldn't
shoot because what ammunition there was was needed at the front.

Dave and I were in the machine-gun company, commanded by a
handsome black lieutenant, an American from Ohio named Walter
Garland. Had we suddenly been transported to the continental United

States, the idea of white troops being commanded by a black in 1937 would have caused mass apoplexy among the entire student body of West Point, and long speeches by Southern congressmen about the imminent fall of Western civilization as we have known it. The volunteers hardly noticed.

There were four machine guns, each different, each requiring different caliber ammunition—which wasn't available in any case. Dave and I were assigned the newest gun, a World War I German-made Maxim. We named it "Mother Bloor" after a legendary union organizer. It was water-cooled and heavy, even for two men to pull, but when we were allowed a rare test-firing, we found it had an authentic machine-gun voice, not like the French Colt or the British Vickers the others had, both of which sounded like a five-horsepower outboard motor at low speed.

By day we went through a respectable parody of traning, and in the evening we mingled with the villagers, making friends and flirting with the *señoritas*. War correspondents from all over the world came to interview us. For the press, it was an ideal war—about the right size to be comprehensible, colorful, good climate, all battlefields within reach of good hotels and bars, and casualties on both sides they really didn't give a shit about. It even had celebrities. Paul Robeson came and sang to us, his rich bass filling every corner of the village church, which was now a storage place for the grain and farm supplies of the village cooperative.

In the house where we stayed, Dave and I had asked our host why all the churches had been stripped. "The high church and the landowner were like this," he twined his fingers. "The church did not serve God. It served the oppressor. Now it serves the people." He continued, "When the fighting began, the bishops ran away but our priest remained here with us. Religion lives in the heart [hitting his chest], not in a pile of stone."

But I had noticed that the curses that liberally salted many conversations among Spaniards were both religious and rather personal. "*Me 'cag' en Dios*," literally translated, is "I shit on God." Quite often they did the same to the "twenty-four balls of the twelve apostles." These expressions were remarkably lacking in rancor. They were said when one hit one's finger with a hammer. Without religion and sex, I thought, profanity would wither rather badly.

It was a pretty good bet that the politically conscious youth of that time would be stuffy about drinking, viewing it as an insidious habit encouraged by the ruling class to anesthetize workers against subversive thoughts, or any thoughts at all. So it was not surprising that there were only a few serious drinkers of any note in the battalion, or that their presence was conspicuous—Larry and Frank, say.

Former seaman Larry O'Toole and his pal Frank Murphy discovered that Tarazona's only tavern had a glorious wine cellar. The bar, much to their disapproval, closed rather early, a situation they considered a ringing challenge. On one beautiful moonlit night, they went to the mayor and said they brought top-secret news of the imminent bombardment of his charming village by a huge fleet of enemy planes. He was to gather the villagers quietly and they would be led to a safe spot. Silently as shadows, the entire village was gathered and led out of town a mile and a half by Murphy and O'Toole, who had been in the tavern most of the evening and were in a joyous mood.

"Remain right here," they told the mayor. "We will go back and stand guard in the village. When it is all clear, we will come for you. ¡Salud, camaradas!" In the early morning, when the villagers at last straggled back, they found, lying behind the tavern bar dead to the world on a bier of empty wine bottles, their very pied pipers.

Later in the morning, Mirko Markevitch stood in the center of the parade ground with his arms outstretched. With each hand he held by the collar a sagging, disheveled ex-seaman. Anger mingled with disgust in his voice when he called the battalion to attention. But the scene struck the volunteers as highly amusing, and they laughed and made jokes.

"Is NOT funny," said Mirko. He looked disdainfully at Murphy and O'Toole and held them as if he were handling excessively soiled laundry. "DISS COME FIGHT FASCISM? DISS?"

This time the ranks remained silent. Finally, Mirko let go. The culprits slid to the ground and immediately fell into a peaceful sleep. Mirko need not have worried, though. Free souls they were, tough, resourceful, and streetwise, but they knew why they had come, and they helped many a less rugged volunteer over the rough spots that lay ahead.

On the Madrid front, things were going badly. The first Americans in the line had taken heavy losses on the Jarama front. A ring of iron circled the city with only one road open, the Madrid-Valencia highway, and even that was under intermittent fire. The Republic prepared an offensive to the west toward Brunete to relieve the virtual siege.

By that time, our training was over. We were lucky, since it had been three days more than three weeks (some of us had yet to fire a shot, though; ammo was short). The rest of our training would take place at the front, and the other side would become our teachers. We would learn well; we would become shock troops in every major battle of that long, glorious-tragic war.

It was time to say good-bye to the little market town of Tarazona. Our stay had been brief, but the impact of our presence had been profound. The innate reserve and dignity of the villagers vied with their intense gratitude that these brave young *americanos* had come so far to help them save their land. They even forgave Murphy and O'Toole, and it was clear that the prank would weave itself into the local folklore to be savored, embellished, and retold. The mayor, who owned the pub and had been very gracious about the loss of some of his very best wine, was anxious that there be a ceremony, an opportunity for him to express the feelings of his people.

It was a Thursday, market day, when the farmers brought their produce to the village in two-wheeled carts with enormous wheels, drawn by tough little gray burros. The burros were unhitched and the backs of the carts unloaded and tipped up. The peasant women then sat beside the small piles of onions, tomatoes, and peppers—whatever they had grown—while the men went to the *fonda* to drink. The carts and the multicolored produce filled the inside of the square.

The town square itself was postcard picturesque. It was ringed by very old two-story buildings, with oaken balconies filled with flowers on the second floor and tiny retail stores—the barber's, the tailor's, the butcher's, the *fonda*—on the ground floor. The square was completely walled in except for two gates just wide enough for the small burro carts to get through.

The big army trucks that had come for the soldiers were parked out-side. Inside, the battalion was lined up in a double row reaching around the whole square, just away from the burro carts. The mayor stood on a little platform in front of his tavern, with the entire village crowding around him and filling the balconies. Into this scene strode tall, handsome, immaculately uniformed Mirko Markevitch.

"Pinch me," David White said to me, "so I'll know that Mirko is not the lead tenor, this is not a Bizet opera, we will not sing in the chorus, and Carmen will not come dancing in with a rose in her teeth."

Mirko faced the mayor, saluted, and gave his well-known command for the battalion to come to attention. At this the villagers broke into wild applause and threw flowers. The mayor raised his arms in the time-hallowed benedictory gesture of politicians the world over. He was not by God going to be denied his moment. Then, to the surprise of all, he delivered a brief, thoughtful speech, in which he expressed the gratitude and affection of his village but also his regret that it was war and killing that had forced the Americans to come to his country to sacrifice instead of to enjoy.

When the ceremony was over, the men came to shake hands and the women hugged and kissed us and cried. Tarazona would not forget us. It would be left with emotional ties, many warm memories, and a few unexpected pregnancies.

"Roger Hargrave should be here," I said to Dave. "This is just what he had in mind."

CHAPTER 5

1937

We went quickly to Madrid and through it without stopping; then on to the great escarpment west of El Escorial that overlooks the plain below, dotted with villages and towns set out like miniatures on an architect's rendering. It was evening, and next morning the great offensive would begin. The machine-gun company lounged under an ancient olive tree, nervous, tense, and quiet. We avoided looking at each other directly because it was natural to wonder which ones were about to die. Wrapped in our immortality, each one was prepared to grieve for the loss of another.

Just before dark, mail, which came sporadically, was delivered. There was a letter for me from Laura Saldi.

Dearest Milt,

I love you, I love you, I love you. I will always love you. When you left so much of me went with you. I was destroyed, desolate. But above all, life must go on, mustn't it? And I knew that I must go on, for after all, you may never return. I really don't know how to say this but sometimes great grief leads to great joy. Not long ago I was invited to Chicago as a guest player in the university symphony. The violinist who sat next to me, Phil, was a wonderful, understanding young man who resembles you in many ways. Many evenings he helped me overcome my sorrow, and yes, last week we were married.

Please, please try to go on without me. Someday you will surely meet someone who will replace me in your heart. Goodbye, my darling.

Your Laura (Mrs. Phillip Ellison)

Without a word I handed my "Dear John" to Dave. When he finished reading it, Dave asked, "Do you mind if I read this to the guys? Might do some good."

"Sure," I said, "Go ahead. Laugh at my tragedy."

Dave got up. "Listen, comrades," he said, "not all of us are fortunate enough to get mail from our loved ones at a time like this. So pay close attention." He gave the letter a reading that milked dry all its dramatic potential, and long before he finished, the tension had been replaced by very raucous laughter. David handed the letter back. "Your Mrs. Ellison may never know," he grinned, "what inherent genius she has for building morale at the very moment she is sure she is destroying it!"

The hours just after dawn were deceptive. Dave and I pulled Mother Bloor along behind us on its two iron wheels. It was a peaceful walk across the rolling plain, except that the temperature rose quickly into the nineties and ahead of us we could hear the low rolling thunder of distant artillery.

Then it came without warning, just in front of Villanueva de la Canada. WHOPP! WHOPP! WHOPP! High, very high, invisible in the shimmering sky, German bombers circled at their leisure and dropped sticks of bombs that made the earth leap and tremble. Each soldier, lying helpless on the ground, could hear the scream of the bomb as it fell and knew that it was aimed at the very center of the small of his back. When the bomb hit and the explosion came, it made a sound we had never heard before, ear-splitting and totally terrifying.

Dave and I had managed to pull our gun into a small gully where we lay and hugged the ground. "T. S. Eliot got it wrong," said Dave, "the world ends not with a whimper but with one helluva bang."

"Where the hell are our fighter planes?" came a wistful complaint. Where indeed? We would discover that for every plane of ours, the Fascists had fifty. For the three 75-mm guns in the John Brown Battery, the other side had a hundred, and the same for tanks, and supplies, and manpower. Well, what the hell. We had known that going in, as soon as we had cut through the smooth-talking diplomatic bullshit in Geneva to the nasty fact that Franco, Hitler, and Mussolini were to get a free pass in Spain.

It seemed forever, but the bombers left quite soon. No one was killed, miraculously, but slight-to-serious shrapnel wounds cost us half a dozen of our slim forces. We reached Villanueva de la Canada and

Sister gun of Mother Bloor,
with the firing speed of a
five-horsepower outboard
motor. At left is Oliver Law,
first black commander of
white American troops.
Killed in action shortly after.

knew that the fighting had gone on ahead, because corpses already
bloating and beginning to smell badly were lying in ditches along
the road.

We continued on toward Brunete but not very far. The enemy had
set up a line of resistance. The machine-gun company spread out behind a low wall and began to return the enemy fire. Fighting became
intense. Both Dave and our water-cooled Mother Bloor ran dry and
overheated. The gun showed signs of jamming.

"We need water," said Dave. "Where in hell can we get some water?"

"There's only one way," I answered. "We must pee in it." We did
but it wasn't nearly enough. We shouted for the soldiers lying near us
to crawl over.

"You must pee in Mother Bloor," I said. "She needs you desperately." The first soldier made his contribution. The next one refused.

"I can't," he said, "it's sacrilegious. My father reveres Mother Bloor. He would kill me if he heard."

"About two hundred yards from here are several hundred Moors very anxious to do that ahead of your father," said Dave, "Pee, dammit!"

Very suddenly, as we lay as flat as we could while raking the opposing line with machine-gun fire and receiving it too, we heard behind us wild shouting and the thunderous gallop of many horses on the dead run. In utter astonishment, we ducked for our lives as Spanish horsemen, wearing broad-brimmed hats bedecked with the flamboyant colors of the Republic and brandishing sabers, leaped high over our heads and raced crazily forward into the teeth of the enemy's chattering machine guns as though engaged in some timeless, existential steeplechase.

"What in the goddamn hell is that," I said.

"If I am not mistaken," said Dave, "THAT is the Spanish Cavalry famed in song and story."

"They'll be massacred," I worried. "I can't watch."

But by a miracle, they weren't. The Fascists were equally astounded. Before they could react, the cavalry began to cut them up and they broke and ran. The offensive continued. By nightfall, eight or nine towns had been taken. For a few days it went better than planned, and then we came to Mosquito Ridge.

A rocky rise far higher than the surrounding terrain, it easily dominated the area for many miles. To defend it, the enemy brought massive reinforcements of men, artillery, and tanks. The British on their left, the Americans, and a Spanish brigade on their right took heavy casualties in repeated attempts to storm the heights. The machine-gun company was becoming exhausted. Every day we had losses, both dead and wounded, and we needed replacements. A mortar shard had lodged in Dave's hip. The medics checked him over and said, "Best place for you is the American Hospital in Villa Paz."

"Take care of Mother Bloor," said Dave. "She does get thirsty you know."

"I'll miss you, Dave, because in spite of your upper-middle-class background, you do make pretty good talk," I paused, "maybe a little heavy for me at times. And speaking of that, will you please take your damn book back. In the next war, how about bringing some light verse—the collected works of Ogden Nash, or better yet, Edna St. Vincent Millay."

We embraced, but neither of us wanted to show how very much we would miss each other. We could buck the political code but not the manliness code. We left it at "Take care of yourself."

Around 2 P.M. on the day David White was wounded, I was posted with Mother Bloor directly across from where a Fascist counterattack was expected. As a precaution, I called for extra ammunition to be brought up.

Renaldo Martínez, the Cuban ammo-carrier, came loping up with his quick, long stride and dropped down beside me, sharing my cover behind the trunk of a large olive tree. Everyone was fond of Renaldo, who had never been known to refuse a request, no matter how unreasonable and no matter who asked it. His attitude was unfailingly, almost defiantly, sunny. He could run like a deer, and knowing what his job was to be, he had had made for him in Tarazona the finest pair of high leather boots in all Spain. They were soft as goosedown, and he oiled and brushed them lovingly every morning. He took a lot of kidding about his boots, but he didn't mind. We knew he had them for a good reason and not for pride.

"How goes the battle?" I asked, after Renaldo had a chance to catch his breath.

"Not bad, Milt, not bad. But each one asks for more ammo. Something is expected."

"The activity will keep you in shape. Keep you from putting on excess weight in the hip area," I said.

"I don't need the exercise," said Renaldo, "especially in this ninety-five-degree heat. Could you spare a shot of water before I go? I'm fresh out."

"Sure," I said, "just save me a drop."

Renaldo lifted the canteen I held out to him to his lips, threw his head back, and swallowed.

As he did I watched a small, perfectly round hole open in the center of his throat. A stray bullet had fired at random, perhaps even accidentally, and Renaldo's life spilled out red on the ground. It was over in seconds.

Inured as I had become—as all the volunteers had become—to sudden endings, I stared at the lifeless body and was sick to the pit of my being. The waste, the pointless, random, insane waste. The man who fired the shot had no idea what had happened to his bullet, what an easy, soft, vulnerable spot it had found. What would he have thought if he could have known? Certainly not that he had killed a decent, caring, admirable young man, perhaps much like himself. More likely he would have celebrated the death of another Red and asked for the military commendation due him. What ancestral, manipulating genius had first discovered man's fear and hatred of what he perceives to be different, as well as the boundless profitability to which such knowledge could be put? For a long while I lay flat behind the olive tree. Some bullets came whistling by low overhead with the distinctive whine that close ones make, and they brought me back to the world of the briefly living.

My eyes wandered down to Renaldo's boots, his beautiful shiny boots. My own *alpargatas* were worn through. Would it be a betrayal, a desecration to take his boots? Someone would surely take them, one of our side, or maybe one of theirs. Would they bring bad luck? They looked cold and insolent lying there unharmed on Renaldo's twisted and lifeless legs. If they *were* bad luck, how many other soldiers would they outlast?

If only I didn't have to take them off. Renaldo had laced them neatly and tightly, right up to the calf. What would my comrades think if they saw me wearing Renaldo's beautiful boots? Would they understand that the boots were useful, impersonal tools, like a rifle or a pistol? No one thought twice about those.

Who did I think I was kidding. They would look at the boots and be reminded of Renaldo. They would despise me as a ghoul, and I would despise myself even more. It didn't make sense, of course, but then again, in war, what did?

So the stray bullet I had dreamed about so long ago had come pretty close. Only now I knew that all the bullets were strays and all their targets unimportant accidents, and that in the end the only winners were the bomb makers and the cannon makers and the casket makers.

In battle, ten minutes can be a day and a day can be forever. One thought takes over—if they would only stop bombing, only stop the shelling, just for a while. Just so there can be a little rest, a chance for the nerves to get back to the inside of the skin, a chance to eat whatever it is they bring without diving for cover.

Loyalist Spain was running short of food too, along with the other things. The Americans learned not to inquire too deeply into what was being dished out of the big pots they brought up to the front. Goat for sure, and horse and burro when that ran out, and dog, and cat. Mexico supplied the staples—garbanzos, known to Bronx housewives as chick-peas, and lentils. Some swore they would never again enter any room that had lentils in it, but I learned to like them.

The stalemate dragged on, so the psychological-warfare people offered to lend a hand. They reasoned that the Moors, who had been exploited for centuries by the Spanish monarchy and had been dragooned into the war by Franco, would be ripe for desertion. The plan was simple. Between the lines was a grove of olive trees. During the night, fresh loaves of bread would be left under them. Loudspeakers were brought up. Then, when the bread was in place, they boomed out:

> Moors! Come over to us. We will feed you well and treat you with dignity. Go to the olive trees. There is a message for you.

Nothing, then we heard movement out where the bread had been placed. Perhaps it was working. But in a little while *their* loudspeaker came on.

> *Rojos* (Reds), we too have a message. Come to the trees.

It could be a trick, but volunteers went out to see. In a few moments they were back. The bread had been thickly buttered.

> *Rojos*, you have little. We have much. Come to *us*.

The enemy laughed into their microphones and then punctuated it with artillery and machine-gun fire. American battalion officers used harsh words with the psychologists, including suggestions that their ancestors were not of the highest rank, intellectually and socially speaking. Anyone could tell that they would not be asked to return.

Two days after Dave White was wounded, the front moved back and forth in attack and counterattack. Ahead of me I saw bullets sewing patterns in the earth, and I tried to find cover. Before I could, I felt my leg burn and hot metal dig into my left elbow.

Medics helped me down off Mosquito Ridge. I was dizzy from loss of blood and the heat. Five hundred yards to the rear, there was a shallow river bed where Dr. Mark Strauss had set up an aid station. And assisting Dr. Strauss, with the sure skill of one who gave the appearance of having had years of training, was Roger Hargrave.

Roger spotted me first and hurried over. "Hi, eastern-Jew Commie-bastard," he said, throwing an arm around my shoulder, "how bad are you hit?"

"Never mind that," I said, "first you waltz around the goddamn ship with a one-hundred-percent Aryan floozie; then you desert your old pals and buddies the minute you hit Paris. Is that what they taught you in your Methodist Sunday-school class? I'm willing to listen, but talk fast."

As he talked, Roger was examining my wounds, dusting me with antiseptic, and applying temporary bandages. "I got thrown in the slammer for assaulting an officer of the *gendarmerie*. Four of us were arrested. We sacrificed ourselves to create a diversion so you could have your way with the Paris dance-hall girls while we rotted in jail for six weeks. You're a fine one to mention desertion. When we got out, you were already in Alès."

"How did you wind up with Doc Strauss?" I asked.

"He was bringing two ambulances to Spain, both donated, and one of the drivers got sick. They asked me, and I figured it was better than climbing the damn mountains. We drove in through Port Bou."

"Who gave the ambulances?" I asked.

"One was the faculty and students of Harvard University. The other was Ernest Hemingway."

I was surprised. "Didn't think he ever got that involved."

"Maybe," offered Roger, "it's a compromise—a way to do something political without saying anything political."

"So how did you get to be a medic?"

"I learned a lot about bandaging when I was boxing. No one else even knew that much. I got along good with Doc Strauss. He insisted I should stay, that he would teach me what I needed to know. He is very good people." Roger finished. "Your leg will be pretty good in a couple of months, but your elbow may give you a lot of trouble. Don't try to bend it."

"That may be very bad for drinking," I said. "Where do I go from here?"

"If you can get over that hill," said Roger pointing, "there's an ambulance that will take you to a Madrid hospital, probably the Palace Hotel."

Roger and I were very glad to have found each other again. We embraced, and then I was put on a mule for the ride up the steep slope to where the ambulances were.

The top half of the hill could be reached by enemy fire. I was reminded of country carnivals where you paid a quarter to shoot at moving ducks. The Spanish muleteer told me to lean down on the far side of the mule. Then he used his whip, and we went up the slope at a dead run, with me hanging on to the short mane with my good hand. Bullets ricocheted off rocks with the sound of angry hornets, the frightened mule bounded, and I could feel Roger's bandages coming off. I was bleeding again, but I had to get to the top, which I just managed before sliding off and watching the mule run down the road with the muleteer after him.

A dozen wounded were loaded into the small ambulance. The Spanish soldiers had kept their rifles when they were wounded, and when we bounced too much over the potholed roads they stuck their rifles into the driver's compartment and threatened to blow his head off if he weren't more careful. This was quite effective in slowing the driver down.

We did go to the Palace Hotel, which was now one of the better hospitals, but only the most serious cases remained there, and I was transferred to the Princesa. They found that the leg wounds were clean and would heal, but a chunk of metal had lodged deep in my left elbow joint. The doctors were afraid to remove it because of the possibility of immobilizing the arm permanently.

At about this point of the war, Italian air force Caproni bombers joined the Luftwaffe's Junkers at the island base of Palma on beautiful, touristy Majorca. From there they introduced their unique contribution to the culture of Western man, the bombing of civilian populations. Madrid, Barcelona, and Valencia were favorite targets. It might strike some as ironic that the techniques developed came in mighty handy a few years later when the Allies did it to Dresden, Berlin, and Munich.

The bombing had almost the opposite of its intended effect. As everyone emerged from the shelters, called *refugios*, and saw women and children being buried in rubble as their city crumbled into dust around them, the million disparate *madrileños* became as one. Determined to resist, they created the slogan, "Madrid shall be the tomb of fascism."

When the all-clear sirens blew between attacks, the streets bustled with people rushing to do their work before the next alarm. During one lull, Edwin Rolfe, a promising, young New York poet with a skimpy body and a face like a starving sparrow, found me at the Princesa and said he had bad news about Roger Hargrave.

"How bad?" I wanted to know.

"Bad enough," said Rolfe, "come on. He's at the Palace. I'll tell you on the way."

Buses and streetcars moved people about, but they were so crowded that the passengers looked like overripe fruit clinging to trees in great bunches. I was using one crutch and my arm was in an "airplane" sling; since everyone was overly kind to the wounded, we had no trouble making our way.

Rolfe told me what he knew about Roger. "Mosquito again. Roger was in the middle of it doing an incredible job. Hans Amlie, the company commander, was wounded, and Roger went out under very heavy machine-gun fire and brought him in. He tried to bring Ray Steele in, you remember big Ray, but he died before Roger could manage it. On the last day of battle, Roger went into the field of fire time after time until he lay down exhausted to rest. Ten feet away an artillery shell hit. Hot steel caught both feet, both knees, his hip, and his forearm. Gangrene was already setting in by the time they got him to an ambulance."

We found Roger in the intensive-care section of the Palace, a pale skeleton dangling from the wheels and pulleys of a complex traction device. He was unconscious and his breathing was uneven and shallow. When the doctor came he said that Roger by all rights ought to be dead, but that he seemed to have a powerful will to live, and with people like that you could not predict.

It was almost a week before I could get back to the Palace, and the change was remarkable. Roger was still in traction, but he was awake and color had returned to his face.

"Where ya been?" he croaked.

"I was here but you were rude enough not to notice. Sleep always did come first with you. So what do the doctors say?"

"I will never bend the knee to anyone again," said Roger, "at least not the right one. Nor the right wrist. Both fused. Theoretically it might be possible to get some movement in the fingers of the right hand. Possible, not probable. Otherwise I'm terrific. Know any *señoritas* who would like to get laid by the good half of an Iowa farmer?"

"Not right offhand," I said, "but I will check with the Commissariat of Public Charity. How long do they say you'll be here?"

"Depends on how fast I mend, but they do speak of sending people up to Sagaro. They need the space here for the fresh meat."

"Sagaro?" I asked. "That's way up above Barcelona on the Costa Brava. It'll be impossible for your friends to visit."

Roger looked at me for a long, silent minute. "See you in Iowa City, pal," he said finally. "Take care of yourself, and keep a diary. I intend to ask questions."

I leaned over and embraced Roger very gently, feeling as I had earlier with David White that we were both victims of the virulent machismo that compels "real men" to behave like strong, silent idiots bereft of emotion. And so, knowing that we would not see each other again for a long time, if ever, I walked to the door and waved good-bye.

Roger waved back and we both smiled, like regular all-American assholes.

The next day I was sent to the British Hospital at Huete, about ninety miles from Madrid. It was an enormous twelfth-century building with three-foot-thick walls surrounding an inner courtyard. It contained a huge church and many small rooms that had had various uses when it was a seminary but were now wards for the wounded.

The hospital was run by Nan Green, a brisk, efficient, dedicated, no-nonsense woman of beauty and intellect. It was staffed by Czechoslovakian, British, and Spanish doctors. The nurses, who were British, were assisted by young Spanish women whom they were training. The trainees were learning with a rapidity that Nan said she had never experienced before and that had to come from very strong motivation. Only two American wounded were at Huete, Jerry Cook and me, and no one knew why, because the American Hospital at Villa Paz was only four miles away. We both preferred to stay where we were.

Life at Huete was pleasant. My leg was almost healed, and while I still could not straighten my left arm much more than halfway, pieces of shrapnel gradually surfaced at the elbow and gave promise that most of it would one day come out. The war seemed remote except for the new wounded who arrived regularly in the four large Matford ambulances assigned to the hospital. In the afternoon, Jerry and I and George, Nan's husband, who had been first cellist in the London Symphony, would climb the hill back of the hospital and talk about politics, history, music, literature, the war, and our hope for a future, hazily defined, that would see society develop free of war, poverty, and oppression.

George was nearing the end of his convalescence. From somewhere he had obtained a cello, and he began to practice. Sitting in the center of the cavernous, empty church as the late afternoon sunlight filtered through the ancient stained-glass windows, he made sounds that were so unutterably sad and beautiful that anyone who heard would stop and not breathe or move until the last note was lost in the silent air. Months later, when George's wounds were healed, he rejoined the British battalion and was killed the first day back by a mortar shell.

When my leg healed, Nan Green made a request. "I know," she

said, "that you still have trouble with your arm, but I think you are quite capable of driving. One of our ambulances was strafed on the Valencia road yesterday. The driver was hurt badly, and we have no replacement. Would you please take it on?"

"What do you want me to do, Nan?"

"I would like for you to take over the big Matford. There are ten ambulatories here that need to be transferred to Madrid. Better take Nati with you—she knows where to go and she's a good nurse."

Nati was short for Natividad, a lovely, sophisticated *valenciana* of wit and charm with whom I was on intimate terms, as Nan Green, who knew everything, already knew. Before we left, Nan arranged for me to get a *salvoconducto* (safe-conduct pass) that gave me unrestricted entree to all areas and top priority for gasoline.

The Matford was a big, boxy, ugly-looking English Ford that carried four stretcher cases and twelve "sit-ups." As soon as I sat behind the wheel, I recognized that this was a position that could be fully appreciated only by infantrymen who had been condemned to walk the earth loaded down like mountain mules, with a view of life limited to the muddy heels of the poor bastard immediately in front.

No wonder the sons of the rich—when they chose, occasionally, not to be public relations assistants to bellicose senators—opted to be carried to their wars on a ship, or in a plane, or behind the wheel of a general's command car. Mobility meant freedom, wider horizons, creature comforts, and always a place to sleep, dry and warm. One could carry a small gasoline stove to make hot coffee and fry the breakfast bread in olive oil, and could store possessions and trophies. I tasted the heady wine of privilege and felt like a bird must feel when it discovers it can fly.

Next day Nati and I delivered the wounded to Madrid, sat out the bombing raids in a café just off the Puerta del Sol, and registered for two rooms at the Hotel Inglés but used only one.

Very early in the morning, we groped our way through a dense fog to the Matford and started back to Huete. I couldn't see past the end of the hood. Nati got out and with her hand on the right front fender called directions to me as she walked along and felt for the curb with her foot. Madrid sits high on a ledge of the Guadarrama Mountains,

placed there by the conceit of a king who insisted that his capital be
built in the exact geographical center of Spain and that his subjects
embarrass the language rather than him by lisping as badly as he did.
(He died, the lisping goes on, the language continues debased, and
beautiful Madrid has the worst year-round climate in Spain.) On the
outskirts of the city, the fog began to lift slightly, enough to make out
dim shapes forty or fifty feet away.

We were running along a raised highway, with muddy fields ten feet
below us on either side. Coming toward us were misty shapes assigned
to the business of war—tanks, artillery pieces, and trucks. Lulled
by the lifting fog, I was caught completely off guard by what happened next.

We slammed into a patch of fog thick as a wall, and before I could
slow down I made out the shape of a truck loaded with a huge mound
of oranges coming at us dead head-on. Some automatic reflex made
me swing my wheel to the right with all my strength. A miracle made
the truck driver swing to *his* right simultaneously. We kissed in the
middle of the highway like parting lovers.

The ambulance sailed through the air and landed axle-deep in the
muddy field below. The truck flew off to the left. Before it left the road,
it tossed its entire load of sweet, ripe Valencia oranges in a lovely high
cascade that covered the highway for a hundred yards. Nati was bruised
and shaken but not, as far as we could tell, hurt seriously. Her forehead
had hit the top of the cab, and a blue-purple lump was beginning to
form rapidly. I had had the wheel to cling to and was better off, except
for where the rim of it had dug into my stomach and rearranged my
internal organs. Nati said she was all right, but she was clearly worried
about her looks. I climbed out and looked back up toward the road.

A big party was going on. All traffic had stopped, and tank drivers,
soldiers, truckers, and private-car passengers were merrily chasing the
rolling, golden fruit and stowing it into their pockets, inside their
shirts, and wherever else ingenuity suggested. What was so noticeable
was that the mood was so relaxed and carefree, almost childlike. Many
times before I had noticed how eagerly the soldier grasps at the slightest
excuse to make reassuring contact with a saner, less sinister activity,
with almost anything that will remind him that even in a world of

strangers not everyone outside his small, safe circle is necessarily an enemy.

With mud sucking at my shoes, I scrambled my way up onto the road and saw among the stalled, sprawling traffic three tanks, and near them, his pockets already bulging, the young tank commander.

"*Salud, Camarada,*" I said.

"*Salud, hombre.*" Considering that he held two large Valencias in his right hand, the tank commander made a recognizable effort to return my clenched-fist Popular Front salute. I pointed to the ambulance sitting belly-flat in the mud.

"Can you, *por favor*, use one of your powerful tanks, of which the whole Spanish people is rightfully proud, to restore us to the highway?"

"*No es posible*," said the commander, shrugging his shoulders. "We must continue to Madrid. Those are our orders."

"Comrade," I said, "the ambulance is very important to the Republic, and sitting within it is a somewhat injured but still very beautiful nurse."

"She is truly beautiful?" he asked.

"She truly is," I said, "and devoted to those who fight for our cause."

The commander held a swift conference with his men. Then he climbed on the apron of his tank and shouted to the crowd, "Clear the way! Everyone must help!"

This was more unexpected fun—a rescue mission complete with fair maiden, for by this time Nati was leaning out the ambulance door, smiling into imaginary cameras and enjoying herself hugely. The commander's tank reeled in the ambulance as easily as though it were a flapping fish on the end of a pole. The only hitch was that when the commander had sent his men out to fasten the chains around the rear axle, many of the spectators on the road became hysterical and shouted (when they could catch their breath) obscene suggestions to the poor soldiers.

When they were gathering oranges, the troopers had thought of what then seemed a brilliant idea for increasing their take. They had tied the bottoms of their trousers tightly around the ankles and stuffed oranges in them almost up to their belts. They had managed somehow to waddle out to the ambulance, but when they lay down to work the chains around the axle, the ripest oranges became gummy juice. In their misery, the soldiers buried themselves in their work, so to speak, for as long as they could. When they finally came out, they looked like very filthy, totally incontinent baggy-pants clowns, and everyone but they thought it was very humorous. When the ambulance was back on the road, the commander bowed deeply to Nati, handed her an orange with a gallant flourish as the crowd cheered, and strode off, happily stuffing Nati's hastily scribbled Huete phone number into his pocket.

My life for the next few weeks was busy and pleasant. Often Jerry Cook was with me as we carried wounded to Madrid, Valencia, and Benicasim, the main International Brigade convalescent center on the Mediterranean coast. At night, Fascist fighter planes came in from the sea and strafed the coast roads, firing multicolored tracer bullets that shot by the ambulance and danced along the road in a hail of deadly confetti. Once when I was very, very tired, I hallucinated the tracers, jammed on the brakes, and jumped into a ditch, feeling silly and ashamed because before I hit the ground I knew it was not a real attack but only in the brain, behind the eyes; the wounded I was carrying had been bounced around and terrified for nothing.

In Madrid, I would stay over a day or two, sometimes with Jerry, and one night in Chicote's Bar we met Ernest Hemingway and his drinking friend, Vincent Sheehan. We were invited to the Hotel Flórida where Hemingway had a very large and expensive rear apartment. The front of the hotel faced up the Gran Vía to University City where the fighting was, and enemy shells came down the wide avenue with not a few coming in the windows of the beautiful upper-floor suites, which now went for bargain prices.

Like an irresistible magnet, the war had drawn the world's artists, poets, playwrights, journalists, and photographers to Spain, and more particularly to the Flórida, and more particularly still to the endless Hemingway supply of fine scotch. He had become a fierce anti-Franco partisan and had developed great liking and admiration for the American volunteers. And almost all of them who met Ernesto (it was a time when he enjoyed being called Ernesto) liked him too, although it is possible they liked Martha Gelhorn better. Ernesto was married to Pauline Pfeiffer, but everybody said that that was over and it was Martha

Gelhorn who was always with him. Gelhorn was a magazine writer with a breezy open manner, a down-to-earth vocabulary, and a belief that if one was going to write about soldiers one ought to do it from the front. She despised Francisco Franco, and it didn't hurt her popularity that she was extremely attractive.

Even in a roomful of big egos, I noticed that Hemingway's presence dominated, and it wasn't just physical, although his six-foot height carried his two hundred pounds well and he looked bulky only up around the chest. He had an impressive black mustache and lots of dark hair on top of his head, flecked with white specks that set it off. He appeared to be living in high gear, savoring the taste of where he was and what he was. All his guests felt welcome and included and not in the least embarrassed when they drank excessively of his miraculous supply of whiskey.

I joined the cluster at the bar in a corner of the large living room and was surprised that when I picked up my drink, Hemingway noticed my bent left arm and asked about it. I told him about Mosquito Ridge and Roger and Renaldo.

"He died well," said Ernesto.

"He died fast," I said.

"Did you know that I also drove an ambulance in a war?"

"Sure do. I read *Farewell to Arms* twice."

"The Americans who are fighting here are very brave," he said, lifting his glass. "I drink to them."

"Actually," I said, "we are scared shitless most of the time. Maybe we keep at it because we have a larger fear—the fear of not living up to a commitment."

He laughed. "Bullshit," he said, "you are very good soldiers."

"Maybe," I said, "but I see that it is better to be a good soldier with a nice big motor up front and four wheels to roll around on."

Hemingway grinned. "Smart. Come here whenever you want, whenever you can. The door will be open."

On the way back to Huete with a full load of wounded, Jerry and I talked about our evening among the literati. We noted the different perspectives of those who *are* the event and those who report *about* the event.

"When I read what they write," I said, "I see that their truth is different from my truth. So whose truth is true?"

"Maybe nobody's," said Jerry, "and maybe in another way, everybody's."

"It's depressing to realize that old Henry Ford may have had something," I mused, "when he said that history was horseshit."

CHAPTER 6

1937

1938

Besides the hospital at Huete, the British Medical Unit maintained a reception villa on the shore of the Mediterranean just north of the port section of Valencia. The area was bombed almost nightly, but only a rare stray bomb came near the villa. Incoming medical supplies, food, and new medical personnel were dispatched from the villa to Huete and to frontline medical stations.

When a shipload of doctors and nurses came in, ambulances and lorries would gather to transport them, there would be a big emotional party into the night, and in the morning we would all go off to the war. Often there were attractive, ruddy-faced nurses from New Zealand, Australia, and Britain aglow with Florence Nightingale dreams of humane service, self-sacrificing anti-Fascist zeal, and romantic visions of darkly handsome Spaniards making wild and intense music on flamenco guitars.

It is one of the malicious attractions of war that its backdrop of danger heightens all the senses like a multistrength aphrodisiac, suspending norms of behavior and freeing otherwise severely inhibited people to behave with the abandon of the temporarily insane. All of us veteran drivers were connoiseurs of this phenomenon. We exploited it without compunction, drinking, flirting, and maneuvering to lure a partner out onto the moonlit beach for as much of a sexual encounter as could be managed.

It happened that one night I was the winner of this peculiar lottery and found myself with a bottle of red Sangre de Toro wine in one hand and a nurse I judged to be Australian in the other. She had arrived that day, looking rather wonderful with a large floppy straw hat, golf clubs, and a tennis racket, and when I first saw her, I wondered what kind of war she could possibly have had in mind. At the beach, she spread out a blanket she was carrying and began methodically to remove her clothes, which turned out to be a grievous error because I noticed for the first time how much larger she began to loom than I had imagined her to be.

I had never thought much of rating myself as a lover, but when I did I suppose I fell somewhere in the median percentile for white American atheist males. As far as I knew, I had only one hang-up—bigness. I had also never learned to cope with the curious belief of British women that if they made love standing up they would not become pregnant. Unless one is in top physical condition, it is a method to be avoided at all costs. Even then it can be very hard on the lumbar vertebrae of the spine, which I attempted to ease by hanging a belt over one shoulder and looping it under one of my partner's knees. Not a pretty sight, but a fairly workable solution nevertheless.

Far back I had discovered that bigness, however, was for me the equivalent of a long, icy shower. And this young lady was big. I made a feeble attempt to caress her, but all I could think of was a line from Baudelaire that went something like, "He lay beneath her breast like a village nestling under a hill." It was no use.

"Listen, Beryl," I said, "I'm really sorry, but I think I must have had too much to drink or something."

Beryl was very sweet. She kissed me lightly. "That's OK, Milt. Don't worry about it. I have a slight headache myself. Let's just talk."

And we did, for quite a while. Then I asked her why in God's name she had brought golf clubs and a tennis racquet to a brutal war in primitive Spain.

She looked distressed. "I know how ridiculous it must seem, and I didn't really expect to play. Except maybe a little tennis? I guess I just wanted to have them for my morale, to remind me that it's not all blood and guts. I guess it was a mistake."

We put out our cigarettes, shook the sand out of the blanket, and started back up toward the villa. "It was no mistake," I said. "Hang on to your golf clubs as long as you can. Maybe if we're all lucky, you will get to use them."

I didn't like going to Valencia. There were restaurants and bars full of Fancy Dans and slickly dressed women. There were prostitutes and hustlers and black marketeers, and there was an atmosphere much like that of any place in the world obsessed with the profit motive. Perhaps it was because it was a port city, visited by cynical, unfriendly strangers. It wasn't like that at all in the rest of Loyalist Spain. In the villages and towns and cities, especially Madrid, there was an incredible, self-sacrificing unity of purpose that filled the population with a generous spirit so palpable it could almost be breathed.

For centuries, Spaniards had borne the crushing weight of an army structure bloated with 847 generals, a degenerate, thieving aristocracy, rapacious absentee landlords, and a church hierarchy entwined in a corrupt partnership with the worst elements of the ruling elite. Before the Loyalist government was voted into power with an overwhelming majority, eighty-seven percent of the population was illiterate, hunger was endemic, and sanitation unknown. Thousands of families still lived in caves, and medical treatment was reserved for the wealthy few. The notorious Guardia Civil, a paramilitary police infamous for un-restrained brutality, swung its iron fist at the merest hint of protest.

During its short seven months before the Fascist uprising, the Loy-alist government unlocked the pent-up energies of the Spanish people and released a creative explosion. Thousands of acres of land were taken from absentee landlords (at fair prices) and distributed to the peasants. Schools, hospitals, and clinics were built in what seemed al-most a frenzy to make up for lost time. Every form of free expression was encouraged. Theater, dance, music, and art flourished, and new magazines and newspapers sprang up throughout the country. Vil-lagers in their sixties came in from their fields in the evening physically exhausted and sat at tiny desks in schoolrooms, all of them fiercely de-termined to catch the elusive magic of reading and writing.

It was just a little more than a year since Francisco Franco, the gen-erals, the mercenary Moors, the Mussolini Blackshirts, and the Ger-man Nazis had on July 18, 1936, begun their crusade to save Spain for God by annihilating the Spanish people. Not so strange when one re-membered that this was the country of Torquemada and the inquisition.

The decision to make a sacrificial commitment to a cause can come rather easily in a moment of high moral resolve, or when you've been moved by an eloquent appeal, or when you see a child in a burning building, or when you've had a little too much to drink. But sticking with it, as day after day the hardship and danger and tension grow, is quite another matter. Like everyone else I had bad days. But if I had ever thought of volunteering to go home as I had volunteered to come,

Typical of the many brilliant
posters done by Spain's great
artists during the war.

I would have been shamed out of it in a hurry. The matter-of-fact
courage, dignity, and comradeship of the Spanish population inspired
resolve just as much as did the atrociously reactionary objectives of the
enemy.

One day in Huete I received a disturbing letter from John Gilloti, a
University of Iowa student anti-war leader. He enclosed a copy of a
Merle Miller front-page newspaper column suggesting "that Roger
Hargrave and Milt Felsen had become 'disillusioned' and that in the
face of nasty reality idealism had turned to ashes."

Merle's star was rising. He was now managing the local radio station
and had a regular front-page column in the *Daily Iowan*, with his
carefully air-brushed picture on it. I guessed that his remarks were
motivated at least partially by an attempt to rationalize his own failure
to come with us, but that didn't make it any better.

I wrote him a strident and self-righteous letter saying I was disillusioned all right, especially with the cynical nonintervention farce being led by the U.S.A. at the League of Nations meeting in Geneva. And with the oil companies that were happily providing the fuel, on credit, to supply the German Nazi and Italian Fascist submarines and warplanes to bomb Barcelona and Valencia. And with all those professed lovers of freedom who refused to consider the consequences of a Hitler-Mussolini victory. I couldn't guess that history was looking over my shoulder as I wrote.

I also made an attempt to explain why, in the eye of one of this century's more violent hurricanes, I felt so calm and at peace with myself. Usually, I wrote, we are aware that vast unseen forces act and we, blindly, react. This time I made the decision. I chose the arena. And I can tell you one thing, Merle, I wrote, it is much more comfortable to read history than to make it.

On the other hand, I acknowledge, I have also temporarily escaped from the lifelong prison sentence of having to make a living, of compromising between what I would like to be doing and what I have to do. Here I feel integrated, in harmony, free. It feels real good, Merle. I added that in Spain, at least for the moment, the population was being magnificently Utopian. Maybe it wouldn't, couldn't, last, but I would be glad to wait till I got back home to venal, corrupt, sordid business-as-usual to be disillusioned.

When I finished the letter to Merle, Jerry Cook came by and said Nan Green wanted to see us in her office. Her husband, George, was there and Nan, looking serious, poured tea before she got to the point. "There is word," she said, "that the winter battles have cost us heavily in casualties, especially at the cliff town of Teruel and on the northern fronts. The government is asking," she continued, looking at George, "that all wounded soldiers who have recovered enough should cut short their convalescence and return to the front."

George was a great bear of a man with a rumbling twinkle in his voice. "I confess, Nan," he said, "that I've been vaguely troubled by a sense of guilt for some time now. Well, for a couple of days, anyhow. So, my dear one, since you know how I detest overdrawn parting scenes, will you mind terribly if I arrange to leave in the morning?"

Nan loved George desperately and had always thought to herself that squeezing an oversized musician approaching middle age into a uniform as a frontline soldier was an outlandish and dangerous idea that could end only in tragedy, but she was incurably British. All she said quietly was, "Of course, George."

Jerry and I spoke up and said we would rejoin the Lincolns as soon as we could find them.

"Fine, Jerry, but not you, Milt," said Nan.

"Why not?"

"Because you are a fine driver, and frontline ambulances are idle for lack of drivers." Nan shuffled some papers on her desk and picked one up. "I have a report from the Ministry of Transportation," she continued. "There is a critical shortage of mechanics and chauffeurs. At Teruel there was a near disaster. Fifty new trucks were given to a graduating class of Spanish *choferes* and loaded with supplies. They drove all the way from Barcelona in first gear, almost ruining the transmissions before they reached Teruel. Then it turned very cold and snowed. No one had taught them about antifreeze. It's hard for us to realize that they have absolutely no mechanical background." Nan looked up from the paper. "Their first request is for frontline ambulance drivers," she said, "but they are pleading with the international volunteers for instructors as well."

"I get the point, Nan," I said, "and you know what they say. Those who *can* drive and those who *can't* teach. I'll get Evelyn to deliver me."

Jerry and I went down to the church part of the ancient pile of red sandstone with its three-foot-thick walls, the fortress that Nan's energy, skill, and devotion had made into a credible hospital. We found Evelyn Hutchins deep under the hood of an old Dodge six-stretcher ambulance.

Evelyn and her brother Les had volunteered from Toronto for the Canadian MacKenzie-Papineau battalion. Five feet two inches tall with long blond hair and blue, blue eyes, she had had to fight what she called endemic male chauvinism from day one. While she was the first to say she hadn't licked it completely, she had, and no one would deny her this, more than held her own. They had barred her from carrying a rifle at the front, but she had driven and repaired trucks and ambulances all over Loyalist Spain. She had been made a lieutenant and was in charge of the maintenance, repair, and assignment of the cars, trucks, and ambulances at Huete.

"*Salud*," we said and then explained our needs. (*Salud* was a very important word. It meant, among many other things, hello, good-bye, your health, long live the Republic, I await your orders, good to see you, and together till victory.)

Evelyn was not surprised. "I know about the situation at the front. Matter of fact, I won't be far behind you. The Fascists have been counterattacking at Teruel for weeks now, and the Lincolns, what's left of them, are about due to be pulled back for a rest. One of the British *camiones* is heading up that way either tomorrow or next day, Jerry, and I'll put you on it." She turned to me. She wiped some grease off her face with her sleeve and grinned. "If you're not too uptown to drive a Chevy, Milt, there's a four-stretcher ambulance that says on its side that it was donated by students at Harvard University. It was sent here by mistake last week, and it belongs at the front. The keys are in it."

It was an ugly little thing. It looked like an oversized grocery carton on wheels—unwieldy, top-heavy, and no match at all for the devastating potholes of the Spanish roads.

"My dear lieutenant," I said, "we both know this monstrosity doesn't belong at the front of anything. It's a Trojan ambulance sent by devilishly clever Harvard right-wingers, but what the hell. Everything for the cause."

The headquarters of the Servicios Sanitarios, Sección de Evacuación del Ejército del Ebro (Medical Services, Evacuation Section, Army of the Ebro), was on the Paséo de Gracia in Barcelona. It took a very long time to get the simplest things done. Even getting a new *salvoconducto* was tough because the air-raid sirens kept us running down into the shelters. Cursing the *aviones* (airplanes), we came up to see new rubble, women crying, and buildings ripped open and spilling their contents like broken shopping bags. After a considerable delay, I was assigned to a Spanish division fighting on the northern front near Huesca.

First I wanted to eat, but I was bored with lentils, garbanzos, and tough goat. I called the Hotel Majestic where some guys stayed who put out the *Volunteer for Liberty*, a sporadically printed newsletter eagerly read by all the Internationals. "I'll give you an address but keep it under your hat," said a man I had met casually a few times and knew only as Frank.

The address was just off the Ramblas de las Rosas in a neighborhood known as the Barrio Chino. Up one flight of stairs over a nondescript luggage shop I met Shlomo Krantz. Officers and war correspondents sat around at the few tables, and they barely looked up as Shlomo maitre d'ed me to an empty one.

"So, what's to eat?" I asked.

"What there is you'll get, wise guy." I was in the only orthodox, black-market, kosher restaurant in all Spain and maybe all Europe. I had matzoh-ball soup, salad, chicken with rice, strong tea in a glass, and sponge cake. It was a genuine miracle, and I knew better than to commit the gaucherie of asking the price.

Irv Goff and Billy Aalto came in while I was lingering over the tea. I had met Goff briefly in New York just before boarding the *President Harding*, but I didn't know Aalto. He was a tall, good-looking Finnish-American, and I found out that they had been chosen as the only two Americans to lead guerrilla warfare behind Franco's lines.

They were in a convivial mood, almost festive. Goff explained that they were just recovering from a successful mission on the southern front, where they had led thirty-five Spanish guerrilla fighters in a raid on a prison fort that held among its prisoners more than 350 Asturian miners scheduled for execution. They had overwhelmed the guards, freed the prisoners, and headed them out an escape route toward Málaga. Irv, Billy, and two Spanish guerrillas were covering the rear, but they did so a little too long and were seen and pursued by Fascist troops. They'd had to make a dash toward the Mediterranean Sea.

That part of the coast is rocky, with high overhanging cliffs. With no other alternative available, all four dove in and headed for Africa. As it got dark, the wind came up strong. The two Spaniards drowned in the waves. Irv and Billy shed their clothes and swam most of the night.

When it got light, they hid under an escarpment and could hear the voices of search parties. It took more than twenty-four hours to make their way to Loyalist lines, and then to Shlomo's place.

One war later, Billy Aalto, Irv Goff, and I were together again in

Just back from a mission
behind Franco's lines,
probably late 1937. Far left,
Billy Aalto; far right, Irv
Goff. Next to Aalto, a
Spanish guerrilla fighter, and
next to Goff an American,
names unknown. Both were
killed in the next action.

Washington, training for underground warfare as members of the
Office of Strategic Services under General William Donovan. By then
we were very close, as only old comrades can be. And as "premature
anti-Fascists," a pejorative term of incredible internal contradiction,
we felt somewhat exposed, vulnerable, and nervous with our military
associates. For all our sophistication, we were amazingly naive, tend-
ing in our near paranoia to be ultracorrect. When we were warned in
lectures that the vulnerability of homosexuals to pressure rendered

them unfit for intelligence work, Irv and I accepted it as revealed gospel and proceeded to destroy the life of our dear comrade, Billy Aalto.

One Sunday night early in the summer of 1942, Irv, Billy and I had dinner in a downtown Washington restaurant. When we finished Billy seemed anxious to leave, saying he had some personal chores to do. When he did go, Irv said, "Come on, let's tail him."

I was startled. "Why, for Chris'sake?"

"I'm pretty sure he's a queer," said Irv. "Come on."

Billy headed for the honky-tonk area and went into a sleazy bar. In about twenty minutes he came out, his arm around the shoulder of a sailor in a U.S. uniform. They walked to a nearby hotel and went in.

The next morning we were in General Donovan's private office, emotionally in turmoil but determined to stab our dearest friend in the back for a higher cause. The general seemed genuinely sorry to hear about Aalto, whom he liked and admired, but he assured us we had by all means done the right thing. Perhaps the strangely quizzical expression he wore throughout the meeting reflected his knowledge of the ironical fact, which we didn't know, that a third of the officers in the OSS were what in those days was termed "swishy."

Donovan was skillfully diplomatic and kind with Billy. He told him there was an urgent request from Camp Meade for a temporary loan of instructors experienced in demolitions, and since Billy was considered one of the best the general was sure he wouldn't mind doing the favor.

If Billy suspected anything he gave no sign, and we said so long, see you soon, with big false smiles, feeling inside like the despicable shits we knew we were being.

Six weeks later, Billy was teaching a class in the use of grenades when one of the soldiers pulled the pin and froze. Billy reacted automatically. He grabbed the grenade out of the soldier's hand, but before he could throw time ran out and it blew his hand off at the wrist. Not much is known about his life after that except that he attended Columbia University and became a poet. Some say he lived with W. H. Auden and that he died a suicide only a few years after the end of the war.

But on that long-ago night at Shlomo's, we were younger and things were less complicated. We savored the moment, enjoying the food and celebrating Irv and Billy's feat. After dinner I said good-bye, got my ambulance loaded with patients, and drove north.

The northern front was ill-defined, and when a bullet went through my windshield I realized I had passed it. I did a very fast turnaround. I was carrying five stretcher cases and six sit-ups, and it was my turn to have rifles pointed at my head with colorful instructions to avoid bumps if I didn't want it blown off. I learned that those who complained the most vocally were not in such bad shape; it was the silent ones who might die before I got them from the frontline tent to the forward hospital near Barbastro.

Ambulance drivers are privileged to witness the ingenious methods that science and technology, working hand in hand, have devised to dismember the human body. It is very instructive to watch a couple of doctors dip into the stomach cavity and haul out yards and yards of a man's large intestine. As they run it through their fingers looking for cleverly designed metal shards, they find innumerable unpatchable holes, bloody tribute to the efficiency of the weapons industry. All over the world people spend their days making arms, and on Sundays they go to church and pray to a loving God.

Sometimes the gods of war have a sense of humor too. I once picked up a Spanish soldier who had worn a thin, World War I French-type helmet for protection. A sharp piece of shrapnel had pierced the center of the helmet, entered his skull, and turned the torn edges of the helmet under it so that the helmet was pinned down over his ears like a comical, tight-fitting hat. Remarkably, he seemed to feel very little pain, and he walked around with the shrapnel sticking up out of his head like a small Excalibur, enjoying his first taste of notoriety. The doctors were baffled. There seemed no way to remove the helmet without removing his head, so that's what they finally did. They cut a complete circle on his skull, lifted it off, and then replaced it as good as new, except for the metal plate in the center.

From just north of Barbastro in the Aragon, you can see the peaks of the Pyrenees wearing patches of snow like carelessly flung ermine. The countryside lays itself out in pastoral landscapes so beautiful as to seem deliberate invitations to be painted. The Fascists chose this spot to open a furious offensive, and as I carried the wounded and bleeding

away along the poplar-lined roads, war's ugliness and stupidity stood
out in even more brutal relief than ever. We were short of ambulances
and medical personnel, so I worked round the clock for three days and
nights until, very near total collapse, I was ordered back for a rest.

An American medical unit under the command of Dr. Bush was
stationed along the Mediterranean just south of Tarragona. A wide
driveway led to the villa that housed the temporary wards.

Dr. Bush took one look at me and said, "Park along the driveway
and get some sleep. When you get up we'll talk about your new
assignment."

My head was under the steering wheel and my feet stuck out the
window of the cab. The sun came in caressing and warm, and I was
deep in a dreamless tomb when I felt, dimly, a blow on my feet.

"Fuck off," I murmured without opening my eyes, not yet awake.

Harder blows. Repeated. They stung.

"I said fuck off," I yelled, struggling out from under the wheel, rub-
bing my eyes, and trying to get a look at the stupid son of a bitch who
was harassing me. When I sat up and my head cleared, I made out
four men staring at me in what I interpreted to be very high dudgeon.
Three wore officers' uniforms, sidearms, and shoulder insignia. The
fourth was in civilian clothes, wore a beret, and had a large, florid face.

"SALUTE!" shouted the civilian in an accent I decided was French.
He had what looked like an officer's baton under his arm, which explained my stinging feet.

"I don't salute fucking civilians," I said starting to lie down again.

The civilian let loose a sputtering tirade in French. I managed to get
the general message, which was that the Americans had sent over a
bunch of rich degenerates and undisciplined lumpen who were a disgrace to the anti-Fascist cause, and that I was a prime example—lying
around slovenly and lazy and probably drunk while the Republic bled.

Unfair attacks provoke response and my mind organized a crushing
counterattack. But then I thought, the hell with it, muttered a "Fuck
you, too," and lay back down under the wheel as they marched off.

Twenty minutes later a frantic nurse was shaking me awake.

"You gotta get out of here right now," she panted. "Dr. Bush says to
tell the dumb bastard there's no time to lose. He meant you."

"Why?"

"Because you insulted André Marty, the supreme commander of all the International Brigades, and he has ordered you to be shot."

"Why?"

"Because you're a disgrace to the uniform, I think."

"What uniform? I don't even have a uniform. Nobody has a uniform."

"Will you please get the hell out of here and stop arguing!"

Thirty-five kilometers to the west in the picture-postcard village of Constanti, an International Brigade ambulance-evacuation group was headquartered in a very old, very large church. On the way I thought about Marty, the legendary hero of the French Black Sea revolt, and about heroes generally, about all those heroes that sit on bronze horses in public places throughout the world and are shit upon by very wise pigeons. We have an irrepressible urge to elevate certain individuals into icons and then to recoil in shock and anger when they begin to believe what is being said about them. Naturally they become bureaucrats, tyrants, megalomaniacs, and in general the very opposite of what they were initially revered for. Don't ever be mistaken for a hero, I told myself; strive for anonymity—an achievable goal and one worthy of respect.

CHAPTER 7

1 9 3 8

It was the beginning of April, and in Catalonia the countryside was lovely, fresh, and green, very different from the barren, treeless, harsh plains of La Mancha. I was still very tired, but I was recovering strength and looking forward to a new assignment. I drove slowly, waving at the long processions of burro carts, their drivers all in peasant black except for their *alpargatas*. They looked calm, unhurried, serene, and detached. War, peace, victory, defeat, they would still get up before dawn, face a long day of back-breaking labor, and go to sleep hungry.

I got no cheery welcome in Constanti. The news was bad. The Fascists had mounted a broad offensive all along the Ebro River and had broken through our lines using planes, tanks, and massive ground forces. Our retreat was becoming a rout. Americans and British were being overrun and decimated. Those taken prisoner were summarily shot. South of the Ebro, the enemy was pushing toward the sea to cut off Madrid and the south from Barcelona and all of Catalonia.

Joe Meyer limped into the church where the drivers were frying bits of bread in olive oil, boiling rancid chicory coffee, and agonizing over the rumors and news of defeat. He was German, an anti-Nazi, and after being wounded at the fighting in Madrid he'd been put in charge of the Servicio Sanidad de Evacuación.

"Orders," said Joe. "We are to use every ambulance that will run, every driver. You know what's going on up there. We will run along north of the Ebro and pick up all the sick and wounded we can and bring them to Mataró and Sabinosa." They were two large hospitals on the Costa Brava.

"We hear thousands of our guys are still south of the river. Why don't we cross?" asked a driver, voicing what many of us were thinking.

"Because the bridges are being blown up by Stukas. We wouldn't get back."

"What the hell is a Stuka?"

Barcelona, Spain
June - 1938

One thing about ambulance
drivers, they get a chance to
pose for pictures, usually
leaning casually on a fender.
Mine was probably dented,
so I came away with this.

"It's a new German fast-bomber," said Joe. "It dives down on a target using the plane itself as an aiming device, and it's deadly."

The evacuation ambulances were huge, ungainly. They looked like Mexican commuter-buses. Some were fitted for stretchers and others had only thinly padded seats. Mine had six stretchers and had been nicknamed, for reasons no one could remember, the 88.

The towns and villages along the Ebro were being bombed into rubble, and the roads were being strafed. Retreating soldiers had to cross the river, swollen and swift from heavy spring rains, the best way they could. Strong swimmers made it, others drowned. They emerged from the riverbanks and olive groves singly and in small groups. Some were naked. Scratched and bleeding, eyes staring and blank, they moved mechanically, uncertainly. They had been through more than they could bear, and most were in shock. I picked up as many as I could—Americans, British, and Spaniards—and ran them back to Sabinosa.

Near Falset on one trip I tried to get fuel. The town had been flat-tened (it was a few miles from the river), but a gas station was still pumping. In the waiting line of cars one flew a correspondent's flag from the front fender. In it were Herbert L. Matthews, the *New York Times* man, and Ernest Hemingway.

An air-raid warning wailed and everyone went for the *refugio*. When we came out, I was introduced to Matthews, whom I hadn't met but of whom I had heard a lot, all good. And I had read some of his stories.

"We've been up and down the river," said Hemingway. "It's real bad."

"Ran across Freddie Keller," said Matthews. "He was wounded in the hip but he swam the river twice. Brought a man over who could barely swim."

"Too many will not get across," said Hemingway. "Too many will die because a superior cause is not a match for superior fire power."

I could see that they were depressed and worried. They were not hiding their feelings behind the detached, cynical, phony-objective pose adopted by most of the army of reporters who hung around the Majestic bar in Barcelona. I liked them very much for that.

"Will the Republic be cut in two?" I asked.

"Yes, if it hasn't already happened," said Matthews. "But not at

Tortosa. Probably Vinaroz. They were only a mile away from the sea as of yesterday."

"In Geneva," Hemingway grunted, "the Republic is being cut into many pieces. League of Nations, my ass. League of connivers. Austrian Anschluss, Munich Pact—Hitler scowls and Chamberlain feeds him another country."

"Speaking of feeding, got any chow?" I asked. "My stomach is so empty a sardine would feel like a striped bass."

"Not much here either," said Matthews, rummaging through a bag on the back seat. "Can let you have some rice and a tin of cocoa."

"Bless you. I will personally put in a good word with whoever it is you pray to."

I didn't feel embarrassed at all asking them for food. Everybody did it because everybody was hungry all the time. Even lentils and garbanzos had begun to taste good.

Thousands of retreating soldiers continued to filter out of the scraggly hills and olive groves of the Sierra Pandols. The Lincolns had fought their way back all the way from Belchite and Caspe through Maella to Gandesa, and then, scattered and broken, they had crossed the river wherever they could from Mora de Ebro to Flix. By April 12, they could count no more than forty Americans remaining of the 450 who had left Belchite together. The others had been killed doing hopeless battle against overwhelming odds, or had been captured and summarily executed, or else had drowned.

I made a last trip up to Flix, picked up a full load of casualties at the emergency medical station, and this time took them to Mataró, a seaside hospital near Tarragona. Strafing and bombing had now subsided somewhat, but the charred and broken landscape was a nightmarish reminder of scenes from *All Quiet on the Western Front*. Man is so much more efficient at destroying than at building—years of mature, creative sweat to build, seconds of button pushing macho to blast and burn. And while I was thinking this, the talk in the ambulance behind me filtered through. It was dejected, defeatist, gloomy talk, as it had to be from men whose bodies had been mercilessly battered, but the worst wounds were deep in their heads.

"*Finito*," I heard one say. "For us it's over. I think we should go home."

That was how they felt. They had fought well on many fronts. But now, with only a handful left, wasn't it merely quixotic to stay?

"Militarily," said one, "we mean less than a hair on a gnat's ass."

I could see the point. No one wants to die, least of all meaninglessly, least of all as some romantic gesture. We were real veterans, and heroics made us throw up.

I expected criticism of the generals, commanders, officers, and politicians who had gotten us into this costly disaster, and there was some. But we agreed that defeat was not the fault of Madrid, or the general staff, or our own officers, but rather of Geneva, Washington, London—and maybe the fault belonged not even to them but to what was behind them. Again I felt that great unseen forces were at work, taking charge of history and manipulating it, mocking our agony over whether this or that personal decision would be most true to our own self-portrait.

Armed conflict is not an exercise in justice. The winners have the most guns. Chaplains ought to explain to the troops that God understands this. He has to be practical; it just wouldn't do for HIM to wind up on the losing side.

The wild fighting from Belchite to the Ebro River must have exhausted the Fascist side too, because most of the front quieted down. May, June, and July were marked by fierce but localized skirmishes. The ambulance base was no longer at Constanti but had been moved north to a vast wine-making estate near Villafranca del Panadés.

There we found deep cellars with giant vats full of wine. It was better than water for drinking where plumbing is primitive, but it was also, ironically, an appetite stimulant that we didn't need, not with a dwindling food supply.

There was time to rest and talk, to speculate. Some of the other drivers had also been dragooned into the ambulance service from early convalescence and had wounds now healed or nearly so. They could manage to carry a gun. We all knew that the Americans were at rest and were miraculously being reborn near the village of Marsa. One hundred and sixty partially trained Americans, the last to arrive from the States, had crossed the river to the north just days before Franco cut the Republic in two, and together with hundreds of very young Spanish draftees they were being integrated into the battalion. The Lincolns, or what was left of them, were getting ready to fight again.

The estate kitchen was huge. In the middle was a great oaken table furnished always with decanters and tall, dark wine bottles. When we talked, we sat around it in heavily carved, massive chairs.

"Maybe we should quit this shit and rejoin the Lincolns up at Marsa," I said.

Sid Lavine, a student from the University of Southern California, gasped as though he had been kicked in the solar plexus by a burro. "You buckin' for the crazy medal?" he asked with heavy sarcasm. "We've all had a gutful. What are you trying to prove?"

"Don't get mad," I said. "I'm trying to sort this out for myself too. I seem to remember that when we first got here we didn't think of driving. We came to shoot and to be shot at."

"Things were different then." Moe Domes was older, and usually silent. It surprised us that he spoke. "There was no army—just people grabbing guns and storming the barricades. The Internationals came along with some military sophistication, training, and discipline. People saw a hope, not only to defend themselves but to win. Now they have a real army, their own Spanish army."

"So if our job is over why don't we just get the hell out of the way and go home?" asked Sid.

"I didn't say it was over," said Moe, "just different. And politically, if you're an anti-Fascist you belong here, no matter what."

"You guys must have rocks in your head," Kenny Graeber joined in. Kenny was pure Kansas. Blond, blue-eyed, round, and baby-faced, he would look like eighteen when he was forty. "Don't you pay attention to the casualty figures? By percentages we have had more of our guys killed, wounded, and captured than anybody. This is not a picnic; it's tough and it's by God dangerous."

"You know you're right," said Sid. "Come to think about it, we can't get enough drivers to handle the lousy ambulances we have now. And this is the first we've had a rest break in months. We're used by the whole damn army. If there's action, we're in it. I think I know every pothole on the Iberian peninsula, and the Iberians, as we all know, lead the world in potholes."

Joe Meyer came in, and we accused him of eavesdropping because he said fighting had broken out near Lérida and that Moe Domes should get on up there.

When it was my turn I was sent to the small hospital at Reus to transport soldiers who had survived surgery to S'agaro, a convalescent center on the Costa Brava north of Barcelona. Just before you got there, you went through San Feliu de Guixols, a village so ridiculously picturesque as to be almost offensive, with its balconied, red-tiled, snowy white houses facing a beach carpeted with fishing nets laid out to dry, some draped artistically over double-ended dories and attended to by leathery-faced fishermen from central casting. There was, however, a supremely redeeming factor that those of us who had discovered swore a blood oath never to reveal—the ordinary-looking little cafe in the center of the village served the most succulent, delicious, melt-in-the-mouth fish dishes in all Europe. Inevitably, years later, the village succumbed and became a postcard.

S'agaro itself, high up on a rocky escarpment, was a collection of villas that had been owned by the nobility and the super-rich. Cantilevered mansions clung to the seaside cliffs like the stilt houses that hang from the Hollywood Hills. Some had small, glass-enclosed elevators so that if you suffered from vertigo you could proceed directly to catatonic panic. Many of the wounded soldiers hated the place and felt uncomfortable in it. Then they would drink too much wine and get into fights, using their airplane splints as battering rams and rebreaking their bones.

S'agaro was a front-row seat in the evening for watching the Italian Caproni bombers flying in over the sea from their base on Majorca to bomb Barcelona. The bombing had been random and round the clock, aimed not just at the dock area but at the central plazas, apartment houses, schools, and shops. There were many thousands of casualties. Barcelona was my favorite place, a rakish, cocky, debonair city. It hurt to see it mutilated.

On the way back to base, I wondered if the other drivers were as

troubled as I was by the conversations we had been having, conversations that got down, I supposed, to the role of the individual in modern
mass society. What can one person do? Does it matter what one does?
Can it have any real effect? It certainly matters to me what I do, I
thought. We all have to come to terms with ourselves, decide who we
are, what we are, and then act on it. If I cross another man's picket line
because my kids are hungry, then I'm a scab, and all the rationalizations are still rationalizations.

Besides, in the midst of battle one does not dream of an old-age pen-
sion. If someone you knew well dies, you think, too bad, he was a good
guy, and you go on. There is grief for the loss, but not regret. Everybody dies, but not everybody knows the joy of living by their own
script.

The other part is harder. How much does it matter to the cosmic
plan whether or not I, personally, am in Spain if at the same time
Neville Chamberlain is off making a disastrous deal with Adolf Hitler?
Conscripts don't worry about such things much; volunteers think
about them all the time.

On the southern front, Madrid and Valencia, cut off from help from
the north, began to come under tremendous pressure. Valencia particularly was a Franco target. On July 25, the Republican government
ordered a wide-ranging attack on the northern front to relieve the pressure on Valencia. Government forces, including the Lincolns, were to
recross the Ebro and penetrate as far as they could into Fascist-held
territory.

Franco was taken by surprise, but not because he didn't know about
the planned offensive. In fact, he knew all about it from his intelligence agents and aerial observation. He just couldn't believe it. He
could not imagine that the Loyalists would have the temerity to throw
themselves against his overwhelming superiority in planes, tanks, artillery, and manpower.

So for the first day or two it was a walk in the country. After that, the
fighting was as fierce and murderous as any in the war, perhaps worse,
because aerial bombardment and strafing went on without pause, hour
after hour, day after day.

All ambulances were ordered to the front. "Take 88 and Antonio up to the Thirty-fifth Division's Sanidad headquarters in Mora la Nueva," said Joe Meyer. "They'll assign you from there."

Antonio was Antonio Ascaso, a twenty-year-old from Alicante I was training to eventually take over the ambulance on his own. He was small but very strong, and he had no trouble holding up his end of the stretcher even when the wounded soldier on it was twice his size.

His father, a metalworker, had been killed the first day of the uprising when, unarmed like the rest, he had joined in storming the pro-Franco Guardia Civil barracks. His mother then became a volunteer nurse's aide in the Alicante military hospital.

Antonio had been an apprentice metalworker from the age of seventeen and was about to become a journeyman when war came. He was delighted to have been assigned to the Internationals, and especially to the *americanos*. He liked jokes, laughter came quickly to him, and he was a quick learner. Two things had the power to transform him. He hated Franco and everything he stood for, and he became inarticulate with rage when Franco's name was mentioned. He changed also when he sat behind the wheel. He grabbed it fiercely like the throat of an enemy, stared straight ahead, and jammed the accelerator to the floor. Years later travelers to Spain from the corners of the earth were to note in their diaries this same characteristic of Spanish drivers.

From Mora la Nueva we crossed the Ebro on a rickety pontoon bridge and bounced along the rutted and shell-pocked road toward Corbera and Gandesa, hearing always the booming artillery barrages and constant aerial bombardment. We crossed the rocky, wooded hills, and steeply terraced ridges until we came to a first-aid station, a small adobe house in an olive grove just off the road, where doctors and nurses moved about among the wounded, who were lying all around on stretchers. They gave injections, stopped the bleeding, and bandaged arms, legs, and heads—only enough to prepare their patients for the trip farther back to a hospital. It was there that life-preserving surgery could be performed—the amputation of gangrenous limbs, or the removal of torn stomachs, livers, and kidneys—there where all the advances of military science could be tested against the advances of medical science, more proof, if any were needed, of the creator's genius in maintaining the delicate symbiotic balance of nature. After Antonio and I transferred those who could travel to our ambulance stretchers, a very young Spanish nurse tried to clean the station's clotted, blood-soaked stretchers for further use. She couldn't make much headway, which made her cry.

Between Gandesa and the river there are a series of high, steep ridges. Along the eastern face of one ran an enormous crevice hundreds of feet long and extending deep into the almost flat, coal-black rock. Protected from both artillery and air, it was a perfect site for the Division Hospital, and there for the next three weeks, as fighting increased daily in intensity, we made our grisly deliveries.

We had been lucky. As targets, ambulances were not immune. They were shot at, strafed, and bombed. On a moonless night on the way up to the front, Antonio and I had talked about our good luck, and I said it never lasts forever. We had to run without lights, even the ones that were blacked out except for a tiny, horizontal slit in the center of the headlamp, because as we came over the top of a ridge we would be clearly visible to the enemy.

The road, like all the roads, had been shelled repeatedly. Even now shells came crashing over. Antonio opened the door and leaned out. On his side the terraces of stunted olive trees rose steeply upward. His job was to keep us close to them because on my side the drop down through the scraggy trees was precipitous and deep. The road itself was bleached white, narrow, stony, and potholed, hardly a road at all—more a trail.

I felt my left front wheel dip sickeningly. A shell must have torn out most of the road. Old 88 was born ugly, unwieldy, and top-heavy. It began to roll over. "Hang on!" I yelled to Antonio. They were words I was to regret forever; he should have jumped. "Sí, Mealy Tone," he answered. He sounded happily excited.

I hung on to the wheel in the suddenly spinning darkness. We rolled completely over, jarred, shuddered, seemed to rise in a dizzying leap, rolled over again, hit, and bounced. I felt the spinning, disembodied, floating sensation and then the black, hurting-all-over end of the fall. I was lying on my back on the inside of the driver's cab.

Our 88 had turned over three times on the way down and was lying on its side, wheels still spinning in the air. I was in pain but I could move. It took a few minutes to work my way out, and when I did, even in the darkness, I could see that 88 stretched halfway up the hillside. It had come apart like a child's toy, its insides spilled and scattered over three levels of terraces. Stretchers and seats lay about, and from an old, stunted olive tree a blanket hung like a flag at half-mast.

Antonio. Where was Antonio? I called his name and listened, and there was only silence. Then I started searching in growing fear of what I might find. I didn't see him till I got almost to the top. He had been leaning out the open door and must have been crushed on the first rollover. His body lay broken and twisted, and I knew he was dead even before I felt for a pulse in his limp wrist.

I tried to stand up but was overcome by a wave of nausea and dizziness. I sat down next to him, drained and empty, and I wept.

I don't know how long I sat there, but it was a long time. The nightmare feeling of rolling and falling through the dark kept playing through my head over and over. Then the guilt came. Why Antonio and not me? It was the universal guilt of soldiers who see their comrades die and who grieve but cannot suppress relief and joy and surprise to still be alive themselves.

I had been resting my chin in my hand and it felt wet. It was blood. There were cuts and bruises over my eye, near my left ear, and in other places. I remembered that I kept a first-aid kit in the ambulance and started down toward the driver's cab. The first light of dawn was breaking and I could make things out better. The carcass of the ambulance looked more dead, more ugly. There seemed to be something lying on one of the upturned wheels, but how could that be? Approaching from the uphill side, I could see that there was something. I reached over and got it. It was a book, a new book that had just come out. It was by Elliot Paul and was titled *The Life and Death of a Spanish Town*. Shit, I thought to myself, no one will believe this; I don't believe it. I decided never to tell anyone about it, and I never did.

Daylight came and with it military traffic on the road above. I caught a ride with an ammo carrier back down to the cliff hospital. One of the American nurses, it was either Anne Taft or Ruth Davidow, I think, clucked sympathetically, dressed my bruises, and asked what I would do next.

I was still in shock about Antonio. Inside I felt nervous and shaken, but I made what I thought was the required stab at macho insouciance. "Oh," trying to be airy, "I suppose I'll go back and grab myself another ambulance."

I went down the steep cliff-path towards the Mora road trying to analyze the effect my remark had had on the nurses. Was it quiet, respectful admiration for gallant courage, or had I detected a hint of amused tolerance for the irrepressible need for males, in the presence of women, to act like jerks.

I wasn't paying much attention to the incessant rumble of artillery, but as I reached the road another all-too-familiar roar ravaged the air. Bombers, enemy *aviones* with pilots who I was sure had seen me and were aiming their screaming bombs at the small of my back. I saw a culvert and dived for it. Other soldiers were already there, grinning and making crude jokes as I rolled in.

"Hi, Milt, you old fucker," said a voice. It was Jerry Cook. I hadn't seen him since our convalescent time in Huete, a time already as distant as childhood. When there is action, two weeks ago is only dimly remembered. The present moment is all-consuming, compressing experience into an intense concentration. There is little room for thought or contemplation, only for the moment itself and for the underlying mental pinch: You and I, we're still here—goddamn.

"This where you hang out?" I said. "In sewers? Progressive anti-Fascist mankind the world over surely does not picture you sitting in a fuckin' ditch. Drinking tea yet."

Of the dozen who had sought refuge in the culvert, three or four were from the British battalion, and they had, somehow, made tea. The British always made tea. It is their historic way of asserting the existence of sanity, despite so much evidence to the contrary.

Jerry laughed. "I was up in the hospital. Came down just ahead of you, I guess."

"What'd you do, get hit again?"

"Not serious. *Mucho* blood but no broken bones. A shard or two of shrapnel, mostly in the hip. What about you?"

I explained about the ambulance, and Antonio.

I was offered tea in a tin can that used the bent-back cover as a handle. It tasted delicious. One flight of bombers left but another one came, so it was hard to talk.

"Old George Green got killed," said Jerry.

"I heard. I think Nan went back to London."

"We had good times in Huete."

"Almost too good. Sex, music, good talk, tea in real cups. Good we left before we got completely corrupted."

"They say," said Jerry, "that all the Internationals will soon be pulled out and sent home."

"Yeah. I heard that too. Makes me nervous. Nobody wants to be the last casualty."

"Gets your name in the papers. Joe Blow, last American killed in Spain with a Nazi bomb up his ass, courtesy of our hero, Franklin Delano Roosevelt."

"He needs the Catholic vote."

WHOPP! WHOPP! WHOPP! There weren't that many targets left, so what the hell could they be bombing? Maybe they had a quota.

"In the next war," said Jerry. "a lot of Catholics will pay a price for those votes."

The bombing finally stopped and we crawled out. We looked back up at the hospital, but the cliff overhang had kept it safe. There was a dead burro with an overturned, two-wheeled peasant cart still hitched to it lying in the middle of the cratered road, but no sign of the driver. Otherwise there were uprooted trees and deep, jagged craters.

"When you get back to Corbera," I said as Jerry and I embraced, "say hello to the guys for me."

"Won't take long. Not that many left."

It was the first week in September, but the heat shimmered in waves over the road as I watched Jerry trudge away. It had been one of the hottest summers on record, bad news for gladiators. When soldiers fell they began to swell almost at once, bloating until they looked like huge, overstuffed dolls, turning black in the sun and stinking horribly.

I went back to Mora on a Russian truck, but they had no spare ambulances there so I waited for a ride to Vilafranca del Penedes. I expected to be chewed out about losing the ambulance, but Joe Meyer didn't give a damn about that. He was deeply affected by the news about

Antonio. In a very short time we had all become fond of Antonio, and Joe was no exception. He found another ambulance for me, but I don't think he ever quite forgave me for not taking care of Antonio.

I was given a bouncy, two-stretcher Chevy van and a new assistant, Jaime (which in Spanish comes out close to Hymie), who could not have been a day over eighteen but as a streetwise *madrileño* seemed older than Antonio. His darkly handsome face wore a habitually wary expression. I figured him to be a Gypsy from the way he sang flamenco and played guitar. The hoarse, gravelly low notes were followed by the curling Moorish wail in the high register, and the guitar spilled out cascades of throbbing sounds very few non-Gypsies could make. He loved to make his music and I enjoyed listening, never more than very late at night driving along a lonely, tree-lined road with the incessant artillery a faint rumble, like bass drums, in the background.

I didn't tell him about Antonio. There didn't seem to be much point. When we went to the front and the action was heavy he had a matter-of-fact bravery and didn't flinch, but we didn't become close. It may have been that after Antonio I was chary about getting too involved. It's strange that Jaime's memory remains so vivid, because on September 22, after we were together less than a month, word came that all the Internationals were being withdrawn from active duty preparatory to being repatriated.

In Switzerland, near the peaceful waters of Lake Geneva, dignified diplomats with perfectly straight faces had agreed to the Spanish Republic's proposal that all persons on both sides who had come to Spain after July 18, 1936, should leave the country immediately. An official League of Nations Commission led by a Fascist general from Finland would take full charge.

The Americans got the news, but for a couple of days the knowledge itself seemed like a particularly cruel practical joke. At the time we were holding an important outpost under ferocious attack and could not leave until replacements arrived. Under such circumstances, the cliché of the last casualty is no longer a cliché. The troops said sardonically that it was like being goosed by the long, bony, fickle finger of fate.

There came weeks of strange, contradictory, disturbing, and confused feelings. At first, if anyone was honest enough to admit it, we felt relief to be leaving deadly danger, but that gave way quickly to guilt about the brave young Spanish troops, boys really, who were left behind. We also felt guilt about not having done what we had come to do, prove that fascism could be resisted and defeated. The Lincolns were in Marsa again, passing the time in fiestas and farewell ceremonies, but they were just going through the motions and no one's heart was in it. Small groups applied for permission to go to Barcelona where they would do the traditional soldier thing—find a waterfront whorehouse off the Ramblas and get listlessly laid.

The medical services were back up at Vilafranca, where it was decided that it would not be a violation of the Geneva agreement for us to continue rearguard "humanitarian" work. That meant we kept our ambulances and could be assigned anywhere in Catalonia as long as we stayed away from the front. It was good to be occupied. I had run into friends from Marsa, and they'd said they were going nuts sitting around.

There was a hospital northwest of Barcelona in Gerona. It was a small, beautiful city with a river running through it, and the war seemed not to have touched it. It had food, real food, and wine. The air had turned brisk, clean, and cool this early fall in the high, fertile, rich plateau-country of the Pyrenees. If it was possible to wangle a trip to Gerona, I went.

Angelica Muñoz ran the hospital kitchen. Maybe thirty-four or thirty-five years old, she was handsome rather than pretty, her face a shade too strong, her expression serious, with a hint of sadness around the mouth. Like many Catalans she was a little taller than average, but she avoided being statuesque. The young girls, mostly local, who assisted her jumped when she made a request.

On my last two trips I had noticed that she had prepared my plate herself and heaped it high. When I thanked her she smiled a very shy smile and blushed. About the third week in October, I made a last trip to Gerona. Angelica recognized the ambulance, and when I came in for lunch she brought me a plate covered with another plate. With a little flourish she couldn't resist, she removed the covering plate and revealed an honest-to-god beefsteak sitting in a circle of thin, crisp potatoes.

Very possibly I overdid my gratitude. In any case, when I finished she asked me to help her with a basket of laundry. She held one side of the basket, and I inferred that she was taking it to her home when we crossed the street and started up a narrow stair that led to her small apartment. Without any preliminaries and without a word, she undressed, got into bed, and started to cry.

I was startled and completely confused. With the back of one hand she dabbed at her eyes, and with the other she motioned for me to approach. I couldn't handle it. All along there had been something about her that reminded me of Miss Lazarus, my high-school Latin teacher. The sudden switch to a lachrymose femme fatale struck me as absurd, almost comic.

"*Qué pasa*, Angelica?" (What the hell is going on?)

"You look like my husband, Angel."

"Where is Angel?"

"I do not know. For almost two years I have had not one word." She wore a rather large cross around her neck on a heavy gold chain, which she now fingered nervously. "Dead. I am sure he is dead." More tears.

Shit, I thought, I'm a stand-in. She doesn't give a hoot in hell for me. She aches to embrace a memory. Recognition of her pain only made the situation worse. The last thing I wanted, or felt able to do, was to act out her fantasy. I searched my mind desperately for a way to leave that would not be cruel.

Three weeks later in Ripoll, when I related this incident to Jerry Cook, I asked him what he would have done.

"Easy," he said, "I would have screwed her and hung around for some more steak."

"No, you wouldn't," I said.

"No, I guess I wouldn't at that," he said. "So tell me already. What *did* you do?"

"I asked her what outfit her husband was in, and when she said she wasn't sure but thought it was the Fifth Regiment, I told her to relax—that meant he was with Col. Lister and he was the best there was. She was still sobbing, so I put an arm around her shoulder, kissed her ear, and came up with one of those lies that are at times so much better than the truth. I told her the reason I was driving an ambulance was that I had been wounded in a place and in a way that I preferred not to describe but that made former male interests academic at best.

"What happened next I was completely unprepared for. '¡Ay, qué lástima!' she cried out (what a bloody shame) and acted like earth-mother of the year. She forgot all about her own troubles and I was awash in her sympathy for mine. Luckily she didn't ask to see the evidence. She enfolded me in a motherly embrace, and I felt within an inch of being suckled. 'Pobre chico' (poor boy), she kept repeating. When I finally got to the door she managed a little good-bye wave. I know she was feeling much better when I left. Did I do such a bad thing?"

"I don't know," said Jerry, "let me see your wound."

During October and early November all the Americans were being rounded up and sent to Ripoll, on the Spanish slopes of the Pyrenees. But on October 29, a glorious sunny day, all of Barcelona turned out to pay tribute to the departing International Brigades as they paraded with flags flying along the wide Diagonal. Streets, balconies, and roof-tops were packed with cheering, shouting, weeping men and women. Children ran out to the marchers with great bouquets of flowers, and the soldiers were embraced, wept over, and kissed.

Dolores Ibarruri (La Pasionaria), the most eloquent voice of Loyalist Spain, addressed the emotionally charged mass of humanity below her platform, speaking first to the women. "When the years pass by and the wounds of war are stanched, speak to your children," she urged. "Tell them of the International Brigades. Tell them how these men gave up everything—their loves, their country, home, and fortune—and they came and told us, 'We're here because Spain's cause is ours.' Thousands are staying here with the Spanish earth."

Then she spoke directly to us: "You can go proudly. You are history. You are legend. You are the heroic example of democracy's solidarity and universality. We shall not forget you, and when the olive tree of peace puts forth its leaves again, mingled with the laurels of the Spanish republic's victory, come back."

Her voice, her words, her beautiful, strong Spanish face, the flags, the cheers, and the tears would live deep within me for the rest of my life. No one could escape being affected by the emotional impact of that day. Even the cynical, hardened press corps felt it deeply, and many of them said so in their reports.

For all the volunteers from more than fifty countries, it was a great, unforgettable day. But it was also a difficult, disturbing, contradictory day. One part of us rejoiced that after almost two years and everything we'd been through we were finally going home, alive and in one piece. But another part said, the war is not over; tomorrow someone else will die in your place. You have not done what you came to do. Franco is winning, and fascism is winning. Has all the sacrifice, the dying, been for nothing?

Those thoughts, and the deeper issues that underlay them, continued to haunt the volunteers as we sat around at Ripoll with nothing to do but wait for the head of the Geneva Repatriation Commission, or as we referred to the illustrious leader, "the Fascist fuck from Finland."

Before long, trucks came with civilian clothes. When we finished answering the Commission questionnaire, we were outfitted. We were back to cheap suits, ill-fitting shoes, and berets—at last coming full circle.

On the surface we expressed optimism. The Republic was united and determined, and it was growing in military sophistication and efficiency. The people, the fabulous Spanish people, would not succumb. That's what we said, but what we thought was different.

We had learned the awful lessons of military arithmetic, the higher math of guns, planes, tanks, and aircraft. The words of diplomats may be smooth and noble, but if you want to know what they mean, pay attention to where they send their guns, and most of all, to whom. If the politics did not change, the Spain we had come to love was doomed, and we knew it.

Why? Why? Why? Munich was still fresh in the news. I asked Jerry Cook what he made of Neville Chamberlain and the pact in Munich.

"A bribe for Hitler to go ahead and attack the Soviet Union—everybody knows that," he said.

"Do you think that, as some say, all great events since 1917 are

Jerry Cook, Ripoll,
November 1938.

joined by one thread, the intention of capitalism to undermine and, if possible, destroy communism?"

"I'm not sure. But let me put it this way. The rise of Mussolini in Italy, Tojo in Japan, Franco in Spain, and Hitler in Germany—all certified anti-Communists you notice—would not have been possible without heavy financing and diplomatic support from the advanced industrial countries."

"Then why don't the Russians send more help here to defeat Franco? I've been here almost two years and I've never even seen a Russian."

"You've seen planes, tanks, and guns, and food, and trucks. If they sent men it would soon be a Russian war, not a Spanish war. Why not ask why France hasn't sent help? Or England?"

"My big problem," I mused, "is to decide what I'm for. I have no trouble defining what I'm against. Francisco Franco. Adolf Hitler. They make it easy."

"I know what you're for," said Jerry. "You're for an ideal world where the darker side of human nature is eliminated with a socially uplifting enema and everyone makes nice to everyone."

"Something like that," I laughed. "Some of your best friends could turn out to be enemas."

On December 2, 1938, nearly two hundred Americans boarded the bravely decorated train that was to take us fifteen mountainous miles to the French border at Puigcerdá and then across it into France. The night before had been full of meetings and speeches of farewell, and a tiny *carabinero* brass band had marched through the cold, snowy streets back and forth until three in the morning. Our transportation home was provided, and we had been given a small amount of mustering-out pay.

At 10 A.M. the train pulled into the tiny station at Puigcerdá. We were two hours ahead of schedule, but the mayor and the entire population were ready. He made his speech, and the crowd cheered and raised their arms in the Popular Front salute as we crossed the border to the French village of Bourg-Madame.

Jerry Cook and I got off the train together and stood looking back at Puigcerdá, and Spain. Less than a mile away, it was already becoming a happy-sad mythic mirage deep in our beings. And as we stared, we heard the familiar, pulsing, ominous roar of heavy bombers. And then we saw them, dark as vultures in the sky, two full squadrons of German Junkers coming in over the little town at the exact hour our departure had been scheduled.

In horror, all the Americans stood and watched the bombs drop and the smoke begin to rise. The bombs that were meant for us were now blowing to bits the sweet, simple people who had come only to say good-bye.

I looked at Jerry. His face was a grimace of pain and anger. "A perfect Fascist valentine," he spat out. "Good-bye. Remember us. We are the people who kill. You no longer fight? We kill you anyway. Killing is what we do."

"I wonder," I said, "when the God who gives the Generalíssimo his instructions told him to do that."

"Must have been last night," said Jerry, "before God had a chance to revise the train schedule."

CHAPTER 8

1938

Right-wing accommodation to Nazism was already entering the bloodstream of French politics. People had gathered at the station to cheer us, but the police herded us into ancient boxcars and shunted us off unceremoniously toward Toulouse. We didn't know it, but concentration camps were already being constructed along the icy cold beaches just north of the Spanish border. Six months later Senegalese guards would herd hundreds of thousands of Spanish refugees behind their barbed wire to suffer starvation, indescribable degradation, and death. At St. Cyr there was not one latrine for 25,000 people. No Lincoln vet was in the least surprised when two years later France fell to Hitler without resistance. The fruit had long been rotten.

At Toulouse the three decrepit cars into which we had been jammed were hooked onto the rear of the Toulouse-Paris express, the fastest train in Europe. The train jerked out of the station with such speed that the possessions we had stowed overhead came tumbling down about us. Somewhere Milt Wolff had managed to acquire an enormous, ugly brown leather suitcase.

Wolff, beginning as a private, had risen to the rank of major in command of the Lincolns. He was very tall, popular, and led a seemingly charmed life, having survived every battle unharmed. Comments on his suitcase had been distinctly unflattering, and when it hit him sharply on the back of the head, Jerry Cook put an arm around his shoulder.

"Wolff," he said, "this is how it's going to be. Nothing could touch you in war but you'll never survive peace. Let's face it, you're a military genius and a civilian klutz. I grieve for you already."

Within ten minutes we were sure we would never reach Paris. The cars jumped and shuddered and swayed. They were built for thirty miles an hour and were doing ninety-five. They would never stay on the tracks. They had cracked wooden benches and broken windows through which the air whistled like a drunken banshee. There was general agreement that the French government had concocted a diabolically clever Gallic plot to dispose of us.

We had no idea where we were going, except somehow, sometime, back to America. Word of the train and its strange cargo of "International Revolutionary Adventurer-Desperadoes" must have been spread in the press because at the one or two brief stops, nuns and Red Cross women tried to hand us bread and cheese. They were turned away roughly by gendarmes standing all along the tracks with rifles at the ready.

We were truly surprised to reach Paris, but the train was our prison and we were not allowed to leave it. We remained cooped up in the railroad yards overnight. An American correspondent for the Paris *Herald Tribune* came out and shouted to us that they were trying to find a ship that would take us back to the States, but there was fear that we were lawless roughnecks and would rape the passengers and destroy the ship. However, rumor had it that the *Normandie* would take a chance. Most of the vets were furious at the distortions being circulated about our characters and our records in an anti-Fascist war. Some reacted rather differently.

"I'm worried," said a little guy named Lou from the Lower East Side whose last name I don't remember. "First Lincoln—living up to him was bad enough. Now they expect Errol Flynn?"

True. The *Normandie* would take us. We went to Le Havre, but at the train station there was a grand confusion. The crew of the *Normandie* had gone on strike that morning. A delegation of mariner strike-leaders came on the train to speak with us. Would we sail on a scab ship? Fuck no! Pandemonium among the French officials in charge of us. A true *contretemps*.

After a time, new instructions were phoned from Paris. Take the damned Americans to the Hill. Fine. But first we were offered, and gladly accepted, the honor of leading the strikers back down to the docks for impossibly long but rousing speeches about international solidarity that would win historic victories for the workers in an industry that would all but disappear in less than twenty years. The Hill was a walled and fenced-in compound that served as a French Ellis Island for immigrants and emigrés waiting to be processed. It no longer exists;

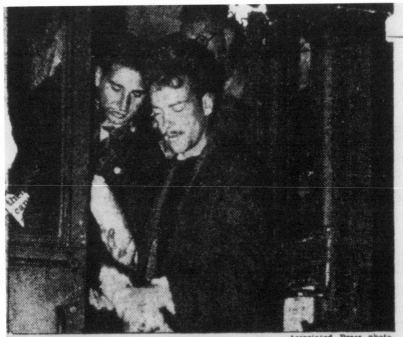

—Associated Press photo.

In a special "sealed train," 326 Americans who have been fighting with the Loyalist forces in Spain, arrived at the Gare d'Austerlitz, en route to Havre where they will be transported back to America. Insert shows food being served the group by nurses.

Spain Veterans Still Are Held
Under Heavy Guard in Havre

326 Americans Denied Freedom While Awaiting Vessel
Home; Declare They Will Not Travel on Any
Ship Manned by Strikebreakers

HAVRE, Dec. 5.—Still completely ignorant of whatever plans have been made for their departure from France refused to let them enter the barracks or to allow any of the confined veterans to approach the gates to meet them.

December 5, 1938.
Foreground, with mustache,
Jerry Cook; left, holding
bread, me.

the German Nazis blew it to bits in World War II. For us, in bleak pre-Christmas days of 1938, it was prison. We would stay till a ship would take us, and with our public image none would.

Physical conditions were not bad—cots, blankets, and boring cafeteria-level food. There were card games and listless talk. And there was the irritating, frustrating, demeaning fact of confinement. That was what was so bad. After two years of horrendous war, a leading "democracy" had thrown us into a stinking jail!

After two days Jerry Cook said to me, "Let's get out of here."

Jackie Shafron was with him. "Yeah. Let's blow the joint."

"How?"

"I think," said Jackie, "I found a spot where we can make it over the wall."

"When?"

"What's wrong with tonight?"

"Not so good," said Jerry. "More guards at night. Better tomorrow about noon. French guards get sleepy at noon. They're well known for that."

At noon the next day we strolled over to Jackie Shafron's spot, tilted a long board we'd found the night before against the wall, and scaled it easily. There wasn't a soul in sight.

We started down a street that curved sharply down toward the center of Le Havre. The raw December wind blew right through my suit jacket, but I didn't mind. To our right was the open sea, and up close we could see great freighters lying at anchor.

"It seems so strange," I said.

"Of course," said Jackie. "The signs are in French. The people wear French clothes. These things happen all the time in France."

"I don't mean that," I said. "I mean I don't hear artillery. I don't hear guns. Don't you feel it? The quiet? Is Spain out of you so soon?"

"Spain isn't out of me," said Jerry. "I think it will never be out of me, out of any of us. But we're out of Spain, that's the fact. We're out and we're going back home. Now if you want something scary, that's scary."

We came to a small bistro. "Drink?" suggested Jerry. Sure.

"Very nice hot rum toddy," suggested the waitress, smiling and trying out her few words of English. "Good. Very, very good. Warm and friendly all the way down."

"Keep 'em coming," said Jackie. "We've got a big empty hole to fill up."

"Easy," said Jerry. "Time to go. Gendarmes will be looking any time now."

But in town we couldn't help it. We overdosed on food-shop windows packed with meats and fowl; *boulangeries* piled with brioches, croissants, and fruit tarts; *charcuteries* with mysterious-smelling sausages; and the bold glistening colors of fresh vegetables.

Jackie stopped in the middle of a street. "I don't have to look anymore," he said. "All I want to do is close my eyes and smell."

We turned a corner and saw three or four gendarmes coming along the street. They appeared to be searching.

"Time to split," said Jerry. Jackie ran up a narrow alley. Jerry and I ran in the opposite direction. The streets were narrow and twisted. On a corner there was a blue enamel sign with white lettering, Rue de Coq. We were in the sprawling red-light district, at that time one of the biggest anywhere in the world. Girls in doorways saw us running and divined with a sure instinct that the *flics*, the common enemy, were involved.

"Ici! Ici!" they cried out. "Venez, venez ici!" One of the houses had a large double doorway that a girl was holding open, and we made for it.

As soon as we were inside she closed the door and motioned us to a broad, carpeted stairway. We crossed a foyer furnished with rather elegant turn-of-the-century chairs and sofas and climbed a long flight to the reception room. Half a dozen young women chattering and laughing met us at the head of the stairs and led us to one of several huge, overstuffed sofas that ringed the large, softly lit room. There were large pictures on the walls of barroom nudes lying on fur rugs. Lisette spoke some English, and she became the spokesperson.

"Ooh are you?" she asked.

We explained. Excitedly she translated for the others. We were legionnaires from Espagne. Of course they had heard all about us—the whole city had heard. Lisette asked how we had managed to get out.

With, under the circumstances, forgivable embellishment, we told. Word must have spread on the street, for half a dozen more women came in and were brought up to date with lavish detail. Now a conference took place. The chatter rose to an incomprehensible, mirthful babble. Everyone seemed to want to talk and no one to listen.

Jerry and I had time to look around. Clearly we were in a well-patronized brothel. But what surprised us was that the women, whom we judged to be mostly in their early twenties, looked, except for being prettier, so ordinary. Neither makeup nor clothes were extreme. Even the room we were in could have been at first glance a club room for alumni of a small college, though it was perhaps not so somber. There were potted plants and in one corner an upright piano with open sheet music. Heavy, tiered, brocaded curtains covered three tall bay windows. All the room colors were pale blue and ivory. A very large wind-up victrola with stacks of records around it played soft accordion music.

There was a sudden burst of delighted laughter and Lisette came over. "Eet ees decided. You will be our guests. You will stay here."

"*Oui, oui,*" chorused the "girls." "Ere you will be verree, verree appy." They all knew a few words in at least twenty languages.

I looked at Jerry. He seemed lost in not unpleasant thought. "Thank you very much," I said. "You are all very kind, but we cannot stay. First of all, we have no money . . ."

Lisette interrupted me. She seemed piqued, and there was a hint of asperity as she said, "We did not ask for money. You stay as guests. Police look for you. Only here you will be safe. There is room enough. Plenty beds." This last with a sly arch of eyebrow.

Lisette herself was provocatively attractive. Maybe twenty-three, she looked like an art-deco drawing, with very white skin against coal-black hair cut short and curling forward at the chin. She had large black eyes and very red, generous-sized lips. She was tall and moved gracefully, like a dancer.

As she spoke, the circle around us parted and two young women came through carrying large trays. On the first were small, crisp rolls, cheeses, crudités, pâté de foie gras, and fruits. On the second were wines and brandies. Jerry Cook came out of his trance, picked up a bunch of grapes, held them above his mouth as he put his head back and said, "Comrade, you must rid yourself of stuffy middle-class morality and values. Accept gladly what is offered us in a spirit of solidarity by these good people who work hard for a living."

"Never," I said, "have I seen a quicker transition from socialism to sophistry."

For two full weeks we had a very good time, fed and pampered and treated like pets. They couldn't stand the cheap, loud, striped Spanish suits we had been issued, so they shopped for cashmere sweaters and twill trousers. The one thing we couldn't do was go outside. It was a silk-lined prison, but still a prison.

Jackie Shafron had holed up in a hotel for two days and then got bored and returned to the Hill, so everyone there knew where we were and couldn't control their envy. Some hid it by thinking up bawdy jokes. Not that there was no sex—that would have been suspiciously deviant. But abundance breeds discernment, selectivity. And if nothing else, we needed the exercise.

Lisette became quite fond of Jerry, and they discussed many things. She told him the girls considered themselves quite different from the street prostitutes. They had a home and they had visitors, steady customers about whom they knew considerably more than their wives did. All the girls were cynical about, and uninterested in, politics. They knew too much about too many politicians to think of voting for one.

After two weeks, the captain of the *Ausonia*, an ugly, British-registry steamer, agreed to take the Lincolns to New York, third class.

Jackie Shafron and Frenchy Robinson were dispatched to find me and Jerry. They came to the Rue de Coq and began to shout at all the houses. "Milt, Jerry," they screamed. "Come on! You'll miss the boat!" Finally we heard them, and Jerry went to one of the big bay windows. He leaned out and as Jackie came underneath, he yelled, "WE didn't miss the boat. YOU did."

Harassed by police over the years, the bordello district had polished and refined an efficient communications network along which word now rapidly spread that the American legionnaires were about to leave. Up at the Hill the Americans formed soldierly ranks and marched downward toward the ship. Jerry and I were being embraced and toasted and were not finding it easy to say good-bye to a life glaringly deficient in moral standards. We realized that if we stayed even a little longer we might think of a good many reasons to eloquently defend it.

"Stay," said Lisette to Jerry.

"Can't."

"Why not?"

"There are reasons."

"Like his wife," I chimed in, meanly.

"Yeah," said Jerry, "that too. But not only that. I thought about it. Life in a cosy cocoon, heaven for two months, nirvana for six months. But I'm no butterfly, and I wouldn't grow pretty wings. I'd grow big globs of fat, first in the head."

Lisette leaned her lovely body against him and ran a hand gently through his wavy blond hair. "I see you will leave," she sighed, "because you are young, with big dreams." She looked challengingly into his eyes, "But you will not forget Lisette, and one day you will be sorry you did not stay."

"I think you're absolutely right," I said, "especially when he has to work for a living and eat at the automat."

The Lincolns came down the hill marching and singing. Jerry and I went to meet them, and they stopped singing and stared. Le Havre's red-light district had declared a holiday, and we walked at the head of our own bawdily boisterous parade. The prostitutes had dressed quickly, as they have a facility for doing, in their glitziest best—fur wraps, feathers, and flowers—and they danced around us laughing and singing and calling out, "Vive les américains! Vive les legionnaires!" And even, "Vive les soldats antifacistes!"

At shipside, the regular passengers on the *Ausonia* lined the rails appalled and agitated, pointing their fingers and telling each other, see what we're in for! God knows what will happen when we're out on the open sea and at their mercy. If we had any brains we'd get right off this ship. How utterly disgusting for Americans to behave like that. They're probably not even Americans; if you ask me, they look like Russians. Let's give the captain a piece of our minds. We payed good money for this trip, we're entitled. That's what we get for going on an English ship. They treated us like dirt in London; maybe they forgot we won the revolution, not them.

We boarded the ship, waved wistfully at the cheering whores, and began a steep descent toward our below-steerage quarters. As soon as we got there, Wolff announced that the captain wanted to see us in the salon. Shafron predicted we'd all get the bends before we got back up there, so we were not in a receptive mood when the captain said he had a big empty brig, which he would be happy to fill with us if we got the slightest bit out of line. Wolff thanked him for his gracious hospitality, and the captain smiled and said we could have lunch right now before we sailed.

The ship's baker had made hot rolls and was most pleased when he heard we liked them very much. But when we ate three thousand and banged our plates for more he became churlish and called the captain.

"More?" fumed the captain, right out of *Oliver Twist*. "You want more?"

"Even at sea," Wolff explained, "an army travels on its stomach, especially an army that hasn't had a decent meal for two years."

The fourth night out, the vets entertained the ship. Scenes from *H.M.S. Pinafore*, a very good "sextet" from *Rigoletto*, piano and violin solos, and the whole group doing Brigade songs drew an ovation. On the last night a passenger spokesman gave tribute to "a group of young men we have learned to respect and admire."

On the surface it was an ordinary, placid sea voyage. We read and talked and joked and played cards. Fake. My mind was consumed with turbulence. I was hiding my conflicting feelings, as were most of the others too, I think, behind a veneer of hard-boiled Humphrey Bogartism.

I had left the University of Iowa in my senior year. In a few months I would be twenty-seven years old, an old man to be a student. Should I go back? What would they teach me now that I could accept without smiling down cynically from the superior height of my worldly experience? Would college kids accept me as one of them, and would I want them to? There was a bigger problem too, which I didn't want to face at all: I had no idea what I wanted to do or what I wanted to "be." You have some talent, I said to myself, for living, but none at all for making a living.

I sat in a deck chair with a blanket up to my eyes to protect them from the relentless winter wind, and though the sea was calm, the gentle rocking was inexorable and inescapable, like the thoughts that returned and returned. Two years of bullets and bombs, of destruction and death. We had "fought well," but so had they. How we'd fought was immaterial, because it hadn't determined the outcome. Why we'd fought did matter to us, but that hadn't determined the outcome either. Would I be doomed to fight the rest of my life for lost causes? Probably. They may be the best kind.

CHAPTER 9

1939
1941

When the *Ausonia*, a graceless tub of a boat, docked in New York Harbor, dozens of FBI men in blue suits and short haircuts stationed themselves in the main salon behind little makeshift desks. They forced all the vets to undergo an unfriendly grilling before allowing us to land, perfectly revealing the ambivalent American reaction to the war in Spain.

Public-opinion polls from the beginning had shown a majority of the public sympathetic to the Loyalists, and as the war went on the support was overwhelming. But U.S. officialdom—including politicians, the army, the FBI, and much of the press—had increasingly sought to downplay the roles taken by Hitler and Mussolini, as well as the savage and widespread repression and cruelty inherent in Franco's religio-fascism. Instead, they had attacked the Soviet Union for selling arms to the Loyalist government.

Years later when Cold War propagandists like Arthur Koestler and George Orwell were annointed by the West as official historians of the war in Spain, they developed this theme into a science. On the one hand they charged that the Russians had sabotaged the Spaniards by holding back enough support to enable them to win; in the next breath they insisted that the Soviet presence was so massive that it constituted complete control. Twisting the war into an East-West confrontation was meant to conceal once again the real question that agonized us. Why had the democracies followed the sacrifice of Ethiopia to Mussolini by throwing Spain to Hitler?

Several hundred relatives, friends, and well-wishers stood on the pier, and there was a modest parade up Sixth Avenue with people on the sidewalks applauding and friendly. But still on my mind was the great emotional outpouring in Barcelona for our farewell—the impassioned words of La Pasionaria, the vast crowds, the flowers, the kisses, the tears. The volunteers had marched up the Diagonal and had felt Spain enter their bloodstreams, where it would stay.

At Fourteenth Street I went down into the subway and rode out to my mother's cheap little upstairs apartment on Avenue X in Sheeps-head Bay.

After we kissed and she dried her eyes, she reverted again to the suppression of feelings that so characterized our family.

"So what did you accomplish?" was her way of summing up her considered opinion, hidden in one innocent-appearing question, that I was a naive, idealistic jerk to think that a hopelessly corrupt world would ever change.

"I'm not sure," I said. "Maybe it's too soon to tell. It may take the rest of my life to figure out the answer to your question."

"You want some chicken soup?" asked my mother.

"With matzoh balls and pumpernickel bread," I agreed. "OK, so we'll repair society some other time. What's with the old man?"

My mother shrugged. "His mind wanders away. He lives in a dream and waits to die. The doctors say without a wish to live it does not take long."

"And Hank? How is he doing?"

"Another genius. My sons know everything about life except how to make a living. He writes books and he starves. He's just like you; you fix the world, meanwhile you starve."

I laughed. "Don't be bitter, Ma. Do you think running after a buck makes a life? Do you see people on Wall Street laughing, singing, and dancing in the streets?"

"Their troubles you should have," said my mother with a little sigh. "You're not such a youngster anymore. Don't you want a normal life? Children? A wife, a home?"

"Don't panic, Ma. There's time. Twenty-six is serious but a long way from sitting by the window in an old-age home wondering where it all went. I just haven't met the right girl yet."

I could see my mother's eyes gleam. "It just happens," she began, "that my friend Sarah's daughter, a lovely . . ."

"Don't you dare," I cut in. "My ties you can choose, which it so happens I don't wear, but my wife, with your permission of course, I would like the first few tries at myself."

"I'll make tea," said my mother.

I marveled at my mother's equanimity. Her work as a practical nurse kept her nose barely above water, enabling her to live a Spartan but independent life. Her four younger sisters had all done better economically, but in every crisis they turned to her. She calmed them and consoled them, and didn't suspect that her painful fate would be to outlive all but one. Nor would her sons be a comfort; they would grow up and move away. She ought not to have wished so hard for me to seek out a mate. I lived with her till I did, and then I too went off and left her, alone and growing old in a dingy flat in Brooklyn.

"Hi," said Roger Hargrave when I called him from Brooklyn, "when you comin' out to Iowa?" Roger had recovered from a series of remarkable operations performed gratis on his return from Spain by a noted Viennese surgeon. He was well on his way to a doctorate in political science.

"Don't know if I should," I said. "Brooklyn is so *je ne sais quoi*. Besides, I'm getting a little long in the tooth to fully lose myself in the adventurous thrill of a panty raid."

"Don't be an asshole," said Roger. "You've got one semester to go for your degree. Maybe it's crap, but it's a ticket. They don't let you into the system without a ticket."

So for a second time I arrived nearly broke in Iowa City. It was January 1939, and so cold that the snow crunched underfoot like breaking glass. Roger and Merle Miller met me at the bus station, and we went to Reichardt's Cafe to eat and to see if I could get my old job back. Old man Reichardt weighed over three hundred pounds. Every morning for breakfast he ate a dozen huge pancakes topped with a dozen fried eggs over easy. Then he got up, waddled into the back room, and spent the day making the kind of pure-chocolate-covered fantasies he remembered from his childhood in the Black Forest. They drew addicts, heavyset worshipers in a secret sect, from all over the Midwest.

The supply of cheap student labor was down, so my servitude was soon settled. Then we had only to choose my final semester's courses and we could be free to spend the rest of the evening agreeing with each other about the looming, inevitable collapse of a society ever more concerned with shiny exteriors while its insides turned to rot.

Reunion with Roger in Iowa City.

Later generations searching inward would never know how long ago it was all settled. We decided I should take philosophy, political science, educational statistics, and "The Bible as Literature," a bow, perhaps, to the universality of my ignorance.

"Come down to the office tomorrow," Merle said to me. "I'll run a front-page story about you and Rog being together again, and students again, and you can say profound things about the world situation."

After Merle's story appeared, Roger and I were invited all over the state to make brave speeches about Spain, but the war news was bad and everybody knew it. Near the end of March 1939, Francisco Franco marched down those beautiful Barcelona avenues proclaiming victory for fascism, as Italian Caproni bombers and German Stukas flew overhead. Only seven months later on September 1, a jubilant Hitler would send his tanks into Poland to begin World War II.

It was strange being a student again. Except for graduate students like Roger and a few campus careerists like Merle, everyone I had known before Spain was gone. And those who were there had grown disturbingly young, I noticed—practically callow, for God's sake. Part of me envied their playful, young-colt ebullience, and I went along to the parties and the drinking bouts, singing bawdy songs around "big-game" bonfires and taking part in daring, tentative experiments with marijuana reefer smokeouts. But it didn't take; I sensed I was being thought of as a kindly, understanding old fart rather than one of the gang, so I cut it out.

It wasn't only that I was older and had been to war. I was, in their eyes, a wacko idealist, one of those who thought you could change human nature and make the world better. In some ways I had to agree, but why do the so-called realists seem to take such SATISFACTION in emphasizing the greedy, selfish, murderous aspects of humankind?

Meeting "Babe" Moulton got me over the money problem. Babe was a terrific high hurdler and a born entrepreneur. It would not surprise me to learn that he owns Switzerland. In the few months we were friends, enterprises sprang full-blown from his mind like snakes from Medusa's head, and with a few exceptions, like the banana-roasting machine, they were remarkably cost-effective. Especially dependable were the Bible Caper and the Calico Caper.

Sue Anne Langer was a vivacious young lady in charge of house-keeping for the ugly, old, eight-story Jefferson Hotel in the middle of town. For a modest consideration, she kept the "Midwest Bible House Publishers" run by the "very reverend" D. R. Moulton fully supplied with Gideon bibles. Carefully we analyzed the obituaries published over a wide area of the state. Babe would make the final choice.

"OK, this one. Mr. Silas Waggoner, age seventy-six, of a heart attack. Survived by wife, Abigail, and two sisters. Family will receive at home Saturday, 2 P.M. to 5 P.M. Send old Si one," said Babe. "The family will get it and say, Gosh darn. The old reprobate knew he was going and turned to God at the last minute. They'll be delighted to pay our ten-dollar bill."

Calico was a little more complicated. We had to rent an old pickup truck and go down to McCrory's and buy up bolts of their most colorful, cheapest cloth. Then we headed out early in the morning for the farthest backcountry. We'd pass the farmer out in the fields and pull up to the house. Frowsy and sagging from overwork, the housewife would perk up a little at the sight of the bright colors.

"Very cheap," says Babe.

"Don't make no nevermind how cheap," she says. "Got no money at all around here." And with a glance toward her man in the field, "he don't leave nothin'."

"That's OK," says Babe brightly. "You got chickens. Just throw in a few chickens."

At day's end, the pickup's old springs would be banging on the axle when we pulled up at the butcher shop where we had a deal and unloaded our crates of squawking fowl. The butcher robbed us blind, of course, but it didn't matter; we had our share and chicken sandwiches besides.

Toward the end of the semester, the seniors sent out their résumés and got back offers of teaching jobs that ranged from bottom-of-the-barrel to pretty good. I got no replies at all, so I knew I had a secure spot on the blacklist. The political pendulum that swings so spastically in the U.S.A. was well into a far-right lurch in reaction to "the socialistic New Deal measures thought up by egghead professors surrounding THAT MAN IN THE WHITE HOUSE." Fifty years later the conservatives would adopt FDR as one of their own and take credit for his works, but not now.

The veterans of the Lincoln Brigade had come to be known as "premature anti-Fascists," a most curious term revealing a great deal more about those who used it than about those who were its targets. But there was no doubt about the results—we couldn't teach and we couldn't get government jobs. And my education, I discovered, had fitted me for the enjoyment of the finer things in life while leaving unexplained what I was fitted to do to be able to afford them. The Depression still lay heavy on the land and would not end until the heaven-sent boon of World War II would start the profits rolling again. Meanwhile, American business was not dangling employment opportunities in front of radicals with working-class backgrounds.

"You sound bitter," said Merle on the morning of graduation, as Roger and I were having breakfast at his place.

"Bet your ass I am," I said. "I didn't expect thanks, or glory, or parades, but to be lied about is aggravating. I'd almost rather have my balls twisted than my motives."

"Relax," said Roger, "the way things are going you'll get both."

"Are you also implying," Merle said a little reprovingly, "that the broad emphasis of a liberal arts education should be subordinated to *vocational* objectives?"

"Not subordinated to but integrated with. I feel victimized to leave here after four years—six if you count the sabbatical for war—without a single marketable skill. That should be permissible only for certified heirs of obscenely huge fortunes."

"You don't do so bad with women," said Roger. "Maybe you could go into fortune hunting."

"Easy for you to say, Rog," I said, "you being smart enough to ride your Ph.D. up over the blacklist into college teaching. But us plebeians are, as usual, fucked."

"Low blow," said Roger. "Take it out on the establishment, not me."

Merle was distressed. "You guys went through so much together. You are so close. You should not be fighting."

"Schmuck, who's fighting?" said Roger. "Can't you recognise an advanced discussion of dialectical materialism when you hear it?"

But I could not conceal from myself that it was a bad time. I had saved enough from my jobs to buy a 1931 Buick convertible, and when the graduation ceremony was over I stuck the imitation-leather envelope holding my diploma in the glove compartment and headed east on its balding tires. Even atheists have faith in something, and my belief that those tires would last was easily the equal of Bernadette's in her grotto visions.

To this point in my life, it had been a long, rough ride, both mentally and physically. I was an activist, politically committed to what I was sure would be a lifelong struggle for a more humane and peaceful society. But I was not a professional revolutionary, nor did I know many people who were. My Communist friends spoke of revolution and even more often sang off-key, militant songs about being ready to take power. But they were really social reformers engaged in putting people's furniture back when landlords evicted tenants for nonpayment of rent, signing anti-lynching petitions, agitating for unemployment-insurance legislation, and doing the grinding, thankless work of organizing from below the unions that would soon be taken from them by corrupt officials at the top. They theorized about a noble American working class eager for the chance to create a social utopia when the average worker was obviously most eager for a chance to open a small business and escape from the damned mill.

And as I drove along over the lonely highway, I realized that I had been longing for what everyone else was trying to escape—a "normal" life for a change. It had never crossed my mind that I wouldn't be allowed to teach. I had been sure I would be a helluva good teacher, and as graduation neared I had visualized myself inspiring a class with the infectious excitement of learning and accepting the congratulations of colleagues in the faculty lounge. I would have a decent job and a decent salary, and a leather briefcase with brass fittings.

What would I do now? As anger and frustration mounted, I pounded on the wheel and stepped on the gas and got a speeding warning from a motorcycle cop. Why should this happen to me? Unfair! Me, a really good person, possessed of only the finest and purest motives. Oh, bullshit. Buck the establishment, and you pay the price. Stop sniveling. I calmed down and searched inside and tried to find my customary sense of how ridiculously human beings inflated the importance of their transitory concerns.

Philosophy works well on a winter evening in front of a blazing fireplace with a drink in your hand, but out there, headed nowhere on a bumpy road, I concluded judiciously that it wasn't worth diddly-shit. The irony of being blacklisted for fighting fascism before someone fired off the official starting gun had really gotten to me.

My mother had moved to 123A Hart Street on the edge of the Williamsburg section of Brooklyn, an area that was clinging to a fading gentility as it was being engulfed by the spreading slum. She was happy to have me move in.

Before Spain, many of us left-wingers had put in time as voluntary organizers with the Committee of Industrial Organization (later to become the Congress of Industrial Organizations, or CIO), whose chapters were springing up in many industries. The pay was a ham-and-swiss sandwich and a bottle of pop, the office an abandoned store. It was a crusade of the dispossessed for decent wages, dignity, and security.

But then Spain had come along, and some of the organizers went and some didn't. Those who remained inherited an explosion of organizational successes. Unions were recognized, contracts were signed, dues were paid. Ragged-assed organizers became elected directors with large offices with windows on two sides, and they had secretaries who made appointments for a week from next Tuesday. From 1936 to 1939, the CIO grew by more than three million members. At least here, I thought, there would be a welcome—a responsible job on the staff with a respectable, not munificent but respectable, salary.

The Lincoln vets had established a meeting headquarters on Fifth Avenue. There were monthly meetings and an attempt to deal collectively with the financial, social, psychological, and medical problems common to young people who have spent time on the killing ground. I met Jackie Shafron, Normie Berkowitz, Jerry Cook, and some others who had been active volunteers in the preunion days. We decided to go down to the Retail, Wholesale, and Department Store Workers Union, which had become very big and very successful and was led by old pals of ours, to apply for staff jobs.

Arthur Osman was the president, and we were greeted effusively by him and by the heads of three or four main divisions. With much hugging and shaking of hands and slaps on the back, they all said how good it was to see us again and would we like a drink for old times and you wouldn't believe how complicated things are now but as soon as they open up even a little bit—although to be honest that could take a long time—believe me you guys will be at the top of the list but in the meantime about all we can do is maybe get you into this place down on the waterfront because we're having a tough time trying to organize. We managed halfhearted thank yous and said we'd let them know and went across the street to the automat for coffee.

"Piecards!" said Jackie. "They've become sell-out, fuckin' piecards. Corrupt bureaucrats."

Jerry Cook smoked a big curved pipe that made everything he said sound judicious and deep. "Why expect the whole society to be corrupt and only one segment of it to somehow be pure? Unions always turn out to be mirror reflections of the industries that give them birth, as well as the social conditions that give them birth."

"We make them nervous," said Normie. "We remind them they could be us."

"I find this a very stimulating discussion," I said, "but we are ducking the issue. Do we volunteer for the salt mine or don't we?"

"Know any alternative?" asked Normie.

Surplus Shippers, Inc., was on Twelfth Avenue in the forties, in the heart of Hell's Kitchen. It was owned by Mr. Finger, the first Jewish man I had ever come across who was an outright Fascist. He thought Benito Mussolini was the greatest living world leader and said so loudly and often. There was a work force of about sixty, and it was soon clear why, in spite of rampant unemployment, it was no problem to be hired. Few who started lasted out their first day of backbreaking labor in that filthy sweatshop. We worked in a large, one-story, warehouse-type room with bare cement walls and a cement floor. Grime covered the small windows, and there was no heat, no cooling, no ventilation. Bathroom facilities were primitive and the smell was rank.

Mr. Finger's function was simplicity itself. He bought the unsold but predated magazines from newspaper stands and had them delivered to his warehouse. We sorted them, baled them, weighed them, put them into burlap bags, and then heaved them up onto trucks that took them the few blocks to the stevedores who worked the busy West Side docks that were lined with ships from the battery to Fifty-ninth Street. Overseas they went on sale as "new."

For eighteen dollars a week we worked nine hours a day with a half hour for lunch. Everything was done by hand and the bags ready for loading weighed an average of 150 pounds. The floor of our huge workplace was littered with odd-sized bundles tied with twine or baling wire, and foremen with bills of lading ran about shouting, cursing, and pushing to get their quotas filled.

The worst job was loading, and I was assigned to it almost immediately. Two of us stood at street level and together swung the burlap bags five feet up onto the flatbed trucks. I had made the mistake of listing college on my employment application, and college boys, it developed, were one of Finger's pet hates. He called me professor and undertook a blatant campaign of provocation.

He didn't have to try hard since the one thing we shared was antipathy at first sight, which rapidly ripened into revulsion as we got to know each other. At the end of the second week, walking up toward the subway with the other vets, I said I had decided to quit.

"We'll never organize that stinkhole," I said. "My back feels like I've been kicked all day by an army mule. If I stay there two more weeks, you'll have to push me up this street in a wheelchair."

Jerry Cook did a couple of slow puffs on his pipe. "You sound bitter," he opined.

"What makes you think we can't get it organized?" asked Normie.

"It's obvious," I said, "that any poor bastard who would work there has reached the bottom of the barrel and is scared shitless of losing what we so amusingly call a paycheck. People who have been pushed below self-respect don't revolt. The American Revolution wasn't the work of slaves; it was the fierce patriotism of well-off property owners who wanted to keep more of their loot."

"Thanks for the history lesson," Normie said with asperity, "but I don't think we should give up."

"That's just why Osman and the rest of those sly fuckers sent us down here," I growled. "They knew it was a ball-breaker, and they knew we'd fail and go slinking off blaming ourselves and we'd be out of their hair forever."

"You do have a belligerent streak in your nature," said Jerry, "but I believe your analysis is not without merit."

The very next Monday morning my personal problem was solved. Mussolini and Hitler had appeared at one of a series of seemingly endless Franco victory celebrations, this one in Seville, and Mussolini had made a speech promising the imminent downfall of the decadent Western world. This had put Mr. Finger in a euphoric mood, and as I strained to hold up my end of the work, wrestling with the clumsy, deadweight burlap sacks, he stood nearby offering a running commentary.

"Well, Professor, you waste so much time to read books. Isn't it better I pay you to throw books." Big laugh.

"You are perhaps yourself a heavy reader, ha, ha."

"Maybe you read too much Commie stuff like comes from Washington. You think I don't know what you talk? I hear. They tell me everything. You should kiss the floor I don't throw you out from here."

Others had started to listen, and the pain in my back and arms had reduced my boiling point.

"You want something kissed?" I asked. "Kiss my ass, you two-bit Fascist!"

Finger was middle-aged, middle-sized, and ugly, with a big belly. In the Depression, no boss ever heard such words from a worker. Surprise and rage rose up his oversized neck, face, and ears, which made his eyes look to me like black olives in a bowl of tomato soup.

He was so mad he could only sputter, "OUT . . . OUT . . . YOU'RE FI . . . , FI . . ."

"I know," I said, "I'm fired."

"That's what you learned in college," said my mother when I told her what had happened, "how to be a big hero and lose a job?"

"It wasn't that much of a job."

"You know a better one?"

No, I didn't. And I felt rotten, useless, and out of step. It was a bad time, and I came very close to feeling sorry for myself, something I hated in others and swore I would never do. Get some perspective, I told myself, try counting the stars, you'll feel better. Good advice, except that I found that when I felt bad I didn't feel like counting the goddamn stars.

The underprivileged understand the value of relatives. My Aunt Fanny knew a man named Jake Herman, who was the Herman part of Herman and Witt, Inc., fountain-syrup manufacturers who were short one truck driver-salesman. The ways were greased, and I applied for the job and got it.

The syrup plant was in an ugly, depressed, small factory district on lower Broadway in the Williamsburg section of Brooklyn under the elevated train tracks. The syrups were made in giant vats—chocolate, vanilla, strawberry, cherry, pineapple, and lemon-lime—and poured into gallon jugs. During prohibition the syrup makers had all gotten rich beyond their dreams by utilizing two-thirds of their facilities for the manufacture and distribution of bootleg booze. They continued to make handsome profits but still yearned for the good old days. New excitement was in the air, however. With the war on in Europe there was already talk of rationing sugar. With their own vast supplies, the black-market opportunities were clear enough, and they had already established a slush fund to buy the requisite politicians.

Herman and Witt were not the biggest, but they were not far behind Fox's U-Bet, who was.

"You are a college boy?" asked Jake Herman when I was being interviewed.

"Man," I said, "college man."

Jake was just over five feet tall, balding, with an obvious Napoleonic complex. "You think you can drive a big truck?"

"I can drive anything with wheels," I said, thinking of ambulances in the mountains of Spain. Jake knew about me and Spain and was intrigued, but more than a little afraid too.

"We trust you with a lot of money. The main thing is to be honest." I didn't know it then but the last thing he expected was for me to be honest. What he meant was I should only steal within expected limits.

"Your wages will be $35 a week," he said.

Thirty-five dollars! Holy shit, I was about to enter the upper, upper-middle class. I tried to be nonchalant. "I guess that's to start," I said. He gave me a real cold look.

There were six trucks. I was given a big, red Diamond-T. The inside was fitted with triple racks that held syrup jugs and special racks for the jars of walnuts in syrup, crushed pineapple, whole cherries, strawberries, and almonds.

Soda fountains—God, how quaint—were the teen hangouts of the forties, and there were hundreds in metropolitan New York. Each driver was given a route. I had two days in Brooklyn, two in Manhattan, and one in the Bronx.

Jakes's brother-in-law, Ziggy, broke me into the route and into how the skim scam worked. The big stops, the ones that took thirty to forty gallons, were out. They signed the book and payed by check, unless of course a special arrangement had been worked out—but that was not for beginners. Small shops, one to five gallons, usually paid cash, a dollar a gallon. All you did was drop five and mark $3 in the book.

"They count your load," I said innocently, "where do you get the extra gallons?"

Ziggy explained as one would to a seriously retarded child. "You make your deal with the platform man. You get an extra dolly, he gets twenty percent."

The longer I lived the more I learned why the free-enterprise system was so much more successful than socialism. The Ten Commandments were socialism, understood by all to be an illusory ideal. Breaking them was capitalism, which relies unerringly on the lowest denominator to be the most common.

I thanked Ziggy for his collegial spirit but excused myself from membership in the club by saying that I had so much to learn about the job itself that I feared making some stupid error that could put the whole operation in jeopardy. Ziggy accepted this but was cold and suspicious. Outsiders like me were not to be trusted. He suspected the worst. I could be one of those weirdos with ethics. He would have to warn the others to shun me.

Actually I had not examined the deeper socio-moral implications of the dilemma that had been put before me. My foundation in mathematics was very shaky, and when I thought of evenings spent bookkeeping dollars and gallons, I knew thiefdom would have to do without me. For one thing, I had not yet finished changing the world.

CHAPTER 10

1941

Nearly all the soda fountains in the metropolitan area were owned by nice Jewish families anxious—nay, desperate—to marry off at least one nubile daughter. And while doctors, lawyers, and dentists floated through their dreams, standards lowered rapidly as time passed and opportunities narrowed.

Ziggy had screwed me good. He had introduced me to the whole route as a college man.

I would swing briskly into a store with gallons hanging from my fingers and find poppa, momma, and a stunningly coifed and frocked Zelda at the counter.

"We have a special on walnuts today," I would say. "Can you use any?"

It was just a way of breaking the ice because I knew what was coming.

"We'll take one jar. So you're a college man, I am given to understand."

"That was a while ago, Mr. Goodman. Just now I drive a truck."

They wouldn't have cared if I drove a wheelbarrow. Besides, they already knew my age, my salary, and the fact that I wasn't married. I felt like my dossier had been mimeographed and distributed throughout the city and that my current market value was being assessed somewhat in the manner of an investment in pork-belly futures.

Once in a while I would date the daughters, and before the evening was over they would apologize for their parents and break down and cry with embarrassment. After that we would mostly become friends, and when I came in they would have a double egg-cream with a cherry waiting. My mother began to worry about my weight.

My mother also began to fidget about me and girls, and she may even have been panicky about my walking in the door with a young man.

"Coming home for dinner tonight?" she asked at breakfast.

"No. There's a meeting at Webster Hall about the Negro problem. People are pushing the idea that the Negros ought to have a policy of self-determination and be given an area in the South where they are a majority, to be ruled by them as an independent Negro area."

"They already have a ghetto in Harlem, so why do they want another one?"

After a pause. "Don't nice girls ever go to any of those meetings you're so busy with?"

"Sure, Ma. Lots of them."

"So?"

"So what?"

"You know so what. I like that you live here. It's good for me. But it's not so good for you. It's not natural. You're not getting any younger. You should have your own home, your own family."

"Look, Ma, I like girls. Really I do. I enjoy being with them and making love with them. But I haven't fallen in love with anyone. If I do, fine, I'll get married, providing she feels the same way of course. I'm just not interested in settling for less because it's time, or some other dumb reason."

My mother recognized that this round was over, but she usually got in the last punch.

"A nice romantic theory," she said, "but in this life it is sometimes better to fall in love *after* you get married. It lasts longer."

Politics was on my mind a lot more than love. As we "radicals" had predicted, the fall of Spain in the spring of 1939 had been followed by Hitler's attack on Poland and the opening of World War II in September. Then came the Phony War period, the Finnish-Soviet War and the Hitler-Stalin pact. Strange bedfellows were making even stranger politics.

The Finns were led by a self-proclaimed Fascist named Baron von Mannerheim, and the British offered to send him help. But the Germans who were fighting and killing Britons also offered to send help to the baron. Rudolph Hess, Hitler's assistant, flew to England, where under peculiar circumstances he was put in a solitary prison and would remain there for the rest of his life, a living puzzle about just what his mission was. Political debate was furious, emotional, and at times painful. The glue that held the Lincoln veterans together was their hatred of fascism. But what, exactly, was fascism? At the meetings arguments raged.

"How could the Russians sign a pact with Hitler? To hell with them. I've been a Communist all my life, but I'm tearing up my card. Too much for me."

"Comrade, don't be so fucking simplistic. Britain and the U.S.A. created, financed, and fed Hitler. There's a temporary family spat, but everyone knows the real target is the Soviet Union. So the Russians bought some time; I'm glad they did."

"What's all this talk about democracy, fascism, socialism? It's a good, old-fashioned imperialist war over markets and profits, and it's doing what wars are made to do—it's getting us out of the damn Depression. We'll stay out of it and get rich."

"Why, you cynical bastard! We didn't go to Spain to fight Franco. We went to fight fascism, and if we don't get in the war I intend to volunteer to the British, the French, or whatever country will have me."

Involvement in such polemics was for me like daily mass for a devout Catholic. I could not understand how people could go about their daily affairs oblivious to those events that were shaping the world, determining its very nature and makeup. How could they agonize over a Brooklyn Dodger loss and ignore the bombing of Coventry?

At the time, most of my friends had lousy jobs and menial salaries, and they envied me. I didn't feel quite that lucky but I enjoyed the raw energy of New York, fighting its noise, confusion, and traffic, experiencing each day the endless diversity of its neighborhoods in the far reaches of the Bronx, Queens, and Brooklyn, as well as up and down Manhattan.

Jake Herman was satisfied with my work, except for one incident when I fully expected to be fired. Streetcar tracks ran along Broadway in Brooklyn, and I had to cross them both leaving and returning to the syrup factory. The two tracks and a third rail were imbedded between a rounded mound of Belgian paving-blocks that had been sold to the city in a particularly outrageous rip-off of public funds, had not been maintained, and were now a menacing challenge to traffic. I had a favorite spot to cross and usually timed the Diamond-T's springs to the rhythm of the deep bumps. But this day I was in a hurry and made a serious blunder: I crossed where there was a double track and I hit a smidgen too fast. One hundred and seventy-five gallons of assorted flavors danced in their racks, and on the final bump they all soared clear and met each other in midair, sounding like a thousand chimes rung by maddened friars. They then cascaded down on the floor of the truck, where they lay pouring their gooey, sticky, intermingling flavors in the most god-awful mess of broken glass I had ever seen.

The guys on the loading dock got the hoses on it and had it almost cleaned out before Jake Herman got a good look, but he had heard what happened and was beside himself with rage. "OUT! GET OUT! YOU'RE FIRED!" he screamed. He was short but he had a full-sized voice.

I stood quite still. I remember trying to work my expression into one of injured innocence while my mind raced, searching for an out.

"You're still here?" he yelled. "You want I should call the cops?"

"Maybe you should," I said with exaggerated dignity, "and I will explain to them that you think I should not have swerved across the tracks to avoid hitting that little boy on a bicycle. I will explain to the cops and maybe to the newspapers that you think more of a gallon of chocolate syrup than of a life."

I was just warming to the subject, but he had already turned and gone back to the office.

I kept my job, and I liked it. It paid good money and left my evenings and weekends free. I was active in the American Labor Party and worked for the election of I. Philip Sipser to something or other. There were Lincoln Brigade meetings and lectures, movies, concerts, plays, and debates. My friends and I shared the humanizing and socializing practice of participating in group experiences, something that television would take from the world and leave in its place lonely, isolated, alienated, passive, visual drug-takers.

On May 1, 1941, I met Roberta Blatt and on July 18, 1941, we were married. There had been a giant May Day parade with hundreds of thousands marching down Broadway to the speakers' platforms in Union Square and that night there was a Lincoln Brigade dance at Manhattan Center on Thirty-fourth Street.

Jerry Cook was splitting from his wife, Annie, and had fallen movie-romantically in love with Ruth Borgenicht, who at the moment was standing with Roberta.

"Who is that over there with your friend Ruth?" I asked Jerry, over the noise of the music and the huge crowd.

"Her roommate, Roberta Blatt," said Jerry, and watching me watching, he continued. "She works at Macy's book department. Very active in the union. Good kid. Serious."

"Let's go over," I said.

"What about 'Tee'?" asked Jerry. Tee was Bea Turetsky, my date. She also worked in Macy's book department, which Macy's trumpeted as the biggest bookstore in the world and in which it employed more than eighty highly intelligent young women, honors graduates, for coolie wages.

"Tee is in the john, which means I have at least fifteen minutes," I said. "Besides, difficult as it may be for one of your carnal nature to imagine, we share an intellectual relationship untroubled by physical desires."

"Bullshit," said Jerry.

"It's true," I explained. "She takes me to Authors' Teas, and Sunday afternoon chamber-music recitals, and private little soirees with leading critics, and then we go to the Village Tea Shoppe and have an animated discussion, after which I take her home. Her lips have yet to touch mine."

Jerry looked at me as if I had just confessed to an uncontrollable foot fetish. "OK," he said, "I'll introduce you. Then I will leave. I want no part of a tawdry little scene."

"Hi, Ruth," he said, kissing her lightly, to which she responded with ardor. She had black hair, very pale skin with a hint of red showing through, lively black eyes, a full bee-sting mouth, and very white teeth. Her family was very rich and very conservative, and Ruth had decided to dedicate her life to rebellion and romance. She and Roberta lived on Grove Street in Greenwich Village, because anything above Fourteenth Street was too bourgeois.

"Hi, Roberta," Jerry gestured toward me. "This is my very good friend, Milt. You've heard me speak of him."

"Hello, Roberta," I said extending my hand, "nice to meet you. Can I take you home tonight?"

Roberta fixed me with a very cool gaze. She had shoulder-length Kansas-wheat-blond hair that she wore in the modified pageboy style of the day, large blue eyes, and a lovely mouth that just now was pursed in disapproval. I was intrigued most by her bearing. She exuded intelligence and self-confidence.

"Not tonight, and not in the foreseeable future," said Roberta. I noted that she had a pleasantly musical voice. "The whole book department knows you're Tee's boyfriend. Be a decent person. Go home with the girl you brought."

It was not a private conversation. Vets' dances drew fifteen to eighteen hundred people, many of whom knew each other and none of whom stood on formalities. I wanted to ask Roberta to dance but I hesitated, partly because while we were in Spain the country had gone a little crazy for a new dance, the Lindy Hop, and I wasn't sure I could handle it. While I was deciding, someone else asked and away she went.

"I'll call you," I managed to say to the back of her head.

When I took Tee home, I debated bawling her out for advertising our relationship so widely and so inaccurately. But she was very subdued and seemed to sense that I was upset with her. She stared down at her hands and moved to the far corner of the bus seat—it was the time of buses and subways—until I began to feel ashamed of concentrating on my needs and desires to the exclusion of hers. She was not unattractive; there was just something about her that reminded one of school librarians and Latin teachers. I discovered later that she hadn't had a date for so long that her coworkers had begun to wonder about her. I had been a godsend, and it was not surprising that she would embroider the lackluster facts to give her colleagues a zestier tale.

"I'm sorry, Tee," I said. "I didn't pay much attention to you tonight. Some things have come up. Problems on my job. I've been distracted. I hope you didn't have too bad a time."

"Oh, that's all right," she said hastily. "I had a fine time. Really, a fine time."

She seemed relieved that I had spoken, but we didn't speak anymore. And that was, we both knew, the last time we would go out.

I called Roberta every day at Macy's with no luck until after a week when she said that her roommate, Ruth, wanted her to talk to me about Jerry Cook.

"Gladly," I said. "How about a midnight ferry-ride to Staten Island?"

"We'll have lunch in the store cafeteria."

"It will have to be Thursday," I said. "I do New York on Thursdays."

"Make it 12:30 sharp," she said.

Macy's book department was huge. It occupied the Seventh Avenue side of the ground floor, and in the middle of it was a great, round information desk staffed by six professionally pleasant but intellectually intimidating young women, skilled at coming up quickly with informative answers to the most arcane questions. In 1941 B.T. (before television), the public, unaware of the coming blessings of sitcoms, was forced to spend whole evenings with nothing but books.

As I passed through Contemporary Fiction, Ancient History, Modern European History, Biography, and Science on my way to Roberta at the information desk, I could hear whispered asides: "That's Tee's boyfriend." "She's on vacation; what's he doing here?"

Roberta motioned me to wait while she dealt with a young man's request for a signed first edition of H. G. Wells's *War of the Worlds*. I observed her admiringly. She was pleasant, quick, efficient. Attractive, I mused, definitely nifty.

We took an elevator run by a handsome young black man to the mezzanine cafeteria.

"This store is not so bad," I said, making conversation. "At least they hire Negros."

"Sure they do," Roberta said sarcastically, "but only to run elevators and only if they are top college graduates willing to work for $16.25 a week."

"I notice everyone in the store seems to know you. How come?"

"We're organizing the union. There's been a great fear of being fired. The company discovered I was editing 'Union Sparks,' which we distribute to the workers, and they fired me. But it kicked up such a big fuss that they called me in, said they had made an error, and offered me an executive job. I refused, pointing out that if I took it the union could no longer protect me. Now my name is printed openly on the masthead, a big help in organizing."

"You had something you wanted to ask me?"

"Ruth Borgenicht is my best friend, and she's going through hell."

"So how do I fit in?"

"She knows you're Jerry Cook's best friend. Jerry promised to leave his wife and elope with Ruth to Paris or Atlantic City or someplace."

"So?"

"So he keeps putting her off. She wants me to find out from you what he really means to do. She's going nuts."

"I think she should forget about Jerry. No girl should get involved with a guy who is that good-looking, especially one who is married."

"True. I mean about the married part. I guess I'm Victorian about some things."

"Listen, Roberta, enough about our friends. How about us? How about a movie tonight?"

"I can't go out with you."

"Why for Chris'sake not?"

"I told you at the dance. Union reps don't steal boyfriends, especially Tee's."

I explained about me and Tee. We argued. Finally she said OK but that I must not come into the store.

"A disproportionate, one might almost say Draconian solution, but I accept. I have been offered tickets to Carnegie Hall this Saturday night. Brahms. How about it?"

Saturday night it rained. Roberta and Ruth were staying the weekend at Ruth's sister's apartment on Central Park West in the eighties. It was impossible to get a cab.

"Let's walk," I said.

"Sure, let's," said Roberta.

The jackpot! A beautiful, intelligent, progressive girl who would walk thirty city blocks in the rain. I felt myself falling hopelessly in love. We skipped along, laughing and joking like teenaged kids. It was a magic night. About forty years later I asked her why she never took another walk in the rain with me after that one unforgettable night.

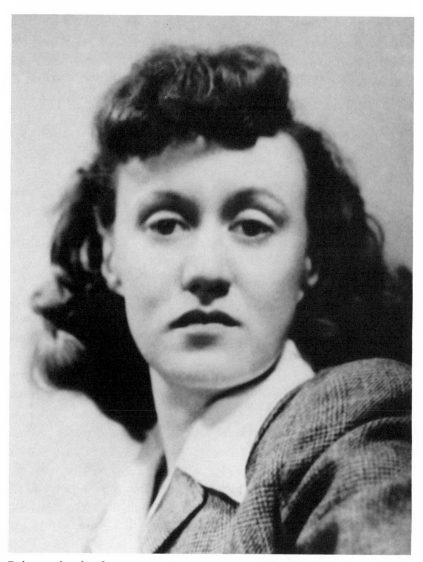

Roberta, shortly after we
were married. The
photographer was a true
genius who succeeded in
turning blue eyes and ash-
blond hair a smoldering
shade of black.

"One gets so damn wet," she replied sensibly.

After the concert I took her home by subway, and before we said good night we explored each other tactilely and were pleased. We went to lectures, meetings, movies, and debated everything. At the end of the fourth week, as we sat at 4 A.M. in a car I had borrowed, I said we needed to have a serious discussion.

"It's definite," I said, "we have a relationship, and relationships do not remain static. They have to go somewhere. That's just everyday basic dialectics. As I see it we have three alternatives."

"Oh? And what are they, as you see it?"

"We could call it off and quit seeing each other; we could have an affair; or we could get married."

"And which, my learned dialectician, do you find yourself leaning toward?"

"I think we gotta get married."

Roberta was silent. I was sure I had blown it. Then she leaned over and kissed me. "What took you so long, lover, what took you so long?"

We heard someone whistling. At 4:30 in the morning someone was whistling the "Internationale."

"It's an omen," I said. "We need a date. We've just missed the fourth of July, so that's out. How about July 18, the anniversary of the outbreak of the Spanish Civil War?"

"But that date marks the beginning of a war," said Roberta.

"Precisely."

"I just changed my mind."

But she didn't, and my mother was excited and very nervous about meeting her. I don't know what Roberta was thinking when she came up out of the Williamsburg subway and I met her. I was still in my syrup-truck driver's uniform, spotted and soiled, and we walked down Hart Street. She had grown up in a middle-class house in suburban Baldwin, Long Island, the daughter of an RKO executive who ran the famous Palace Theater on Broadway. While she had become intellectually radicalized, her background—riding horses, training at Juilliard to be an opera singer, attending junior miss coming-out parties—must have created an emotional turmoil within her as she walked along this semi–slum street on the arm of a jaunty but rather filthy-looking character who smelled from a mixture of chocolate, strawberry, and lemon-lime.

My mother was even more nervous. Her crazy son was for the first time in his life bringing home a girl for her to meet, a girl, can you imagine, he knows for a few days and suddenly it's moon-June and they're ringing wedding bells. Must be some girl.

My mother was a fantastic cook, and she had knocked herself out. She had carved a duck like a surgeon, stuffed it with secret delicacies, deboned it, and sutured it back together so carefully that the surgery was undetectable. And God knows how in that tiny, crummy kitchen, but she had also baked bread and Viennese torts.

We sat down to dinner and I said, "Ma, what are we doing with a tablecloth? We never use tablecloths." Roberta laughed and called me something derogatory, and my mother began to relax and smile at her.

They hit it off real well, and later when they were doing the dishes together my mother told Roberta not to worry about what to feed me.

"Just put a tomato on the table. And for dinner, whatever you're having, make sure there's a bottle of ketchup and he'll be happy. He's a good boy. He just doesn't have any taste buds."

Friday, July 18, 1941, was a Jewish holiday, one of those that forbid weddings, but Roberta's mother was anxious for her daughter to have at least that protection from God. Toots Fajans, one of the Lincoln vets, said he would dress up as a rabbi and we went ahead as planned. As it turned out, it wasn't necessary because someone reached an assistant to Rabbi Wise on Fifty-seventh Street, a rabbi who was so reformed he wasn't sure it was a holiday at all, and we could do it if we made it by sundown.

I had to work that day, but I was sure I could make it because I could use our new car to get there. Roberta's mother had scraped up $250 to buy her a trousseau. When I then asked Roberta what a trousseau was and she told me it was fine underwear I convinced her that underwear was a thing of the past and that what we really needed was an automobile.

We did what the whole world has learned never to do; we bought a used car from a dealer we thought was our friend. We called it OSITQU—Our Stake In The Status Quo. It had the lack of decency to break down on our wedding day, so I got there late enough for Roberta to begin wondering what life would be like in a remote convent. But I did make it. The next week we lent the car to Toots Fajans, and the motor fell out on the Henry Hudson Parkway.

Ruth Borgenicht, Jerry Cook, Toots, and a dozen other friends and vets went with us on our honeymoon to Camp Unity in the Berkshires. We went there because we knew we would have a good time but also because they had lectures and study groups and we could not be accused of ignoring the burning issues of the day in an orgy of self-indulgent concern with individualistic pleasures.

Jerry shouldn't have come. The week before, he had agreed to Ruth's suggestion that they meet at midnight in the middle of the Brooklyn Bridge and elope to Paris. Then, deciding he couldn't do that to Ann, but without a word to Ruth, he didn't show up. We differed with his decision but we kept our opinions to ourselves.

Married, we needed to find a place to live. Jerry and Ann Cook, who were still together, needed a place too, and we searched together. Knickerbocker Village, a huge apartment house on the Lower East Side we heard was cheap, but there was nothing much available. As we were leaving the agent had an idea. There was a three-bedroom penthouse apartment with a wrap-around terrace we might like to share. The rent was $75 per month. We grabbed it, and later Irv Goff and his wife, Sophie, moved in. It was a financial success and a social disaster.

We vets shared a close bond. Our wives would not have been friends if they were stranded on a deserted island together.

To add to our domestic tensions, we all had the feeling we were dancing on the edge of a precipice. War was getting closer and we would be in it, we could feel it. On June 22 the Germans had launched a massive attack on the Soviet Union. German panzer divisions were approaching Leningrad and Moscow. On the western front, too, resistance to the Nazi advance was crumbling. An attack on England seemed inevitable.

Again the dilemma: war was insanity, an obscene waste; but Hitlerism, we knew, would leave us no choice. And soon enough it didn't.

CHAPTER 11

1941
1942

The Lincoln Brigade Vets' office was on the third floor of a nothing building on lower Fifth Avenue.

"Meet me there," said former Commander Milt Wolff late in November 1941, "Saturday morning around ten."

Half a dozen of us were there when Wolff showed up—Irv Goff, Vince Lossowsky, Billy Aalto, Al Tanz, Jiménez, and me. Wolff wasted no time.

"I've been approached by British intelligence. They want certain of our guys to volunteer for their Special Forces units. It will be dangerous underground work. I don't have to bullshit you; things, as you know, are going very badly in the war. It's up to you, but it's a chance to get one more crack at Hitler."

We talked it over. We wanted to know more about it than he could tell us. We gathered he had been contacted by Vincent Sheehan's wife, Diana, who we suspected was close to, if not part of, British intelligence. We all knew Sheehan and liked and admired him very much, and not only because he had brought a case of champagne to our internment camp in Le Havre in that long-ago spring of 1929.

"You don't have to decide now," said Wolff. "You will be contacted by a man named William Stephenson. Decide after you talk to him."

Stephenson was the notorious "Intrepid" of postwar spy fiction.

We would wait for him, we said, but it was only going through the motions. The decision had been made years earlier by all of us when we clambered over the icy boulders high atop the Pyrenees. Preparations for us to leave for London got under way, but the Brits moved too slowly. They let December 7 come along, and Pearl Harbor, and the U.S. entry into the war.

In Washington, Colonel William J. Donovan was head of the Office of the Coordinator of Information, the COI, soon to metamorphose into the Office of Strategic Services, the "Oh So Social" OSS. He had been buddy-buddy for some time with the very same William Stephenson, and his ears had twitched when, during casual after-dinner cigars and brandy, Intrepid let drop a reference to the half-dozen rather expendable Yanks he was on the verge of shipping off to Special Forces duty in London.

Donovan considered it a dirty-pool grab for Americans. He didn't want able-bodied veterans with very special and up-to-date military know-how to be snapped up from under his nose by limeys—friends, but still limeys. That night he called Milt Wolff, and days later, Irv Goff, Vince Lossowsky, and I found ourselves sitting in large armchairs facing Col. Donovan (soon to be General) in his jumbled Washington office in the Apex Building at a corner of the Federal Triangle.

"Listen," said the colonel, "I know who you guys are. Left-wingers, radicals, maybe even Communists, but I don't give a damn. I want you in this outfit, not in England. You're Americans, not limeys. We're in the war and you belong here."

"Why, knowing our backgrounds, do you want us in a super-duper outfit like this?" I asked.

"Because I've been put here to win this war," said Donovan, "and I will use anyone and anything I can to do it."

We looked at each other. We had caught the word *use*, and the faint aura of menace that hung around it was not lost on us. Later, in the lounge of the Congressional Country Club with our feet up on the overstuffed furniture, out of earshot of our weird-looking colleagues, we discussed the ambiguous position in which we found ourselves.

"I like Donovan," said Irv. "I think he's straight. His politics are probably right up there with Genghis Khan, but he seems to hate the Nazis somewhat more than the Democrats. I think he'll try to give us a chance to do something worthwhile in this war."

"I agree," said Vince. "His history shows that brave soldiers give him an orgasm. As long as Hitler lives, so may we. After that, look out!"

I thought a while. "Kleenex," I said, "will be more carefully expended than us, but we haven't much choice. If we turn this down we would go ahead and volunteer for the army and most likely wind up doing KP in some Mississippi boot camp for the rest of the war."

Next morning we met in Wild Bill's office again, and then we piled into a limousine and drove about thirty miles to the top of a mountain northwest of Washington. In an opening in the forest there was a pool, a lake, and many small cabins.

"This was a rich kids' camp," said Donovan. "We plan to make it into the main training area, and I want all your ideas, everything you learned about guerrilla war and underground operations in Spain."

"Will there," I asked, "be instructors from other sources too, like Army intelligence, the FBI, etc.?"

"We have a two-front war," replied Donovan, "one against the Axis, the other, more deadly, against every son of a bitch in the other branches who would rather share information with Hitler than with us."

We spent the next few days at the camp watching old Hollywood spy movies, racing each other in the big swimming pool, and laying out obstacle courses, target and demolition areas, lecture rooms, and communications and code rooms. The area was soon to be used for FDR on weekends, and someone gave it the name Shangri-la. Later Dwight Eisenhower redubbed it Camp David.

When the weekend came, we jeeped to Q Building, collected our pay envelopes, raced to Union Station, and tried (as we talked about our extraordinary pay envelopes) not to look conspicuous. This was not so easy, because the COI-OSS had not decided if we should look like civilians, which we were, or like soldiers. The compromise was to issue nondescript, rumpled khaki clothing, which made us look like neither and which had the effect of causing puzzled stares in our direction by everyone in our crowded train compartment.

"Now what do you suppose Colonel William J. Vanderbilt, former governor of Rhode Island, had in mind giving me $1,095," I mused out loud, "while both of you got $195?" For a few minutes all three of us stared at bills we had never seen—two crisp hundreds and one unbelievable thousand. "Perhaps these ruling-class-types do have a keen nose for the potential brilliance that lies in some of us rough diamonds," I said finally. "Maybe he can spot a leader of men at one hundred paces."

"Bullshit," said Irv, "it's an obvious test." Pontifically he added, "They wish to see how we will react, what we will do with the money, and whether we can be trusted."

"What do you mean 'we'?" I said. "It's my damn money, and if it's a test, it could be that I don't necessarily care to pass it."

During our few days in the COI-OSS, we had already seen whole buildings crawling with rich playboys, expatriate princes and dukes, captains of industry and finance, nutty professors, Hollywood directors, Wall Street lawyers, Mafia dons, and other staunch pillars of the United Status Quo. In this zoo it would be wise to move warily. The train also was crowded with briefcase-carrying bureaucrats, so we continued to discuss earnestly but guardedly what we ought to do with that thing with all the zeros. We were quite aware that we were already American spies with a duty to be circumspect and not look directly into the eyes of our fellow passengers, lest we arouse suspicion.

Still, Vince could not help breaking security. "Stop fondling that bill like it was your pet puppy," he growled, loud enough for heads to turn.

"Fuck you, you under-scale spook," I said. "Apply yourself, and maybe someday you'll earn a raise."

"You have to give them back their lousy thousand bucks," said Irv, ever the upholder of socialist morality. "Do it in New York. Some jerk in Q Building told me the outfit occupies the whole twenty-fourth floor of the RCA Building."

"OK," I agreed, "but let's have some fun first. Let's tell the gals we're rich and they won't have to work anymore."

"Darling," Roberta greeted me, throwing her arms around my neck. "I got a raise!" We had been married for six months.

"How much?" I asked.

"Not bad! I went from $16 to $16.75 a week," said Roberta proudly, showing me her pay envelope.

"Throw that junk away." With my best attempt at insouciance, I threw my $1,000 bill on the sofa.

For a moment she stared at the bill. "Oh my God," she said, and began to sob uncontrollably. This was the last thing I had expected.

"What's wrong?"

"I can see your poor corpse already," she cried. "How long do you think they can afford to keep you alive for this kind of money?"

Irv rushed to explain why she could multiply her estimate by ten. Next day we went to the twenty-fourth floor of the RCA and returned the money to a man named Russell, who looked at us curiously and shrugged his shoulders, thinking to himself that the outfit he was in was a good deal more unusual than he had thought. Naturally, the first thing I did on our return to Washington was to barge into Vanderbilt's office.

"So what's the big idea, Bill? Couldn't you guys think of a more sophisticated test than to stash that bill so crudely into my envelope?"

"What the hell are you talking about?" asked the colonel, raising both of his aristocratic eyebrows.

I explained. Vanderbilt appeared faintly amused. "So I may have made a little mistake. What are you making such a big fuss for? Forget it," and placing an arm around my shoulder, he led me out the door.

I raced to find Irv and Vince. "We are in a strange world," I said, "and we had better learn the language."

In the early spring of 1942, COI-OSS training was bizarre. From Donovan himself down, notions of who we were, what we were, and what we were supposed to be doing were at best foggy and at worst erroneous. The basic training method was to postulate a hypothetical scenario replete with frightful choices. Say you find yourself friendless and alone in the center of Berlin, what is the first thing you would need? Aladdin's lamp? Yes, but besides that. Karate. Karate? Well, you certainly couldn't call attention to yourself by using a firearm!

The former chief of police of the British Zone of Shanghai was imported. He taught us karate and the kosh. He was a fully qualified sadist who taught by doing, and within two weeks half the men in his class were under various levels of medical care. Karate everyone knows. The kosh is a good trick to have up your sleeve, where it is normally placed. It is a lead ball attached to a handle, at the end of a spring. When the arm is swung, the ball comes forward and if someone's head is in the way, it is difficult indeed to avoid crushing the skull.

"Clearly," I said to Irv, "this son of a bitch has not been told that he is fighting against the Germans, not for them."

To continue the scenario, how would you get to Berlin in the first place? By parachute? Sure, and we must all learn to jump right away. Parachutes arrived. A tower with a wire was erected and we slid down it a few times. A place to practice was arranged for. Field-officer-level brains then went to work. Surely the drop couldn't be at an airfield; it

Spring 1942. OSS
parachute-training group.
Kneeling left, Lincoln
Brigade vets Al Tanz and Irv
Goff. Can't find me in this
photo, but some swear the
fellow with the big ears
standing second from right is
Iran-Contra affair's General
Singlaub.

had to be over open country. Ah, but certainly not in broad daylight!
It'd better be in the darkest night, and to be on the safe side, from the
lowest altitude (to cut down target time, of course). A wise precaution
was taken; for the first jump, young Dr. James would go along on the
outside chance that something might go wrong.

The small military airfield in northern Virginia was dark and almost
deserted near midnight, when we piled into the B-26 and took off. Intense discussion erupted as soon as we were airborne about who should
jump first. Sophistry was raised to a new art form as each explained
why—pantingly eager as he was to take the lead—it would be an

egregious tactical blunder. Silence. Irv broke the sweating tension with a brilliant idea. Dr. James should obviously be the first, since he could then be on the scene prepared to lend his highly professional assistance if something should happen to any of the rest.

Before anyone was ready, the young jumpmaster from Fort Bragg yelled, "HOOK UP." Then rushing air pulled at me at the next command, "STAND IN THE DOOR." And then, "GO." It was like diving into a bottle of ink. Fall. Jerk. Bang. When I came to, I could hear them shouting my name. My head hurt, and I couldn't stand. Pretty soon Irv limped up.

"We've been looking for you for half an hour; you must have conked out," said Irv brightly.

"I think my chute was oscillating. It got caught in a tree and dropped me head-first on a rock," I said. "I need the Doc."

"The Doc needs you," said Irv. "He's got a busted leg. I think the only one who can walk is the little bastard that pushed us out of that door."

We had landed on a remote Allegheny mountaintop. There were no roads, and it took till dawn to get picked up by a severely frightened truck driver.

Later there were more jumps for all of us. The jumpmaster had said that the easiest landing was in water. "Just slip out of the harness about fifteen feet above, and it's like a nice dip in the pool," were his exact words. So Big Dick, who had been a professional wrestler as the "Masked Marvel," made out a nice river shining in the moonlight below him and slipped gracefully out of his chute. Only it was not a river. It was a concrete highway. A week later he was back from the hospital, bandaged and unable to bend both knees but still jovial.

Next to intrigue him was the class on Molotov cocktails, which used old pop bottles and lots of gasoline. When the rest of us were at the lakeside dock studying underwater demolition, he came up with his bottle, lit it, and blew the flames at us, causing us to dive or jump into the water to avoid being burned. That sight made Dick laugh, but the flames reversed and his face and neck were suddenly swathed in flame.

"Jump!" we yelled, "DIVE INTO THE LAKE!" And he did, but where

OSS parachute training. I'm
sure this is Irv Goff.

OSS parachute training. And
Irv Goff is sure this is me.

he did it the water was a bare three feet deep and muddy. So his stiff, bandaged legs stuck out and waved back and forth in a frantic semaphore.

We dragged him out and thought that would be the end of him, but he stayed and became the camp favorite. He was indestructible. No one could ever figure out how Big Dick had become part of the outfit. Whenever he was angry, he slipped into an obscure Slavic dialect that was probably obsolete.

After the sixth jump, all of us, using fictitious names and swaggering like veteran parachutists, headed for home on a weekend pass. But fellow Spanish War vet Al Tanz did not show up at Shangri-la on Monday morning for our Basic Essentials of Clandestine Warfare class.

His wife answered the phone when we called New York and said, "He's in the hospital. Broken shoulder. Parachuting."

"He didn't have one when he left here Friday night," said Irv.

"Well, he's got one now," she snickered, and then she went on to explain. Months ago, just before Al had left for Washington and the OSS, she had rented one of those shiny-floored, neomodern apartments, complete with dropped living room and steps leading down to it guarded by fake, overwrought-iron balustrades. Al had come home flushed, excited, and still full of adrenalin from his last jump. He had barely brushed her lips with a kiss before he was telling her how thrilling it was.

"It's easy," he said, "watch me. When the jumpmaster hits your leg, you go out the door, grab the shrouds to steer, and . . ." So saying he jumped down into the living room onto a throw rug that skidded swiftly out from under him, landed on his shoulder and the back of his head with a sickening crunch, and passed out. We didn't see him again until the day we were leaving Algiers, and since by then we had our own troubles we didn't bother to ask him how his parachute career was coming along.

For the rest of us at Shangri-la, despite our karate and parachuting expertise, the training scenario was not yet played out. Suppose we came across a German motorcycle? Perfect for escape, but not if you didn't know how to ride! Ten enormous cycles came on Monday. By

Friday the damage to personnel and equipment was, by any standard, colossal.

During the hiatus necessary for repairing bodies, headquarters suggested stimulus for the creative minds of this unusual and brilliant cadre. First, indoctrination. We sat in the front row and so had a good view of the slight pot on the belly of the lieutenant colonel from West Point who had taught a class there called Know Your Enemy.

"Forget everything you ever were taught about honor, truth, decency, fair play, or your instinct for ethical behavior," he began. "Your life will depend on being able to lie, cheat, and deceive and to kill quickly, silently, and without hesitation. You must think dirty and fight dirty." In other words, we were to become morally indistinguishable from the enemy. Is it always true, I thought, that you become those you fight?

"So what do you think?" I asked Irv afterward.

"If I read von Clausewitz correctly," said Irv, "it's a good argument for settling disputes other than by war."

There were troubling questions, but on the whole we were having a very good time; our opinions and experience seemed to be highly valued, we were rounding into terrific physical condition, and we were able some weekends to catch a train or an army plane up to New York for quick connubial trysting. But the ground was never steady under our feet. One day Donovan's office asked if we knew of anything worthwhile that could be useful as a text for underground warfare. We suggested Mao Tse Tung's classic *On Guerilla Warfare*, which thereupon became the OSS training text.

Another day we were called to Q Building to view the latest drop capsule intended for the resistance forces in France. Dressed in our usual sloppy semifatigues, we found a roomful of generals and colonels, including Beedle Smith and the *Brooklyn Daily Eagle* publisher, Colonel Goodfellow. Protocol in such a situation being indistinct, we said, "Hi, Generals," and joined in the conversation, which at first was limited to the technical aspects of the capsule's deliverability, capacity, weight, and so forth.

But soon Colonel Goodfellow got down to the nitty gritty by saying,

"We must take care that these do not fall into the wrong hands." I na-
ively thought he meant the Nazis, but I was quickly disabused. "There
are several groups in the underground," said the colonel, "and we
don't want them falling into the hands of the Commies, now do we? If
we supply the far left with arms and equipment, we build the in-
frastructure for them to take over after the war."

"We shouldn't supply them even if they are doing the best fighting?"
asked Irv.

"Especially then," said the colonel.

"Christ," I said later, "here I am worrying about the second front
and these fuckers are already into World War III. Creating a more humane social order may turn out to be tougher than we thought."

Washington in the summer of 1942 was steamy, humid, and overheated. It was also crowded with soldiers, sailors, Wacs, Waves, and
marines, along with sweating politicians up to their ears in patriotic
speeches and arms-procurement deals. At Shangri-la, training intensified even as the hypothetical scenarios crossed the line into the
hobgoblin-infested spy-world of surreality. Naval war in the Pacific was
for real, and John Ford came to the camp and ran some of the incredible footage he had already shot of kamikaze attacks on U.S. warships.

But the government was concerned that the public did not yet themselves feel that the war was much more than a mild distraction from
the National League pennant race. The OSS was asked to come up
with something to test the public's war-awareness pulse. Irv Goff and I
learned that we had been selected as "volunteers," bait for a fishing trip
into the collective subconscious of Washington's wartime population.
We were to don German Gestapo uniforms, stroll around strategic
capital buildings, and see what happened.

"Don't worry," said one of Donovan's aides, "we'll be following
closely in an unmarked OSS car."

"Cold comfort at best," I said. "I fully expect to be shot dead while
you're searching for a parking space."

The sinister black uniforms were correct to the last details of the SS
insignia, although they were perhaps a touch off-center to a sophisticated eye.

Irv was built like a role model for the proverbial brick shithouse. He had grown up on Brighton Beach in Coney Island and had spent long periods of the Depression unemployed, perfecting acrobatic and muscle-building skills. At one time he and a pal had actually built a vaudeville act and toured the country tossing a variety of eager young ladies into the air between them and, not invariably, catching them. ("Stage struck" was a too painfully apt description for the poor dears.) I thought it would be a small miracle if the shoulder seams of his new uniform would hold. He decided not to swing his arms, which gave his walk what he said was an authentic Prussian stiffness. I said he looked like ten pounds of fertilizer in a five-pound bag.

Not that I fit Richard Wagner's dream-vision of Tristan either. A former University of Iowa wrestler, a shade below average height, green-eyed and dark-skinned, I looked more Neapolitan than Teutonic.

The OSS car dropped us off at the edge of Lafayette Park across the street from the White House. We were sure we wouldn't get past the first cop or the first American officer. It was a beautiful day, the sun shone, the streets were crowded, and not a thing happened. Most people hardly glanced at us.

Then we saw a group of soldiers coming our way. They looked uncertain, as though they would like to avoid a problem by crossing the street. So we headed straight for them. The GIs saluted. Salutes were returned.

"I'll be goddamned," I said. Irv suggested we try for some officers. Near the entrance to a well-known restaurant, we spotted a navy admiral with an army captain. Again, mutual salutes.

Irv looked at me. "Tell me," he said, "are my swastikas on straight?"

"Listen," I said, "we haven't heard the radio for a couple of hours. Maybe the war is over."

We went back to the OSS car to talk about it. America may be at war, we decided, but Americans aren't. We called Q Building for instructions. "Continue the experiment but deepen its character," they said.

"I feel good," I said, "we're beginning to learn real spy talk."

This time we walked directly to a corner news-dealer. "Poddon us!"

said Irv in his best imitation of a German accent. "Ve are straindgers in Vashington. Could you maybe perhaps tell us vare ist de main telephone building?"

For a long moment he stared silently at the two black uniforms with the silver swastikas. Ah, we thought, he is wondering how he can hold these two Nazi bastards till he can get the cops. One should never lose faith in the little people. In them is our hope for purity, decency, and courage; they are the reservoir of our hopes for a better world, the real cause for which we sacrifice and fight.

But then he spoke. "Sir," he said to Irv, "I was trying to remember. I'm pretty sure if you go straight down this street to the second traffic light and make a right, you can't miss it." And so it went.

Donovan made a full report to President Roosevelt. Word leaked to Congress and the press. There were speeches and a couple of editorials. Then the incident sank out of sight under the weight of the dank, steamy heat of Washington's worst summer in twenty years.

By early September it was clear that something big was on. We were assigned to the Spanish Desk, run by one of Donovan's favorite agents, Donald Downes, an Ivy League literature professor, a fat-and-forty intellectual who had been immersed all his life in the thrilling derring-do of fictional, larger-than-life characters. He was witty, charming, and emotionally unbalanced. Secret operations were his playground for free-form fantasies. To be in his command could be highly amusing and extremely dangerous.

It came time to be organized into mission groups. Captain Jerry Sage, a tall, improbably handsome ex–football star from the University of Oregon, was put in charge of Group Eight. He was totally innocent of military knowledge, but he was not a dope. When he learned of the fighting we had done against German, Italian, and Spanish Fascist forces, the captain would not make a move without checking it out first with us, and our respect and liking quickly became mutual.

For a while, Sage tried to pass on what he learned from us about up-to-date German and Italian equipment and field strategy to the brass in Washington, who were still struggling to comprehend what had gone on in Château-Thierry in 1918. Those who were most kind ignored him. The others convulsed the Officers Club with their wittiest barbs, guaranteeing many thousands of needless U.S. casualties in the field of battle.

Donald Downes called Group Eight to a meeting in Q Building. Excitement made his eyebrows flutter like a hummingbird scenting nectar. "Can't tell you much," he said, "and what you hear you must forget. I see in your future a long sea voyage. I see much sand. I see desert. I see a mission you would die for. I mean figuratively, not literally, ha, ha. Get you all forthwith to Shangri-la and use each moment well. Your asses may depend on it. Irv and Milt, remain with me." Normal conversation for Downes resembled the script for an Errol Flynn movie.

When the others had left, he turned to us. "Do you know Abercrombie and Fitch?"

"Of course," I said, "my very favorite store for items of the hunt. They have fly rods truly beyond compare." Neither I nor Irv had ever remotely imagined entering what we deemed a toy store for excessively wealthy but socially retarded grown-ups.

"Go," said Downes, "buy whatever you think we might need in [whisper] the desert."

We shopped carefully, pecuniously, and diffidently—a compass here, a hunting knife there. When the stuff got to Downes he was furious.

"I presume," he said, giving scorn his best Harvard accent, "when you run short in the Sahara you will skim through the A and F catalog, which you may have considerable leisure to read in some German Kriegsgefangene Lager."

"We weren't sure of the budget," I said.

"We don't have a budget," said D.D. "We have needs and we fill them. Now get your socially conscious, psychically inhibited asses back up there. Perhaps in your case you will be comforted by Lenin's dictum 'To each according to his needs.'"

This time a bowing and scraping retinue of Uriah Heep clones followed us as we indicated with a lofty wave or pointed finger daggers, pearl-handled guns, wrist compasses, purest-down sleeping bags, and leather jackets and boots almost sensuously rich and soft. We couldn't know that, later on, this beautiful and in some ways ridiculous equipment would come within a hair of costing me my life.

Through September and October the mission took shape. We were to train and arm agents to infiltrate Franco's Spain, to sabotage his plans and later to lead a revolt should he enter the war against us. At that moment the generalissimo was publicly declaring neutrality and privately fueling Nazi submarines at Cádiz. If he decided to enter the war, the entire Mediterranean would become a German lake.

Downes came up to the camp and joined Group Eight for lunch. We were seated at one of the better tables. You could not, in truth, call it a mess hall—not with damask linen tablecloths, Waterford crystal goblets, Queen Anne's lace silverware, a menu presided over by a former instructor at L'Escoffier, and meals served with impeccable skill by waiters who glided around in utter silence. They were silent because if they spoke the uncontrollable hatred they felt for the OSS cadre they served would come pouring out. All of them were regular army draftees called out of their units and sent to the OSS on the basis of brilliant academic backgrounds; they were demonstrably the finest minds in the country. Since Q Building didn't quite know what to do with them, the perverted logic of military intelligence ruled that they should meanwhile perform as an underclass of indentured servants, personal lackeys to the OSS "students."

Over the second cup of steaming Himalayan coffee I asked, "Where are we to get agents of a sufficient caliber to carry out such a delicate and dangerous mission?"

"There are thousands of ex–Spanish soldiers in North Africa who fought against Franco," said Downes. "You must convince them to volunteer."

The cool cynicism of this suggestion made me want to throw up. He was right about their being there, by the thousands in fact, in stinking, disease-infested concentration camps, all their days spent building the trans-Sahara railroad in brutal, unending desert heat. When the Spanish Civil War ended in March of 1939, the Spanish navy, which had remained with the anti-Franco Loyalists, had loaded as many ex-combatants and their families as they could onto ships and escaped to presumed freedom in French North Africa. In a preview of Vichy's collapse and collaboration, the French colony greeted the refugees, who had earned parades and cheers for their achingly brave years of anti-Nazi resistance, with rifle butts and encircled them with ten-foot-high fences of barbed wire.

I stared for a minute at the trace of oil that had gathered on Donald Downes's chin as he gnawed the bone of his double-thick butterfly pork chop au Mornay clean. "I think," I said, "you have just given the word *chutzpah* a new and deeper meaning. They will refuse us, as they have every right to do!"

But I was wrong. When not many weeks later we reached the first camp thirty miles south of Algiers and suggested to inmates that they volunteer for a mission that had every chance of ending in almost certain death, not one refused.

Like most military preparation, every possible contingency was envisioned and meticulously planned for except those that actually occurred. We were all given two 45-caliber army automatics, unlimited ammo, and instructions to shoot, shoot, shoot. We were told to be daring and inventive like real underground agents, so we blew up each other's cabins with molotov cocktails and the general's jeep with the general's wife in it when she visited on a Sunday.

Thirty-five sons of the king of Siam (Thailand) joined us for code training. They spoke little English and smiled a lot. It was mostly dots and dashes, so it didn't matter. Everyone liked them and realized that they would soon be running their native land, which they are, although they are probably no longer on the payroll of American intelligence, not all of them.

It was almost time for the final training exercise. Most of the rich, playboy types had turned out to be useless and were gone to upholstered chairs in procurement offices. Their special contacts in Rome, Berlin, and Prague were, while well-placed, thoroughly devoted to the defeat of America. At Shangri-la, President Roosevelt began to visit on weekends. Something was in the air.

We leaned over crude drawings. "This is Camp Meade," said Captain Sage. "Over here is a radio tower. Irv, Vince, and Milt, you will land from the deck of a submarine, hide your boat, infiltrate, blow up the tower, and get back here by dawn." Sage then turned to me. "Draw up your plan and let me see it. Make it simple. An outline is enough."

So I did. It went like this:

1. 10:00 P.M. Move the *Marsyl* (the submarine) to longitude 77.16.25, latitude 38.24.
2. Assemble foldboat on deck of *Marsyl*. (I pictured moonlight, not a black, lashing gale.)
   10:25 P.M. Leave *Marsyl*.
   10:45 P.M. Land. Reconnoiter.
   SIGNAL: striking of rocks together twice sharply will indicate "stand by for our return" if mission impossible to accomplish.
3. Take boat into woods. Disassemble and bury 100 feet from shore.
4. Proceed from landing point on azimuth of 35 degrees to road. Stay in woods and follow road almost to crossroads. Then on azimuth of 240 degrees to tower.
5. Expect to reach highway at 11:10 P.M. Blow tower at 11:30.

"Want the return trip?" I asked Sage.

"Nah," said the Captain, "just set off your firecrackers. After that the show's over."

He was right, of course. Just the same, I didn't like being reminded of my expendability.

We dragged our foldboat onto the narrow, slanted deck of the sub at midnight in the middle of the Potomac. It was raining. The foldboat was in two bags. It had slotted-end bamboo rods for a frame and a rubber cover stretched tight over it. If you could get it together right, it made a fair sort of kayak. Doing it in the rainy dark was a test of how far human beings could push themselves without a shattering of nerves and a proof of how dumb the theory of military training could be as related to anything that ever happened in real life. Somehow the three of us made it into the kayak built for two, and somehow it stayed afloat, but where were the paddles? Half of one paddle was found. Good for going in circles. I suggested that perhaps we should call it a fruitful learning experience and try again some other time.

"Can't do that," said Captain Sage. "Camp Meade knows a little about this exercise and has posted extra guards. Matter of fact, they have been issued live ammunition. And as you know, they hate us worse than anybody. Anyway, if you guys are as good as your reputation, what's to worry?"

Sailors pushed the kayak off into the black river.

"Sage, you prick," shouted Irv, "all three of us are Jewish and if any of us gets shot the ADL will have your ass."

We got to shore almost an hour later and buried the kayak at least a mile from the planned spot. We would never find it again.

"Fuck the kayak," said Vince, "let's blow the goddamn tower."

There were close calls with the Meade guards and once, as we crawled through the wet forest, Vince wanted to surprise one with half a pound of dynamite. Around 3 A.M. we made it to the radio tower, laid the dynamite in the right places, set the timed detonators, and started back to camp.

We were bone weary, but we couldn't resist temptation. Below Thurmont, through a postcard-pretty bucolic valley, ran a single-track railway, and in the far distance we could hear, as they say, "its lonesome whistle." Quickly we set impact detonators in our remaining five pounds of TNT, fixed it with admirable speed to the rails, and retired swiftly to the woods. The explosion was really quite satisfactory. People ran about shouting, waving their arms, and finally discovering that the small engine had been partially derailed.

"Well," Irv observed, "I think we have drawn their attention to the fact that there is a war on, and for that alone we deserve commendation."

"Let's not mention it just yet," I suggested.

The word finally came: "Go home, say good-bye, come back on Monday, we're going over."

Roberta had moved us to a basement apartment at 67 Jane Street in the West Village. Street passers-by, if they bent down, could see into the living-bedroom and observe that its floor slanted down to a tiny fireplace. Roberta had a feeling of foreboding when I came in and we kissed longer than usual, which was pretty long. Two small boys watched intently from the sidewalk and one shouted, "That's not the soldier who was here last week!" Children in New York develop a mordant sense of humor.

For those active in the left-wing movement, the city, the whole country in fact, was full of friends. A wealthy young woman we knew had a cabin on the estate of Roger Baldwin, the head of the Civil Liberties Union, in the northern New Jersey woods. Four couples were invited up for the good-bye weekend. Besides Roberta and me, the Irv Goffs, the Cooks, and the Fajanses came. It would be two years before Jerry Cook and Irv Fajans, both Spanish vets, would be in the OSS in Italy.

Our host, Ms. Kaufman, suggested that we play some tennis. The women declined, and when Ms. Kaufman strode out onto the court they were glad they did. She was amply endowed, a fact that was emphasized by her being also topless. We all thought of ourselves casually as revolutionaries, but in point of fact we carried a full load of middle-class bourgeois baggage, including but not limited to the usual sexual hang-ups of the day. The women retreated from view muttering, but the men made a stab at nonchalance—not a very good one since her bobbing boobs drew magnetic focus, making us not care about the shots we missed, which we might have anyway. She was a very good player.

When we were sweated up good, she took off the rest of her clothes and dove into a nearby stream. She was very pretty and had a terrific body. She smiled prettily and waved us in. We looked at each other and hesitated. Our wives were viewing from afar, arms folded in the attitude of avenging Clytemnestras. Psycho-sociologically it was an interesting moment. Jerry Cook came up with a compromise solution and stripped down to shorts. We all jumped in happily, sure that our wives would appreciate the skill and delicacy with which we had avoided an embarrassing contretemps. The feeling was quite short-lived since we had been aroused by Ms. Kaufman, and when we stood up our wet shorts were considerably more revealing and provocative than we had bargained on.

Beneath the fun and games of that weekend there was a suppressed sadness, a chilling apprehension. Roberta and I had met in May and married in July of 1941. She would be left, within a few hours, to live in anxiety until I could return from the war. She had not been too thrilled about the weekend from the start. She disliked rusticity and had been unhappy from the moment she discovered the pretty cottages were excessively primitive.

"What do you do when you have to go to the john?" she asked Ms. Kaufman.

"Just go in the woods," was the airy answer.

"What do you do for paper?" For city-girl Roberta it was a painful conversation.

"Just use leaves," said Ms. Kaufman with a trace of impatience.

Sunday night, back home in Jane Street, newlyweds facing our last night together, perhaps forever, Roberta confessed to me that she was in agony, that she had a terrible rash on the inside of her thighs. A doctor friend came and made a diagnosis. It seems the leaves she had used at Ms. Kaufman's suggeston were mostly poison ivy.

Perhaps never in history have an ardent couple expressed their passion with such infinite care. We thought of the old joke about how porcupines make love and laughed.

In the morning, before I left, we talked about the war. On the one hand, we understood and hated fascism and knew it had to be fought. On the other we detested the superpatriotism of business interests that turn the blood of young men into mountains of gold. We had agonized during the Spanish Civil War as the U.S.A., England, and France refused to aid the democratic Republic, thereby giving a free hand to Franco, Hitler, and Mussolini. Why? Why had Hitler been financed from the West? There had to be a logical explanation, and we felt in our bones that we knew it. The Russian Revolution and the establishment of a huge Communist-controlled state had sent a volcanic shock through the capitalist world. From 1918 onward there would be divisions and rivalries among the capitalist states, but there would also be an iron-firm though unspoken alliance, implacably dedicated to the destruction of the Soviet Union. In turn, the Russians would draw their wagons into a circle and develop a fortress mentality in a closed and paranoid society.

To me and Roberta, these were not issues with which to liven up cocktail-party discussions. We had long ago concluded that a society dedicated solely to the pursuit of profit would ravage the fragile earth and leave as its monument a huge pile of human detritus. In a country subjected to a torrent of anti-Communist invective, ours were not popular views and we had paid a price. Calm, objective, analytical discussion of world politics is one thing, but voluntarily laying your ass on the line is another. Moreover, this was no clear-cut, idealistic, white-hats-against-the-black-hats crusade like Spain. It was an uneasy coalition of strange bedfellows, many with murky objectives and some with whom I would rather not be caught dead.

We agreed that for most Americans it was not an anti-Fascist war, because for one thing they had never been involved in serious debate as to just what the precise nature of fascism is. It was anti-Hitler (nobody could stand him), maybe even anti-Nazi, and certainly anti-"Jap." Was that enough to outweigh our basic anti-war instincts? Could we really rationalize our involvement because half a noble cause was better than none and in any case a Hitler victory was an unbearable idea? We fell silent, reluctant to voice the inevitable cliché that so often made old cynics out of young idealists, the choice of the "lesser evil."

Finally Roberta sighed and said, "Do you have any clean socks?"

When it was time to leave, Roberta was crying. I said what all soldiers say, "I'll be back." Like all soldiers, I did not really believe in my own mortality, which is what has always made it possible for old men to send young men to their deaths.

CHAPTER 12

1942
1943

With relative ease, the OSS saw to it that the nucleus of Group Eight—Captain Jerry Sage, Irv, Vince, and I—were in Oran in time to greet the troops landing on the North African shores. There was then a long train-ride to Algiers, during which we were warned not to eat the plentiful dates. I wondered why Americans always got sick when they traveled, especially on food that they paid enormous prices for when it was imported and sold in specialty shops on Madison Avenue and in Beverly Hills.

In Algiers, according to OSS custom, we commandeered a small castle that overlooked the city and harbor. The view was magnificent and the war seemed remote, but we went right to work. In the desert thirty miles due south was an internment camp with many Spanish ex-combatants. They were willing and learned fast. With thousands of troops already landed in North Africa, the danger of Spain's entering the war worried Washington. Spain could easily close the Strait of Gibraltar and leave the Allied Forces stranded, cut off, and helpless.

There was pressure on Group Eight to get agents into Spain at once to organize a resistance movement. Arms would be supplied later if Franco made a move. Meanwhile, there would be communication and the development of intelligence. If Franco stayed out, it would be a paid vacation. The British assignment in this venture, which they had insisted upon, was to deliver the Spanish agents to their home country.

The Brits chose submarines. It worked fine until a double agent aboard tipped off Madrid. The OSS agent was picked up and treated to all that civilized man has learned about how to have a conversation with a prisoner—electrical shocks, nail pulling, cigarette burns on the eyelids, etc. He told about the OSS and all hell broke loose.

Franklin Roosevelt had an unofficial contact with Madrid, a leading Catholic layman named Robert Murphy, who also spoke for the rightist Pope Pius XII. Franco complained to Murphy about the OSS operation he had discovered, and Murphy, ever solicitous about his friend the dictator, carried on hysterically to FDR, threatening that Franco had a good mind to enter the war unless he was assured that the OSS operation and all other unfriendly acts would be stopped at once. Donovan then had no choice, and for a while Group Eight was reduced to watching Harvard anthropologist Carleton Coon make explosive mines camouflaged in the form of donkey shit to be spread on Tunisian roads in the rear of the German forces.

Our unexpected leisure time gave us the chance to wander into the Casbah to watch the finals of the belly-dancing championships. The Casbah was dangerous and off-limits to troops, but Irv and I decided it would leave too wide a gap in our education to miss such an unusual cross-cultural experience. We went and were inordinately impressed, along with the rest of the audience of three thousand wildly enthused Arabs, at the heroic gyrations of the favorite, Fatima. She looked like one imagined Carmen ought really to look, and she danced like Frank Sinatra sang—as if issuing a personal invitation to each one to share with her his, and for that matter her, most unfettered fantasies. The berobed and beveiled audience responded with screaming approval, and Irv and I could not help but applaud too. As we did, a slim, dark boy maybe nine or ten years old appeared out of nowhere and said to me, "Feefty franc."

"For what?" I asked.

"For Fatima," said the boy.

We never spent the fifty francs, tempted as we were. We were not only suspicious of foul play but also chintzy about the money.

Robert Murphy wasn't satisfied with our continued presence. "Get those left-wing lunatics out of Algiers!" he screamed at General Donovan, and FDR hinted that maybe it would be just as well to pacify the son of a bitch. So all of us in Group Eight, padded with ten partly trained Spanish agents, were on our way to the Algerian and Tunisian deserts with only the vaguest idea of just what the hell we were supposed to do except hide.

We were neither mentally nor emotionally prepared to sit on our hands, not with the Brits coming from the east, the Americans from the west, and General Erwin Rommel in between. On foot and with parachutes, we infiltrated the ill-defined lines and blew things up. It was ranger work, not what we had trained for, and rather a waste. Sage, now a major, promised that when things calmed down in Washington the organization of underground work would resume.

We were camped in a cork forest high in the Atlas mountains north-west of Tbessa, and we were burning the cork to keep warm. A British colonel assigned to observe OSS infiltration methods brought word that Rommel had attacked Kasserine Pass and that the Americans were in full retreat. We all jeeped down to the valley to see what was going on. Whole regiments—men, trucks, and artillery—streamed by in retreat.

"We should do something," said the Brit. "I feel like a bit of a shit."

"What do you suggest," I asked, "holding up Excalibur and shouting halt?"

His name was William Hornsby-Smythe III, and he was veddy upper class. He had just come from Gibraltar, where he had had a disastrous love affair, and was actively searching for a romantic gesture to end a life that he no longer felt was tolerable. The day after the retreat, Sage said that the colonel wanted to go behind the lines that night with a group because he needed the experience. Refusal was unanimous, couched in language best described as gaudy. An hour later Sage was back, troubled but firm.

"We are at the front," Sage pointed out, "and the colonel is the senior officer here. He is giving a direct order, and whoever refuses to go tonight will be shot. He means it," added Sage unhappily, "and whether he shoots you or kills himself doesn't seem to make much difference."

Irv, Vince, and I called a meeting and explained the situation to the Spaniards, who were so inured to the arbitrary and absurd behavior of senior officers that they merely smiled at the naiveté of anyone who would expect officers to function any other way. They agreed that the colonel would have to be shot if it appeared he was about to get us all killed as a fitting sacrifice to his lost love over there in Gibraltar. It was a little past midnight when William Hornsby-Smythe III seemed to sense a definite menace in the cold desert air. He suggested that perhaps we should go back to our own lines and admitted that he had not the slightest idea how to do so, since he was hopelessly lost. Irv took the lead and we were back in half an hour.

Soon after, Jerry Sage said he had good news. We were about to be recalled from exile because big things were being planned for Sicily and Italy, but first there was one more small chore. The colonel wanted a friend of his, a Scottish captain, to join us for one more infiltration, only this time there would be planning and a legitimate objective. Of sorts.

The fighting at Kasserine was still intense, and the Germans were finding particularly useful a railroad bridge that had resisted until now all aerial attacks. We would blow it. Rough military maps showed a dried-out wadi running diagonally into the German lines. We could run up pretty close and hide a jeep there for use on the way out. If there was trouble, the British would cover us with light artillery mounted on fast carriers.

The mission was risky, but possible. Sage wanted to go along, and there would also be the two Brits, Vince, Irv, and me. Carrying two inexperienced personnel meant extra precaution in planning details. We decided to wear nondescript army-type clothing with no insignia and phony dog tags. Irv told Major Sage that unless Hornsby-Smythe and his pal agreed to act only as observers, following and not giving orders, there would be no mission. We were all nervous and unhappy, with good reason as it turned out. The plan was to reach the bridge by 2 A.M., do the job, and get out by daylight, but it didn't work. The terrain was difficult and the maps were off by miles. When we got into position, it was daylight; we would have to wait until nightfall.

Then, at three in the afternoon, we noticed absolute quiet. In the intense desert heat there was not a movement of troops or guards. We decided to take the chance. Setting our time-delayed charges, we quickly mined the bridge and made it back into the undergrowth of the mountain foothills. We knew we had to move fast and were able to reach the low hills above the wadi where we had hidden the jeep just at dusk. Irv, Vince, and I looked at each other; by some miracle we had pulled it off.

We had to cross a small gully and then an open ridge covered only

Vince Lossowsky, left, and
Irv Goff in Naples, January
1945. Nearly two years after
the bridge-mining escapade
and still in one piece.

by low sagebrush. On the other side in the bottom of the wadi sat our
good old jeep. For the captain from Scotland, it had all been too, too
boring. He looked back at the hills, and there at the crest of one he
saw, clearly outlined against the sky, a German soldier. He could not
resist. Aim. A quick shot. For a moment the rest of us were stunned.
Then we ran for the ridge that suddenly seemed miles away.

First to hit just ahead of us were heavy mortars, then machine guns,
and finally, from a fold in the hills, the whoosh of 88s from at least two
tanks that we must have unknowingly passed on the way down. We
had gone right through Rommel's Sixteenth Panzers, his crack division.

I turned to see where the heaviest fire was coming from and caught a
bullet that creased my left temple and continued through my ear. The
impact spun me around and knocked me to the ground. I bled pro-

fusely (ears have a generous blood supply). Irv appeared at my side with sulfa and clean white bandages.

"I'm all right," I said. "Let's go!" But wherever I went, machine-gun bullets followed like a swarm of bees. My nice clean white bandage shone like a beacon in the dusk. I began to be hit. Shrapnel hit my left hand, in which I had been carrying the new explosive, plastique. Two more machine-gun bullets in the right leg, then shrapnel hits in the thigh. I went down and tried to bury myself in the sand under the cactus and sagebrush. I felt myself growing weak, but I didn't hurt. Shock kept the pain out.

In a little while I heard voices. The voices spoke German, and they came very near. Then there was silence. I rolled over to take a look. Waist-high was a ring of machine pistols all aimed, quite accurately, I thought, at my head. Above them were unmistakably Teutonic faces, all very grim.

First they noticed my wounds, but then they noticed other things, like my shoes. Abercrombie and Fitch finest-grade-leather jump boots—off they came. Then the 38-caliber banker's specials—one from under the right arm, one from under the left. The Germans began to grin at these souvenirs sure to impress the fräuleins in Berlin. I wondered if they believed all GIs were as elaborately equipped. I was very glad they were, like all soldiers, compulsive collectors; presentation to the Gestapo with such equipment would be a sure death sentence. They continued to strip me, taking the stiletto in my belt and the beautiful wristwatch-compass. I couldn't resist a pang when that went. When I was down to just my shirt and trousers, they picked me up and carried me to a tank. And there was Major Sage. He too had been wounded, although rather lightly in the leg, and captured.

"Don't worry," he shouted as they led him away, "we'll get out of this in no time." Sage, a basically very decent man, had a tendency to say things like that. I was loaded on to the apron of the tank and lashed to the barrel of the 88. When they reached the first-aid station at a frontline airfield, I was only half-conscious. Faces of German doctors were above me and I knew they were patching me up, sewing my hand, removing shrapnel and bullets.

Somewhere in the world a decision had been made that the British and American air forces should at this precise moment choose this particular airfield to bomb. The makeshift operating room began to jump around. Mortally wounded soldiers were being brought in, and I began to feel disgusted with the level of leadership planning, and especially timing, at the Allied Command.

Things got worse when a new and distinctly unhandsome face appeared above me, the face of a Gestapo intelligence captain. Interrogation began: your name, the name of your officers, what outfit are you with, when did you arrive, what was your mission, where is your base, what is your rank, where did you train? I struggled to suppress the desire to give nasty, flippant answers. I knew if the captain even suspected the truth, I would either be shot or wish devoutly that I had been.

"There were all these soldiers on a boat," I said. "Then we got off and went to a camp somewhere and were told we would be replacements. A squad was sent on night patrol and I got lost." I stuck to my basic story, and when the questioning got tough I passed out, which was not too hard since I was on the verge of doing so from loss of blood and residual anger at the dumb Scottish bastard who had got me into this.

The Gestapo man must have grown tired or bored, because when I came to I was in an ambulance passing fruit groves and date palms and cities with strange names—Sfax, Gabes, and then Tunis.

The stretchers were finally unloaded and placed on the sidewalk in front of a Tunis hospital. Other wounded prisoners, mostly British, lay nearby. It was hot, and time passed slowly. Someone brought water. I was wondering what would happen next when it dawned on me that I was no longer hearing German. Soldiers bustled around wearing funny little hats. Then I made out the language, Italian. The wounded were being turned over to the Italians. That had to be a good development. But before I had much time to think about it we were shoved into ambulances again for another ride. This time the trip was short.

We were unloaded on the tarmac of the Carthage airport. Carthage! Bits and pieces of ancient history, from high school and from random reading, littered my mind, but I did remember it as a place of carnage, a place used to being sacked by Greeks, Romans, and other heavily armed crusaders roaming the Mediterranean consumed with the self-righteous desire to bring the benefits of their superior lifestyle to the locals by killing them.

Not much had changed. The German soldiers who had captured me wore belts inscribed "GOTT MIT UNS." God is with us. Well, why not? Of what use is the Judeo-Christian God of love when so many soldiers must be blessed while carrying out their murderous patriotic duties? I was completely baffled by the effrontery of organized religion. Most of mankind did seem to have created various gods convenient to their perceived needs, but looked at objectively they had done a pretty sloppy job. Christ, Buddha, Muhammad. Really! Deify a young, hallucinating Middle Eastern Jew, ignoring tens of thousands of years of human history, and in adoring him justify the cruel anti-Semitism of the Torquemadas, Hitlers, and Louisiana rednecks?

Religion and soldiers. Why were they so linked together in my mind? This was my second war and fifth year as a soldier—quite a lot for an anti-war activist. Not only that, but I had *volunteered* to fight against Franco in Spain and I had volunteered again for the OSS. If I dug under the anti-Fascist rhetoric, did I get a zing out of the excitement, the guns, the big hunt, the killing game itself? Soldiers do not shoot at political abstractions; they shoot mostly at apolitical young carpenters, shoe salesmen, and students, all mostly poor, mostly working-class, and mostly bored with their lives, anxious to try out their manhood, with praises of politicians and priests and the music of stirring military bands ringing in their ears.

Go be a hero in the patriotic war to preserve our civilization. How? Well, the more people you murder, the bigger the hero you are, the more beribboned your chest. A few troubling contradictions there to be sure. I decided to think about it some more, but not just then. Just then I was lying on the tarmac at Carthage among a weird collection of what seemed to be World War I German Fokker airplanes with their motors running, and my wounds were beginning to hurt like hell. Not only that, but the goddamn High Command had authorized another U.S.-U.K. air raid on this airport at this moment. The Italian troops took off and left us all lying there, and again the ground was shaking and jumping. It seemed to go on for a long time, but it probably had not. I noted that our vaunted pilots had not hit much of anything.

Certainly not the Fokkers into which we were loaded, stretcher touching stretcher on the bomb-bay floor. As we flew over the Mediterranean, a British stretcher moaned, "This is the first bloody plane I ever flew in where the wings flapped." It was true. Whatever the planes were, they were very, very old, and we flew so low over the water we felt we could drag our feet in it. It flew like a wounded pelican that had eaten too big a fish. In the open cargo door was mounted an ancient machine gun manned by an Italian boy-soldier who couldn't have been more than seventeen years old and who grinned constantly at some secret joke. Maybe he knew that the fast Allied fighter planes could not possibly get low enough to attack without crashing into the sea.

We landed in Sicily and were taken to a Palermo hospital, which was also under bombardment. I had thought subjectively that it was the other side, not us, who hit hospitals, and so I was for the moment bitterly critical about the whole damn war. The feeling passed when the Italians loaded us onto a train and we rode through the beautiful Sicilian mountains before being ferried across the Strait of Messina and up the spectacular Italian coast through Naples and Rome to Bologna.

The trip was true Italian-style informal. Civilian passengers were crowded into our compartment, and when they found out who the wounded soldiers were, there was constant talk and we were pressed with smelly, garlicky food, full of stomach-destroying sauces. I considered how different the Italians were from the stiff and cold Germans. OK, so national and regional characteristics were charming and interesting and refreshingly diverse, but didn't they maybe lend themselves to easy jingoistic exploitation? Wasn't it all too easy to dislike, and then to hate, and then to be willing to destroy those so menacingly different from oneself? Was it at all possible to retain national characteristics without the dangerous concomitant of virulent nationalism? Not up to now.

The prison hospital in Castel St. Pietro thirty kilometers outside of Bologna had been an enormous religious school run by priests and nuns. Italian doctors had been brought in, and about thirty nuns remained to help with the wounded. The outside of the building was massive, probably fourteenth century. Inside were more than eight hundred wounded prisoners, almost all British taken at the fall of Tobruk in North Africa, including a general and half-a-dozen doctors.

Wards were arranged according to prevailing caste and class distinctions. There were commodious quarters for the general and the other officers in appropriately descending scale, and then the wards for the English, Welsh, and Scottish. Farther away and more crowded were the Australians and New Zealanders, then the Indian Sikhs and Gurkhas, and finally the cantankerous Irish. I was put in with the tough and rowdy Aussies. I was renamed Yank and immediately became inordinately popular because I was the only white who was friendly with the Gurkhas and Sikhs. They were vegetarians and gave me the tins of Spam from their weekly Red Cross parcels, which in turn I was able to trade with the Italian guards for eggs and wine.

I liked the Australians. They were rough, honest, and friendly, and whatever they thought, they said. They did have a primitive sense of humor, though, that surfaced in what they did about the nuns. None of the nuns, it happened, spoke English. So they taught them that "Fuck You" meant good morning and that the sign of the cross was recited "Ace, King, Queen, Jack." The nuns were totally baffled by these wounded and imprisoned strangers who would break up in uncontrollable laughter if you merely said good morning to them. In a little while the Aussies became embarrassed by what they had done, but they could find no way to undo it.

Most of these teaching nuns were young, and some were very attractive. They had welcomed a nursing assignment as a further opportunity in a life dedicated to serving those in need. But no one seemed to have thought through the effect of throwing these young women into close contact with hundreds of scantily covered men, who except for some random holes here and there in their hard young bodies were otherwise rather bursting with normal appetites. Indeed, many wounds had damaged muscle structures that required for their recovery the soothing, reconstructive stimulation of massage.

The bed next to me was occupied by Jim Galt, and we had become friends. In real life he was foreman of a sheep ranch near Melbourne. He spoke not one word of Italian and, for that matter, very few in any other language. He was tall, very tanned, and had caught a cluster of nasty shrapnel in his back. He reminded one of Gary Cooper, so it fit the natural symmetry of nature that the nun assigned to him should be so Ingrid Bergman that when the two were together I wondered how the movie would come out.

At first there was brief eye contact, a blush or two, a just noticeable overstaying of tender hands on the healing but still lacerated back. Not one spoken word ever passed between them, but as time went on everyone in the ward knew they were witnessing a primal and irresistible process. She would enter the room and her eyes would fly to Jim. He would reach out his hand, and as she sat on the edge of the bed, the storm of emotions within her would be reflected in her eyes and her open, mobile face—desire, shame, love, panic, tenderness, and confusion. Jim understood and suffered for her, and the ward managed somehow to leave them to each other. Instinctively they seemed to know that falling in love should be a very private matter, even in a prison.

There are many kinds of prisons, not all with bars, but all with one enemy—time—and prisoners need to defeat it to survive. Conversation had always been a favorite with me, but here it just didn't work. Think of being in the same room with the same people twenty-four hours a day forever. Conversation is good for maybe twenty minutes in such circumstances. The rest of the time we made up games, read, schemed for black-market items with which to bribe the guards in their ill-fitting uniforms, dozed fitfully, and dredged up out of the memory pond in our heads bits and pieces of the past, trying to make some sense, some orderly pattern out of it all.

I fidgeted. I could not let the war be fought without me. I found an Italian phrase book and used precious cigarettes to convince a guard to bring me newspapers so I could learn enough to read the daily war communiqué and either thrill or agonize over it. I also learned to play bridge, which for me was almost tantamount to betraying the revolution. In my zealous early days as a radical, I had scorned cardplayers as decadent, bourgeois time wasters, worrying about whether to double four spades while workers were losing their jobs and going hungry.

When for the first time we were allowed to write home through the

Vatican, I sent Roberta a five-line postcard that she received months later. She had known that I was a prisoner because when Irv Goff got back to Algiers soon after the capture, he had written her on the back of a tourist card that "he had been with Milt till the end." Irv had a gift for the *mot juste*.

All of my and Roberta's friends commiserated with her and said not to worry too much; after all, I was not in Germany where I could get shot, and with my background I would certainly be tortured. (Five months later, though, I *was* there. So much for commiserators.) She had not been upset at all when her OSS contact in New York had informed her that I was missing in action. She had drawn a mental picture of me mischievously sneaking off to an Algerian bar and flirting with some too-attractive French barmaid when I should have been busy with the rest of the agents breaking the enemy codes, or whatever the hell we were supposed to be doing. The biggest worry was that the card came from a hospital. All I had said was, "Over the Alps lies Italy, and so do I. I'm just fine. Relax. Read a good cookbook. I love you." Was it a code? Did I mean I was hungry? This was just the beginning; she was in for a lot more worry and a lot more mystification.

There wasn't much talk of escape among the prisoners. Most of us were bedridden, and even those who were or became ambulatory wore only flimsy hospital gowns. Clothes and shoes had been taken away and stored in a lower room when we were processed in. We were all sequestered on the upper floors far from any entranceway, and there were always armed guards everywhere. The best thing was that we were allowed to circulate freely among the wards, and I enjoyed listening to the tall desert-war stories, decorated with Cockney humor, twangy Aussie slang, and the rolling cadenced burr of the Scots.

The stories were fine and exciting, but they were always about WHAT had happened, never WHY. What was the war really about? The soldiers detested Hitler and Mussolini because their political leaders urged them to and because they were patriots; they understood and accepted that a soldier's basic duty was to die. Fascism was just an abstraction.

My wounds were slowly healing, and I was able to get around fairly well with the aid of a cane. I could see that hundreds had really serious

STANDARD TIME INDICATED
RECEIVED AT

TELEPHONE YOUR TELEGRAMS
TO POSTAL TELEGRAPH

THIS IS A FULL RATE TELEGRAM, CABLE-
GRAM OR RADIOGRAM UNLESS OTHERWISE
INDICATED BY SYMBOL IN THE PREAMBLE
OR IN THE ADDRESS OF THE MESSAGE.
SYMBOLS DESIGNATING SERVICE SELECTED
ARE OUTLINED IN THE COMPANY'S TARIFFS
ON HAND AT EACH OFFICE AND ON FILE WITH
REGULATORY AUTHORITIES.

BY3N —

WUA29 37 GOVT WMU WASHINGTON DC APRIL 5 1943

MRS ROBERTA FELSEN=   B43 APR 6 AM 9 29

101 WEST 60TH STREET NEWYORK NY (RDD) =

THE SECRETARY OF WAR EXPRESSES HIS DEEP REGRET THAT YOUR
HUSBAND SERGEANT MILTOON FELSEN HAS THIS DATE BEEN REPORTED
MISSING IN ACTION IN NORTH AFRICAN AREA SINCE FEBRUARY 24
ADDITIONAL INFORMATION WILL BE SENT YOU WHEN RECEIVED=
              ULIO THE ADJUSTANT GENRAL .

. 24 .

Delay in notification made
the message all the more
ominous.

wounds—the amputees, the paraplegics, and the blind. It made me
think of the rigid physical examination that potential soldiers had to
pass in the U.S.A. and probably in other countries. Flat feet? Out.
Fine perforation of the left eardrum? Out. A trifle hazy on color defini-
tion? Out. Only perfect physical specimens are suitable for the honor
of becoming maimed. And did the rejected ones throw their hats in the
air and dance for joy? Quite the contrary. They slunk back to civilian
life shamed and demeaned, hiding their 4F status like a burning brand
of dishonor. How can one be fit to live if he is not even considered fit
to die? If only it weren't so invincibly ridiculous.

All of the guards were eager to engage in foreign trade. I had thought
of cigarettes only as a terrible habit I would someday have to break, but
now I learned to respect them for their role as a truly international ne-
gotiable currency. I had finally discovered something that could unite
all mankind, a universal yearning for lung cancer.

One of the guards spoke some English, so I began to deal mostly
through him. Not that he could come up with much—an occasional

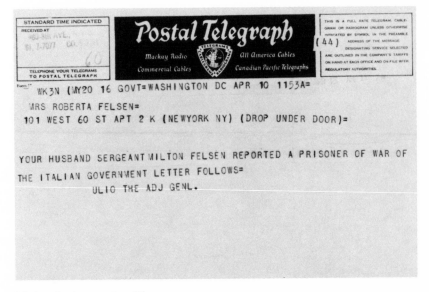

Notice the instruction "drop
under door." They did not
need to add "and run."

egg, a tomato, some wine. His name was Mario, and he was a big pusher
of the local wine Valpolicella, new to me, but I liked it very much.
Mario had relatives in Chicago and had once been there. I learned that
it was difficult to go anywhere in Europe without running into people
who had relatives in Chicago. Mario hated the war and he hated the
Germans, who as everyone knew despised the Italians. But the prisoners also despised and patronized the Italians. The wards were always
full of jokes about what lousy soldiers they were, how their uniforms
didn't fit, and how they couldn't even march in step properly.

I began to be uncomfortable. Why were my reactions the direct opposite of everyone else's? I was growing fond of the Italians, not merely
because they treated the prisoners humanely and with respect but more
precisely because they had the rare good sense to detest all things military. What raises man above the jungle? Love of life, love of music,
love of culture, love of talk, love of love, love of *making* love—nor
should the love of food be omitted. Every attribute was the antithesis of
what makes for a good soldier. But the world was full of good soldiers

trained to shoot straight and ready to march in step over the edge of the cliff. What the world needed was more Italians.

There began to be talk in the air about Italy's quitting the war. The English general had access to a radio, and the BBC nightly broadcasts hinted at a possible surrender. The Allies had been able to hang on to their beachhead at Anzio and were moving up the Italian boot toward Naples against a stubborn German resistance.

I sat down with Jim Galt and two others who were ambulatory for a serious discussion. If the possibility of Italy's leaving the war was now real, what should we do? We estimated that between thirty-five and forty of the prisoners were ambulatory and in good enough shape to have a chance of surviving if they could make contact with the partisans, who were known to be strong in the Bologna area. Then they could remain hidden until the Allies arrived.

Jim and I and a few others had done some preliminary work trying to learn, by whatever means, as much as we could about the surrounding area. Mario had been a gold mine. His home was on a slope of the Po Valley less than forty miles away, and when I showed interest he did a full-press, Chamber of Commerce spiel about it as the most beautiful spot in Italy if not the world. Before the war he and his two brothers had shared ownership and worked a small but successful vineyard. He was worried because they had all been conscripted into the army, and the vines had surely deteriorated.

I asked where his kids went to school, where he bought his supplies, how many villages were nearby, and how far they were from the mountains. Mario was delighted and even drew me a small map. "I'll come back and visit," I promised. With all the bits of information we had been able to gather, we felt we could make a start.

"First thing we'll need," said Jim, "is our clothes, and shoes. How in hell will we find our shoes?" We decided we had better meet with the general. Gordon Forrester was the very model of an English major general—tall and slender, with an iron-gray moustache and a voice so upper-class it was virtually impossible to understand a word he said before he swallowed it. For the six months the prisoners had been there he had sulked about the ignominy of his capture and had rarely been seen outside his private room. Jim Galt undertook the task of peeling through the layers of subordinates. He convinced them that the general's advice and leadership was desperately needed, and as senior officer in charge he owed it to us. A meeting was arranged.

Ever since capture I had tried and failed to understand the European military tradition that mandated prisoners to behave as if they were not prisoners. Foot soldiers had to salute and obey corporals, corporals obeyed sergeants, sergeants obeyed lieutenants, and so on up the line. Their captors, in turn, gave instructions for what they wanted done only to the highest ranking prisoner, from whom orders went back down the line and were carried out without resistance, since soldiers are not in the habit of defying their own superiors. As a system for controlling thousands of men who might otherwise have considered it their duty to continue to struggle in every way they could against the enemy, it was just about perfect. But it had the smell of collaboration about it, like a pact among nations to protect each other's entrenched bureaucratic establishments above all. War is so educational, I mused; they should give a course in some of these things to high school seniors just before they graduate.

The surprise was that when we finally got to him the general was decent and helpful. Jim became the spokesman, and he came directly to the point.

"Sir," he said, "the scoop is that Italy has had about enough of this bloody war and may soon quit. But according to the information that you have given us yourself, most of Italy, including this area, is still held by the Germans. Quite a few of us are well enough to get around on our own. The minute Italy goes, we want out of here. We have good evidence the population is anti-German and would be likely to help us."

The general nodded. "Quite right," he said, "it is the unquestionable duty of every prisoner regardless of rank [here he stared directly at us] to escape and rejoin his unit. I appreciate knowing your plans. But surely there must be another reason for coming to me, mustn't there?"

"Yes," said Jim, "we have no clothes, no shoes. And we have no idea where they are stored. We thought you might know or be able to find out."

"Right," said Forrester, "I do know. But you will want more than that. I will instruct one of the officers to draw a complete schematic of the interior, as nearly as he can, indicating stairways, exits, and so forth." He hesitated. "Report to me please, before you act."

"Yes, Sir." We saluted and left, feeling pretty good.

It was September of 1943. For two weeks there had been only one topic of conversation riding a mounting wave of suppressed excitement. When would surrender come? Should those who intended to make an escape leave singly, in pairs, or in groups? We decided to go in pairs and to fan out in different directions.

Then it came, late one afternoon. Every radio station in the country announced that as of the next morning Italy would be out of the war. Jim and I and the rest of the escape committee called a meeting of the entire group. Plans were gone over. Prisoners who could barely hobble came in and wanted to join the escape attempt. The whole hospital seethed with shouts, laughter, and talk. Even the nuns skipped about smiling and happy. Wine bottles appeared.

At 7:30 P.M. the meeting was drawing to a close. "When we finish here," said Jim, "we'll go down and get our clothes sorted out. We should leave first thing in the morning." He had not finished when General Forrester's aide-de-camp, somewhat breathless, made his way to the front of the room.

"Hold it!" he ordered. "We have new information and General Forrester has issued new instructions." We waited.

"Twenty minutes ago a BBC broadcast carried an official communiqué from the Allied High Command. The gist of it is that all prisoners in all locations are to remain exactly where they are. Special units of the Allied forces are being dispatched immediately to release all captives." The aide-de-camp finished, looked around at the stunned faces, and added, "Orders are to get your asses back in bed." He left.

For a few minutes no one spoke. The planning and the anticipation of unknown dangers we knew would await us on the outside when we made our break had raised our levels of adrenalin too high. The letdown was too abrupt. Slowly, heads down, a few got on their feet and began to drift out.

"Wait just one bloody minute!" It was Jim Galt. "First of all, I ain't a damn bit sleepy and second, in case you haven't noticed, there's not an Eye-Tie guard in the place." True. Minutes after the big news came, the guards had dropped their guns and taken off. (Why hang around when there were wives to be loved, food to be eaten, and Puccini to be sung? Three cheers for the incomparable joys of abject surrender!)

Galt continued, "We've been cooped up in this joint for months. We've been prisoners. Right now there is nothing to hold us here but some promise that the Good Fairy is on his way. Screw the instructions. I'm for leaving right now, as we planned. What say, Milt?"

I thought for a minute. "Right. Looks like a fine night for a good long walk."

Arguments broke out. The reflexive response of obeying official word from above becomes for the soldier more compelling than the bell for Pavlov's dog. The escape committee conferred.

"OK," announced Jim, "them as wants to stay, stays, and them as wants to go, goes." Animosities cooled. We hugged each other.

"Let's go get our clothes," I suggested. But word of our decision had already gotten back to the officers. When we reached the clothing storeroom, there was a guard in front of the door holding an Italian rifle. The guard was an English corporal, posted there by Forrester.

"Sorry," he said, "orders. The store is closed." We pleaded with the guard and appealed to him as a fellow prisoner, as an upholder of the right of democratic choice for which, after all, we were fighting. Assuming he had ever heard of such a cause, there was no sign. There were some suggestions of rushing the son of a bitch. And then General Forrester appeared.

Everyone, of course, saluted. "Gentlemen," he said, "we have no choice. The broadcast was very clear. The armies know exactly where we are, but if the prisoners were to leave they would be in danger of being shot by the Germans, by the Italians, by anyone, military or civilian, unfriendly to us. It would also mean a wasteful, time-consuming effort trying to round up such personnel wandering around at random."

He spoke to an angry, unconvinced audience.

"Sir, how do we know when they will come to free us?" asked someone. "And what if the Krauts get here before they do? We'd sure be in the shit then."

"We are prisoners who have a chance to escape," another put in. "Sir, we want to take that chance. We are supposed to take it. As far as being shot at, that's part of it; that's how we got here. Isn't it part of the job?"

The talk continued, but we all knew it wouldn't matter. Forrester had made a decision as natural to him as breathing: FOLLOW ORDERS. That was the nice thing about orders, in a way. It didn't matter whether they were good orders or bad ones; all one had to do was follow them and one was off the hook. In a little while Forrester left, and we drifted back to the wards, confused and angry.

It became a night of alarums and excursions. Sleep was out of the question. The bed-confined had the worst of it. They begged everyone who passed by for the latest news but were glad to chew on new or even secondhand rumors. They felt a need to visit with each other, to move around, to speculate. The whole hospital was like an anthill stepped on by a giant foot. Even the nuns had stayed, and they moved around nervously telling their beads and trying to understand what was happening, as though anyone had the slightest idea.

A little past midnight there were shots when two New Zealanders tried to force the guarded storeroom. Both were hit in the legs, nothing very serious, but the news of it was devastating. How easily exchangeable are the targets of military leaders, I thought, a prerogative of the uniformed career that confers on starred, bemedaled, and otherwise spindly-legged mortals the power of gods.

I tried to find Jim Galt. We had become separated in the confusion at the end of the session with Forrester. He was not in our home ward. With all the milling about, he could be anywhere. I ran across the doctor who was working on the New Zealanders who had been shot. No, Galt had not been involved. It was nearly 3 A.M. I headed back toward the ward, hoping to catch a little sleep.

I saw them in a hall, Jim and "Ingrid Bergman," headed in an unfamiliar direction. Perhaps she knew of an unguarded way out. Of course, through the nuns' quarters. I had been about to call to them, but then didn't. Not such a good idea, something inside me said.

Better to let them go; wish them well, but let them go. I would never see them again and would never know what happened to our Gary and Ingrid, who had no language but their eyes.

Morning came and still nothing happened. It was a warm, beautiful morning. The sun came in the windows and made almost unreal the nightmares of the long night. Only the sight of English guards, resting on Italian rifles, reminded us that it was all too real. As the morning wore on, those who had counseled obedience to the general gained confidence and began to assume an air of bored superiority over those who had argued for escape, but the luxury of basking in self-righteousness has seldom been so briefly savored.

CHAPTER 13

1943
1944

Precisely at 11:30 A.M. they came, a dun-colored motorcycle with a plump Gestapo officer in the sidecar, followed by a half-track troop carrier spilling mean, tough-looking German soldiers. The Gestapo man climbed out of the sidecar, and as he marched toward the hospital door I could not resist a be-mused chuckle. From a distance it was Irv Goff to a tee in last summer's Washington masquerade. It seemed so long ago.

Now we would be in the hands of the "good soldiers"—the cold, efficient, stone-faced, disciplined, impersonally brutal Nazis. Even the language fit. When they gave an order in German, it was like a rifle butt to the head. No musical Verdi cadences here. It is a language re-markably well suited to the barked guttural command. Consider *Aus! Raus! Schnell!* and their favorite words *Krieg! Sieg!* and *Heil!* Even their word for such pleasantries as thank-you and please has its bite— *Bitte.* How did Goethe ever manage it?

Some of the badly wounded, grown used to a measure of com-passon, reacted to the roughness with disbelief, pointing to their ban-daged heads, their deep scars, in the naive belief that it would make a difference. It didn't. The Germans didn't play favorites, you could say that for them. They were equally indecent to everyone.

So what sort of national characteristic did this little display reveal, I mused. Here was a nation on whom fascism did not have to be im-posed. They had embraced it, gloried in it, sang and marched to it, and were happily annihilating the Jews for it. One had to admit, though, that they made really fine soldiers. It would be hard to think of a country that wouldn't be glad to have them.

Trucks had come, and we were boosted and packed aboard. It had taken less than half an hour to roust us all out.

The BBC broadcast had been a fake. General Forrester had been following the orders not of the Allies but of the North Italian Sector of the German High Command. He would certainly face a court martial when he got back to Britain. As it happened, he didn't wait. He committed suicide in Offiziers Lager XII near Breslau in Germany. It had been a very clever ruse by the Germans, and not only Forrester had been fooled. But modern society expects, nay demands, a certain number of tits for tats.

The trucks pulled up at the railroad station in Bologna and we were dumped out. Collectively, we must have looked pitiful. The Germans, noting the hospital gowns, had opened the storeroom and thrown all the clothes into one big pile. I had been careful to choose British-type army things to wear. I had never told anyone a story much different from the one I gave the Gestapo captain in North Africa. Jim Galt had tried to probe into just how one American had come to be with 850 British, but I had said, "If you don't pry, I won't ask you if it's true what they say about Australians and their sheep." It was very warm, but I had picked out a combat jacket and had rolled up two blankets. I'd learned long ago in Spain that for a soldier, very hot is followed quickly and inexorably by very cold.

We sat, lounged, and dozed until almost dark. There was water but no food. Once in a while, Italian train workers dressed in blue *monos* came through, silently showing in every way they could their sympathy and concern. Dark brought Germans and gun butts. *Raus! Raus!* Why did they have to shout? I wondered if they made love to their wives at the tops of their voices, and whether they approached it in a disciplined and orderly way like they did everything else. (One, left arm around and under right shoulder. Two, right hand on left breast. Three, . . .)

I was brought back to the present with a jolt. Two big soldiers were heaving the prisoners up into the freight-cars. I felt myself being thrown head-first on top of a heavily bandaged Brit who cried out in pain. The cars were rickety and very old, of the type called in World War I "forty and eights" (forty men or eight horses). There were two tiny barred windows high up, one at each end of the car, and double doors through which we were being loaded and which would be locked. More and more men were being jammed in. We couldn't believe it.

"These fuckers must have trained at the Fourteenth Street Station on the IRT during rush hour," I fumed. Finally two galvanized buckets were thrown in and the doors locked. We counted ourselves—one hundred sixteen.

A series of teeth-rattling jerks and the train began to move. We were on our way to Germany via the Brenner Pass, via Austria, and via Poland. Very soon after leaving Bologna we felt the train straining, climbing. The oppressive heat, some from the closely pressed bodies, became cool as sweat dried to an odor. Clanking and squealing, the ancient cars climbed and climbed higher into the Alps, into the snow. Grown accustomed to the Po Valley warmth, most had not thought to bring a coat or even a jacket. Now to survive they had to embrace each other like lovers.

Our industrially advanced, engineering-genius captors had provided us with the very latest in sanitation facilities, the two empty pails. Having been used, the pails were no longer empty. Even those who of necessity had to use them made superhuman attempts to refrain from breathing until they could push the rank container somewhere, anywhere else. Except for the times when they were emptied, about every six hours, those simple, ugly pails came close to achieving perpetual motion.

During the night there was one death. He might have died anyway; we had after all been prisoners for almost six months, and some of those aboard were more seriously wounded than they appeared to be. My own wounds had been stirred by the cold to complain, and I had thrust about all night trying vainly to find a position acceptable to them. But even as I did I sensed that something deeper was the matter.

For the six months in Italy, whatever the physical indignities of captivity, we had been allowed to retain, in large measure, our human dignity. In less than eight hours the Germans had robbed us of it. Our precious individuality, nurtured all our lives, that defined us to ourselves had been tossed into a galvanized pail of excrement. These Nazis, I reflected, had refined the technique of inflicting the most excruciating, the longest lasting pain of all, the utter degradation of the human spirit. Maybe in the long run warfare was obsolete, but for now these bastards had to be beaten.

By morning we were coming down out of the Alps. Standing on tiptoes, we took turns straining to look out the two tiny windows. There, shining in the sun, was Innsbruck. The absurd contrast between our own miserable condition and the Tyrolean travel-poster scene below us was not lost on me and some of the others. We even managed to kid about it.

"I believe," said a voice, "that due to some incredible oversight I forgot my ski boots."

"That's the trouble with you Australians," the voice this time was English, "no proper sense of dress. Comes from slogging around in sheep shit and waltzing with Matilda."

"Don't mention that word. With the stink in here I intend to pray to God for the greatest gift in his power to bestow on us—constipation," from a far corner.

For the four days and nights we were caged in the train as it pulled and jerked toward the eastern end of Austria, we struggled against depression and despair using the age-old soldiers' weapons, self-deprecating humor and irony. Collective hatred of the Germans didn't hurt either. It gave inspiration when all else failed.

When we were removed from the train we fell down. Cramped muscles just wouldn't hold us up. We had grown so accustomed to the acrid stink that now the air smelled funny. We were loaded onto trucks again and driven a ways until we passed guard towers. We had come to Stalag Seventeen.

We would stay only three weeks to be processed, numbered, tagged, classified, divided by nationalities and rank, and prepared for further travel. But we would stay long enough to observe another facet of the mighty Wehrmacht so beloved by the *Deutsche Herrenvolk*.

Stalag Seventeen was laid out like most other prisoner-of-war camps. A huge outer perimeter bristling with guard towers and tall barbed-wire fences surrounded a series of compounds ringed with more barbed wire that separated prisoners by nationality. The compound next to mine held some five hundred Yugoslavs who had been there for some time, were very friendly toward the newcomers, and tried to shout advice to us across the dividing fence. Six feet from the main fence ran a low trip-wire. It was a warning boundary not to be crossed and meant to foil escape attempts.

It was near noon. Several guards were nearby, some lounging idly on their guns. One of the Yugoslavs asked for a cigarette to be tossed to him. It fell just out of his reach inside the trip-wire. He was cautious. He caught the attention of the nearest guard, pointed to the cigarette lying so near him on the ground and indicated with a gesture his request for permission to pick it up. The guard looked at him impassively. So the Yugoslav bent over, picked up the cigarette, and smiled at the guard, who without a change of expression shot him three times in the stomach, killing him instantly.

The hundreds of prisoners who witnessed the senseless execution stood transfixed, not by death—they had grown used to that—but by the act of a programmed, dehumanized monster.

This was the true face of Stalag Seventeen. Many years later veterans of that place would have to be physically restrained from throwing rocks at their television sets as their grim experiences were trivialized by a series depicting it as a postadolescent fun-camp run by fat, jolly German imbeciles constantly at the mercy of happy, clever Americans pulling off audacious capers and enjoying to the full their paid European vacations. "Hogan's Heroes" was a huge commercial success. It made a lot of people a lot of money and sold vast amounts of nationally advertised products. It also sold German fascism as benign, providing welcome relief from those with such a boring attachment to the subject of the Holocaust. The rule seemed to require remembering things from past wars only in a way that would make the next war more acceptable.

Americans captured in North Africa, Sicily, and Italy and those shot down during air-raids over Germany and Europe were being assembled for shipment to Stalag Two-B in Neue Stettin, Prussia, on the Baltic Sea not far from Gdynia, Poland. I found myself in several stalags, on many trains, traveling with a growing number of what all other nationalities referred to as Yanks, much to the disgust of fiercely redneck young men from such places as Louisiana. What I could see of the landscape from the tiny windows were glimpses, especially north of Posen (Posnan), of dreary, almost treeless plains, devoid of people or houses. The somber-looking countryside depressed the natural banter, and we traveled in silence thinking our own thoughts.

Stalag Two-B was called an American camp and it did contain some three thousand Yanks. But its inner compounds also held ten thousand French, five thousand British, and one thousand Yugoslavs.

It was only the end of October, but already the raw Baltic winds ignored our uniforms and chilled our flesh to a discomfort that would almost never leave us. Summertime, it would later seem to us, would last about an hour and a half. The row on row of barracks were a monument to the boundless ugliness that man, if he really tried, could achieve. I tried to imagine the architect's thoughts when he'd planned it and couldn't.

A pewter tag on a chain with the number 80645 etched into it was put around my neck, and I was assigned to Barracks Eight. The Germans, I noted, have a consistent if perverted sense of how to utilize space. Just like the railroad cars, the barracks were designed to house forty men, and they were now crammed with 130, stacked five straw-covered bunks high. At each end of the barracks was a tall, tile-covered stove, theoretically capable of creating a faint illusion of heat, but since no real fuel was ever provided the theory could not be tested.

Every morning poker-faced guards would enter and deposit ten ingots of ersatz coal. It looked a great deal like coal except that it had the truly remarkable capacity of turning into ash without burning, while remaining quite cool to the touch. Another of their triumphs was the ersatz blanket. It looked fantastic, almost an inch and a half thick, with the outer appearance of pure Scottish wool, but it had the warming capacity of aluminum foil. Actually, aluminum would have been better, being less porous. Older prisoners took to greeting newcomers with sympathy for their arriving in such a cold climate with only their skinny (pure woolen) GI-issued blankets and to generously offering to swap one big thick German one for two of theirs. It was a scam that never failed.

November brought the serious cold. Condensation from the jammed-in bodies froze two inches thick on the inside wall of the barracks. A neat dialectic, I thought. The crowding was psychically unbearable, yet without that exchange of life-giving heat, we very likely would have perished from the cold. I hoped that even the Germans had not figured that one out.

In the middle of the night, the first real blizzard came in off the sea, and some of us couldn't stand it. In desperation we ripped out the wooden window-frames, and for the first time the tile stoves blazed with a real flame that made us feel warm and good. But such wood burns out all too fast, so we ran to the outhouse, ripped out all the doors and windows, and got through the night.

At best we dreaded going to the outhouse. We had to leave the barracks and cross twenty yards in the open to get to the long, low building with double doors at each end and twenty crude, uncovered holes on one side plus twenty opposite. The holes were cut in a platform on which we could theoretically sit, but that was impossible. In Germany, as in some other European countries, human waste was, and may still be, a prime source of field fertilizer, so it was let fall in a very shallow trench heavily inhabited by enormous rats, all seemingly infected by the environmental Prussian belligerency.

From the first day of captivity in Germany until the last, everyone suffered from chronic dysentery, a consequence of bad food, bad water, lack of sanitation, and for some, the debilitating terrors of an uncertain fate. I had it too. I tried to observe and remember as much as I could, and I figured I had caught mine in the forty and eight halfway through the Brenner Pass. The night after the blizzard, with the storm howling even worse than it had the night before, I headed for the double doors of the outhouse. But there were no doors and no windows, and I remembered the great fires of the night before.

I reached the entrance, looked in, and wished at that moment to be Francisco Goya. GIs lined both sides. They crouched as high as they could, and each one had a stick or implement with which they pounded the platform beneath them to keep the rats from jumping up and biting their testicles. Freezing snow blew in through where the doors and windows had been. Faces were contorted with the cold and snow that attacked bare bottoms. The scene was horrendous and comic at the same time. How could humankind take itself seriously when it could so easily be reduced to the level of a monkey on a string? Our captors were the direct descendants of the Huns and the Visigoths, and they seemed to sense how thin was the veneer of the social compact and to delight in forcing their victims to despise the ugliness of each other's naked vulnerability.

In the beginning there were plans and talk of escape, and we found that escaping from the camp itself was not difficult. One could get sent on a work party to a farm under the supervision of the older guards who were wounded veterans of the Russian front and who could no longer hear, see, or move too well (although they never seemed to lose the pleasure of shooting). One could slip away.

But where to? The population of Germany supported the war, supported Hitler, and supported nazism. Prisoners on the lam were fair game for anyone with a gun and everyone was armed, including young boys down to the age of nine. These members of the Hitler *Jugend* were upset only about the lack of victory news from the front. Escaping prisoners presented wonderful targets of opportunity on which to vent frustrations. As casualty reports came in, dreams of escape turned to the challenge of everyday survival.

It was much too cold to get undressed, so we wore our clothes twenty-four hours a day and wrapped our blankets around our shoulders when we moved about. Every two or three weeks we were taken in groups of thirty to a shower room and given three minutes under water that made us dance like dervishes since it was either too hot or too cold.

At the rear of each barracks was a huge trough and an imposing-looking water tap with a permanently open valve, since rarely did anything come out of the damned thing. The prisoners learned they had to post a round-the-clock guard to sound the alert, WATER'S ON! The tap had two speeds, spurt and drip, which were as unpredictable as everything else about it.

Like everyone else I tried to be stoic, and I organized my wash-up needs for instant use: soap, toothbrush and paste, mess kit, razor. Water alert came one night at 2 A.M., and I joined the rush to the tap. It was pitch dark but we could hear the water. Desperately, we reached over one another, some trying to wash their faces, some to brush their teeth, some to clean their eating utensil. The water began to spurt and drip, spurt and drip, and I finally was able to fight my way to the tap. Some water fell on my hands and I succeeded pretty well in soaping up my face and neck. The bottom of someone's mess kit hit me on the nose and it felt grimy. I reached again for the tap but heard a collective groan. The water was off. A day and a half later it came on again.

The real killer was the food. The daily ration never varied—one-third of a loaf of bread made of potatoes and rolled in sawdust. It could be years old and rock hard, and to cut it we fashioned primitive saws out of old tin cans. It was good exercise; the sawdust flew till a slice of the near-black stuff was chiseled out. All my life I had told myself I could eat anything that didn't move, but when I first swallowed a piece of this bread, I imagined that I heard it hit bottom with a distinct clunk. I was not surprised to discover later that I had developed a first-class hiatus hernia.

We got an inch or two of what seemed to be a form of *blutwurst* and a small chunk of cheese. Late in the afternoon the main meal was served. Two guards carried into each barracks a black, restaurant-sized pot of tepid "potato soup." There were indeed traces of potatoes if one was first in line. But these were potatoes that were so bad that they had been rejected by the pigs on the nearby farms.

Not many would have survived if it had not been for the Red Cross food parcels. We were supposed to receive one a week. That was the agreement worked out with the International Red Cross officials in Geneva. But the temptation to waylay them long before they got to the prisoners was much too great for mere mortals to resist, so they didn't even try. The parcels were a standard size and came from the U.S.A. and Canada. Maybe one half-parcel a week on the average reached us. Occasionally there were bulk parcels with playing cards, bland books, and some board games.

A full one contained gold in the form of two packs of cigarettes and a bar of chocolate, Spam, margarine (Canadian ones had butter), sardines, some C or K rations, powdered milk, a small can of Nescafe, biscuits, crackers, and canned Argentine beef. Not enough to forego an evening at Maxim's for, but adequate to keep body, if not soul, together.

With the escape option closed, the mass of prisoners formed themselves into a society based on a universally acceptable currency, a more or less democratically chosen leadership, an entrepreneur class, a working class, scattered intellectuals and entertainers, and a large number of unemployed.

Cigarettes were the currency. The unemployed played a lot of cards, mostly draw poker. They bet cigarettes, which as they were piled up and pushed back and forth became pretty filthy and the tobacco would dribble out. Bankers and money changers would buy up the used "currency" at a greatly reduced exchange rate for new "money," reroll the used ones, and sell them back to the players at a rather handsome profit. These thousands of cigarettes were never actually smoked by anyone; after a brief time, they merely disappeared.

I was most baffled by the entrepreneurs. They would first circulate through the various barracks using their cigarette capital to trade, barter, and buy rings, blankets, cigarette lighters, foodstuffs in cans, clothing, wallets, anything they thought someone might possibly buy. They would then congregate along the main walkways, lay this junk out on a blanket, and sit all day flailing their arms against the bitter cold. They were apparently driven by some relentless inner compulsion to amass wealth for its own sake, since there was nothing they could buy with it in the camp and all those cartons of loose cigarettes would be stale and worthless if and when they ever got out.

It seemed to me like a metaphor for the frenetic auctioneering on the floor of the stock market or for the race of the very rich to acquire even more possessions they could never use before they died of a heart attack in the effort and before their pampered children, having nothing to strive for, committed suicide in colorful ways at early ages. The profit system did seem to have its faults.

The worker types too had a need to do something, anything. They figured out services they could perform for a price. They even did laundry. First they had to bribe the kitchen Germans who made the daily "soup" into setting aside hot water. Soap they got from parcels, and when they were ready for business they hand-wrote price lists. Shirt washed (sorry, no pressing), ten (new) cigarettes, and so on. No one else could get hot water so they had a monopoly. The system worked fine, except for the consistent poker losers, the permanent poor, who became the scrungiest prisoners in the camp and everyone knew they were lousy poker players.

The British, the French, and even the Yugoslavs dealt with the German colonel in charge and the prison administration through the usual military command structure; instructions were given to the top sergeants (there were no officers) and passed on down to the men. The Americans, basically civilians who happened for the moment to be in uniform, considered all prisoners created equal and endowed with the right of contempt for their captors.

But even they knew they needed a representative structure to deal with the camp command. Each barracks selected one person to serve as part of a top committee. I was chosen to be the Barracks Eight spokesman. I was three or four years older than the others, and while they knew nothing of my background, I seemed to them to make sense when I spoke. I had also worked at learning to read and speak German from the first day.

At first it was easy to study. Berlin had decided that the Americans were politically naive and vulnerable to being won over. The camps were flooded with newspapers, magazines, and sample English-German "lessons" that peddled their heavy-handed idea of making nazism puppy-dog lovable. With the handful of marks that came my way—issued to us when the Germans put up a few fake shops the day before a Red Cross inspection visit, and then immediately torn down— I subscribed to Hitler's own newspaper, the *Volkesher Beobachter*. It turned out later to be a most intriguing investment.

Americans, in general, believe that anyone in the world who doesn't speak English is hopelessly retarded. The very last thing they wanted anything to do with was the Germans or their language. Moreover, as the war began to go badly, word came down from on high to ban everything lest the prisoners learn what was happening on the fighting fronts.

Everything was then most effectively banned. Not a newspaper, magazine, or anything current got through—except the *Volkesher Beobachter*. It was delivered early every morning to my bunkside by a postal clerk, complete with the official daily war communiqué printed in a box on the front page. The invincible efficiency of German bureaucracy was such that no matter what happened, its branches continued to move independently and automatically, like a worm cut into segments. Within minutes of its delivery every morning, I had translated the communiqué. The rest of the paper I burned. Someone came from each of the other barracks, copied the communiqué, and posted it. Within half an hour the entire camp was covered.

The Gestapo went crazy. They tried everything—bullying, bribing, searching—and they put their own guards, who they knew were being bribed anyway, through hell. As a top committee member, I was automatically suspect. The area around my bunk was ripped and torn apart. All our mail, and there was not much allowed, was censored before it was approved for delivery but not a newspaper from Berlin. It was there every morning, right up to the day in January 1945 when the Russian artillery was landing nearby and we began our long, long march across the north of Germany. At one point I was concerned, however. I received a notice that if I wanted to continue to have uninterrupted delivery I would have to send in twelve marks for renewal of my subscription.

For the Americans, life was tougher than for the other prisoners. Purely by accident, the least politically sophisticated became the most militant guerrilla fighters, all because the German authorities, who were sure we would be the easiest target for pro-Nazi propaganda, completely misread our psychology. It began simply, almost imperceptibly. The colonel in charge of the camp and his staff would walk through on a desultory inspection from time to time. The French, British, and Yugoslavs he came across would salute, as they would any officer. Their training was not to salute men but the uniforms they wore. The salutes were, of course, returned.

Not the Americans. We wouldn't salute our own officers, for Chris'sake, and we sure as hell weren't gonna salute no goddamn Kraut. So we would loll in front of our barracks, and as the colonel approached and began his salute we made an obscene gesture, snickered, and slouched inside. There couldn't be a more offensive insult. Infuriated, the colonel ordered that all Americans who lined up for the daily prisoner count should be kept standing at attention for a full hour. In the angry Baltic wind it was a long time. Men fainted, and many ideas for striking back were hatched.

Work details were selected in the usual meticulously organized style by prisoners' numbers, the ones we wore around our necks. The guards would call out the numbers from a list they had. It was simple because they knew exactly where every prisoner was barracked, in accordance with his number. After the parade-ground punishment, the top committee that had quite naturally developed into the resistance-planning committee, instructed all the Americans to switch numbers haphazardly throughout the camp.

I felt that the result far exceeded anything we had dared to hope. Swarms of guards and their officers jerked the prisoners around roughly, checking their tag numbers against lists they held. Frustration grew to fury as hours passed and nothing matched. To minds other than military-Teutonic, a simple solution would most certainly have suggested itself. Sixty men are needed for work details? Grab the first sixty and send them out. Such a response was not even considered since it would have done violence to rule number one: The method by which something is done is more important than what is done. More natural was to invoke rule number two: If something goes wrong, punish everybody in the neighborhood.

This time the late afternoon "soup" was served when it was already dark, and instead of the usual tepid it was ice-cold. It went on for two weeks. The somewhat ragtag American civilians in uniform were being rapidly molded by their captors into dedicated and implacable guerrilla fighters. The camp commanders had expected trouble from the British, whose cities were being buzz-bombed, and from the French and Yugoslavs, whose countries were occupied and ravaged, but not from the far-removed, politically indifferent Americans. A small failure to accommodate a minor clash had hoisted them very high on their Prussian petard.

The Geneva Convention on the Treatment of Prisoners of War called for humane treatment and had been agreed to after World War I by most countries of the world, including Germany, but Hitler treated it as a mildly interesting fantasy. When conditions were at their very worst for the Allied prisoners, however, and that was very bad indeed, they could still be thankful that they had not fought on the Eastern Front.

Not far from Stalag Two-B there was a Russian POW camp, and we watched in silent horror as truckloads piled high with bodies passed by. We learned that tens of thousands died there; no one knew how many. The German guards explained, lamely, that there was a typhoid epidemic there and shrugged their shoulders, and anyway they were *Kommunisten*, not much better than *Juden, "nicht wahr?"*

I was surprisingly busy. I was stimulated by being on the camp's top committee and enjoyed the sessions where we sat around and noodled plans to fuck up the Germans without getting shot. Occasional meetings with the authorities were tense and unhappy; they consisted of learning of the imposition of new rules even more onerous than the old ones and airing our own gripes. "Many are sick. We have no doctors, no medicine," was met with, "This is not a hospital. We do what is necessary. There is a lazaret. The very ill are removed."

True, there was a lazaret. It was a small building with a male nurse who had a thermometer. Treatment was a miracle of simplicity—aspirin. The dose was administered in direct ratio to the fever reading—one, two, or three tablets. It was also true that the very ill were removed, which they resisted fiercely since it was common knowledge they would never return.

Along with keeping busy, I found ways to visit and make friends among the other nationalities. I had learned to like the British in Italy and admired their affection for theater and the polished skill of their actors. Even in this camp the shows they managed to put on were far superior to any others. They did reveal one characteristic that intrigued me. Their army used profanity to a mind-boggling degree. All armies swear as naturally as they breathe, but it was left to the Brits to develop hyphenated profanity.

"I was born," one would say, "in fuckin' Liverpool in 19-fuckin'-15. We lived in a cold-fuckin'-water flat." The curious thing was that after a while the words didn't exist, like a too-familiar landscape.

It occurred to me that this might be the way to deal with the problem of pornography that offends so many congregations of morally pure churchgoers around the world. Overdose. Forced feeding of anything, even strawberry shortcake, engenders revulsion. Tie the filthy-thought-prone in front of a screen and make them watch over and over again the limited and ultimately repetitive and visually unappetizing ways in which various openings can be filled with various objects. They might well come out more celibate than the Pope.

The French prisoners outnumbered the others ten to one, and some of them had been prisoners since 1941. They were seasoned and cynical veterans, and I found them friendly and knowledgeable. Two of them, Charles and André, I saw almost daily. Charles was a Parisian lawyer and André was a minor functionary in the post office. Both spoke English quite well and agreed to give French lessons to an American class if I would do an English class for the French. Inevitably the sessions strayed far from the conjugation of irregular verbs. We covered the war, history, politics, and our hopes and guesses about the future. There was time enough for talk, and if sometimes the arguments grew warm it helped us forget the relentless cold.

The Jewish question came up early. Our camp committee discovered that when work details were sent to farms, suspected Jews would be taken alone by a guard to an isolated field and be shot "trying to escape." Countermeasures included discarding or altering dog tags stamped with an *H* that identified the bearer as Hebrew.

Deprived of H tags, the Germans relied on their own test, the facial characteristics labeled *Juden* that appeared almost daily in their press in dark-eyed, hook-nosed, beetle-browed caricatures. Here and there in the camp, a bible-pounding, anti-Semitic, fundamentalist American discovered that if a Nazi thinks you *look* like a Jew, then perforce you damn well *are* a Jew.

I was not as shocked or surprised as many of my fellow prisoners. Jews have never agreed on a self-definition, leaving an age-old vacuum most often filled by the enemies of Jews. "If anti-Semitism were to disappear, most likely the Jews would too, there being no further use for them," I argued. Too long in the camp, the others thought, and it's getting to him.

The profundity of the discussions had little to do with the passion of the debate. Arguments about how many tollbooths there were on the Merritt Parkway in Connecticut were as heated as those about the nature and fate of humankind. In the struggle against boredom, I was chosen as the agent provocateur, an assignment I accepted gladly.

"Our U.S. constitution," I postulated, "ignoring the then-prevailing custom of slavery altogether, begins with a series of bald-faced lies. 'That all men are created equal'—rubbish. Clearly some men—and women too by the way—are bigger, smarter, more industrious, richer, handsomer, more talented, and more gifted than others. The founding fathers were shrewd, successful property-owners, and they ducked the problem of dealing with inequality by ignoring it.

"Then we come to being 'endowed by their Creator'—whoever or whatever that is—with a whole bundle of goodies, including life, liberty and the 'pursuit of happiness.' If any of you misbegotten dogfaces have missed out on some of these things, like your liberty," I needled, "you now have someone to blame, your creator."

They attacked me for speaking like an immoral, unpatriotic atheist. I pretended indignation.

"On the contrary," I said. "By guaranteeing forgiveness for every sin conceivable, religion strikes at the foundation of morality—personal responsibility for one's actions. Atheists believe they have only one, potentially beautiful life, to be lived in one, potentially beautiful world, whereas religion promises heaven after death. Atheists cannot comfort themselves with a vision of everlasting life; they are driven by their own relentless logic toward decency and morality. If it weren't for religion, this would be a tough place for sinners."

Tension in the American compound was higher than in the rest of the camp because of reprisals and counterreprisals. It was difficult for the Germans, because once the victims are cold, hungry, and living in miserable conditions, annoying them further in a noticeable way begins to tax the ingenuity even of such devout sadists as they seemed so proud to be. Not surprisingly, some of their attempts were more bizarre than effective.

Abutting the camp was a German army replacement depot where troops were collected for reassignment. Some brain figured out that the all-male American prison population was obsessed with the pain of sexual denial, so German soldiers would bring women close to the outer ring of barbed wire and fornicate, all the while laughing glee-fully. Theoretically, taunting with forbidden fruit has a certain validity, but this try failed miserably on at least two counts.

First, the prisoners were obsessed almost exclusively with their need for adequate and decent food and for warmth. Second, as they watched rather dispassionately, they remarked how uncomfortable it must be for the woman, lying on the cold, uneven cobblestones without as much as a pillow for her head. There was more sympathy than lust.

Another bust was the attack-dog routine. Some unlucky soldiers dressed up as American prisoners, and others taught giant shepherd dogs to tear viciously at the "prisoners" in full view of the Americans behind the wire. At first it was chilling and uncomfortable to watch, but it wasn't long before we were laying bets on which dog would be first to tear the extended sleeves to shreds. The authorities caught on and the dogs were soon called off.

The resistance committee had its own problems. We refused to accept that we were out of the war, but if we were to sabotage the German war effort, we had to do it in a way that did not expose the saboteur to instant execution. Inside the camp we had done well with the numbered tags, and as time went on we even developed a method for making false ones. We also had some costly fun with the daily prisoner count. Each morning we were lined up on a large, bare square and counted. We were ordered to line up in files five deep, so the tallest would stand in front and leave gaps in the file. *Zum fünf! Zum fünf!*, the angry guards would shout. The shorties in back would shuffle back and forth, ostensibly trying to comply while actually creating utter confusion. Trouble was, it kept us all standing out in that bleak, wind-driven, raw cold, and we would usually give up before the guards did.

Forcing prisoners to work in war-related industries is specifically forbidden by the Geneva Convention, but all the prisoners except the Americans were forced to do it. It had reached the point where the intractable Americans weren't trusted inside a factory, so they were limited to the horse center and to the farms.

The horse center was important. The Nazis were running out of gasoline, so they used horses to move their lighter artillery, two horses to a gun. Knocking out horses meant knocking out guns. The horses were collected from all of occupied Europe—France, Belgium, Holland, and Denmark—and shipped by train to Neue Stettin, arriving there in dreadful shape and barely able to stand. The center's function was to rest, feed, and rehabilitate them before they were shipped to the front. The work of the center was performed by the prisoners.

I had grown up on a small farm in upstate New York but was no expert on horses, nor were any of the others on the committee, but I did have an idea. Though Roberta's letters took months to arrive, she was able to have a limited number of censored and safely innocuous books delivered to me from the International Red Cross in Geneva. She was mystified and worried that I might be losing my marbles under the strain of confinement when she got my request to send all the books she could find on the subject of animal husbandry with special emphasis on horses, but she did it. (Most of the fourteen-line letters I was allowed to write each week, about half of which she received, were full of my longing and love for her; but some of them—replete with colons, semicolons, and literary and allegorical references—were, she was sure, coded messages, which if translated and carried out would enable the Allies to open a second front and win the war in a matter of days.)

The committee discovered that horses that had accepted as their lot in life the performance of farm work, as all of these had, were generally docile, stupid, and unbelievably obedient, yet possessed of a constitution as delicate as a hemophiliac Hapsburg princess. They were susceptible to fevers, colics, infections, and diseases without number. Above all, they were somewhat like men, perfectly willing to cooperate in their own destruction.

We set up innocent-appearing classes in animal husbandry, exciting no interest at all from the authorities. After a while reports began to come back from those who had been sent out to the farms and the horse center.

"We had to plow this field," came a typical report to the committee, "so I pushed the plow down real deep and never stopped for a rest at all. The guard was pleased; best worker he ever saw. When the horse foundered and collapsed, he blamed the horse, not me."

Those who worked at the horse center came in with ideas of their own too. They asked everyone to save the sugar from their parcels and to give it to them, not a small thing to ask since it was scarce and prized. Most did. They would exercize the horses till they were lathered up, hot, and thirsty; then they dissolved the sugar, which horses cannot resist, in buckets full of ice-cold water and let them drink their fill. They did this only with "rehabilitated" horses just prior to their being loaded on the trains for the trip to the front. Deadly.

The prisoners had mixed feelings, almost all of them, about what they were doing, and so did I. In war it is accepted, actually demanded, that the humans on one side will destroy the humans on the other, but not furry little kittens. Soldiers ordered to do that would revolt in a minute. The prisoners felt almost the same way about the horses.

Ordinary prisoners suffer the loss of liberty, which is a bad thing, a true punishment. The prisoner of war, in addition, hates his captor and is hated by him. Worse, the prisoner-of-war's sentence is fixed not by time but by the unknowable outcome of a global struggle that could last months or years, that could be won or lost. He is not even sure whether his own fate would be better if his side were to win—that could drive his captors to seek revenge in a final fury of frustration.

I knew that most of the men felt these things subconsciously, even if they couldn't verbalize them, and I wondered why for the most part everyone seemed so placid. I decided finally that it was because their captivity had imprisoned and freed them at the same time. Their talk, after all, was of debts and mortgages, of lousy, low-paying, dead-end jobs, of misbehaving kids and dull, routine, Saturday-night outings, and of all the damn responsibilities, the benumbing burdens, that seize the juice of life and slowly squeeze it dry.

Well, all that had been lifted from their shoulders. They had no more personal responsibilities. Instead, they had the luxury of not having to think for themselves what to do, of being, however badly, fed, housed, and clothed. In a way, it was a return to childhood. Veterans' organizations would later grow and flourish because, aside from providing a lifelong opportunity to tell egregious lies about imaginary heroic exploits, they kept forever alive the cherished memory of the dear second-childhood time when men could crawl around on their bellies playing little-boy cowboys-and-indians games and were as free as birds from the grinding realities at home. The secret weapon of the military was the liberating seduction of war.

CHAPTER 14

1944
1945

The first news of the D day landings in June 1944 set the camp dancing. But when weeks passed and not much seemed to happen, there was letdown and despair. We sat around, absorbed in the daily task of picking lice out of the seams in our clothing. Heads bent down over shirts, we could have been a ladies' sewing circle in Scarsdale, except for the talk.

"This fuckin' war ain't ever goin' to end."

"Why should it? The goddamn generals are havin' too much fun."

"Yeah. They got tired screwin' the English tarts. Now they got Frenchies and Dutch ass."

"Maybe if the Nazis hear how much chocolate the GIs got they'll quit."

The aching cold came in and we blew on our hands.

"Quit?" The voice had been dipped in sarcasm. "They're believers. They think Hitler's holdin' a secret gun and at the last minute it'll be *Deutschland über alles.*"

"I don't give a shit about Alice, but I don't mind saying that secret ray gun makes me nervous."

We talked to hide anxiety. Winning and losing were not the issue to us any longer. At some point we could become a burden to the Germans, a burden to be disposed of. Some of the Germans seemed to sense the end was near even more than we did. The older guards, the same ones who had been vindictively stabbing us in the ass daily with their bayonets, began showing us pictures of their wives and children and talking about how much they hated the war and secretly yearned for peace. "We're just like you," they said. "We want to go home too." Things must be getting real bad, we said to each other.

Throughout the last six months of 1944, melancholy things were happening inside my head too—a near skid toward pessimism, cynicism. I was still sure about despising fascism, but I felt I was beginning to hate not only German Fascists but Germans. There was something so smug, so superior, about "good Germans" that war could not possibly erase. What could any war do except make things worse? Americans carried the virus too. Would we be the next ones who would stand on the world's neck and shout WE'RE NUMBER ONE, WE'RE NUMBER ONE? I didn't mention any of this to my fellow prisoners. I had enough trouble without that.

On January 12, 1945, we began to hear the earth-trembling roar of Russian artillery, and there was no more time for reflection.

It had been snowing steadily for two days and nights, and it was twenty-seven degrees below zero. In Neue Stettin the snow in January doesn't fall; it comes in horizontally under the brim of your hat straight into your eyes, where it is stitched into your eyelashes by the pitiless wind. Everybody has to hunch up and look down at the ground. The prisoners who had spent the months and years accumulating possessions were frantic and fell to knocking slats out of their bunks in a desperate effort to fashion makeshift sleds to drag their security along behind them. The guards pushed and prodded and shouted and tried to form us into a semblance of ranks, while we stamped our feet and shivered and wondered where we were headed and what would be our fate now.

Sam Vitale, John Givens, Freddie Stone, Artie Blumberg, and I stood near each other. We had, over time, gradually formed into our own small unit, reflecting the atomizing process that had taken place throughout the larger group of prisoners and that met in some way the innate need for a family group, dependent on each other, to support and shelter each other against the unencompassable, impersonal mass.

Sam Vitale, son of a Philadelphia wholesale-produce dealer, was our food scrounger. We said he could find an egg where there wasn't even a chicken. John Givens, our banker, grew up on a small Texas ranch. He was one of the best poker players in camp, and his winnings put us in the economically privileged class. Freddie Stone and Artie Blumberg were both from the Brownsville section of Brooklyn and had grown up tough, cynical, and as wary of friends as of strangers. School dropouts, they had lived by petty thievery, numbers running, and small-time extortion. In camp they were chronically restless and had come to know every corner of every barracks. If one of us ran out of wearable shoes, Freddie or Artie would soon "organize" another pair just the right size.

Close as we had become, I can't ever remember a conversation about anything other than how to fill immediate needs for immediate survival. We never talked about the war, what had led to it, what it was about, why it was being fought in just the way it was, or what would be the shape of the world when it ended. They had always accepted life as it was handed to them, without question, without examination. You got drafted; you got captured; c'est la vie. Life was not a bundle of fascinating possibilities but a set of fixed circumstances, dealt out by far off, inscrutable, all-powerful forces that could decide to rain on you at any moment, and the best you could do was to find an umbrella.

Their general view of life was one I had come to consider quite essentially American—that it was something that came in attractive little bunches like a bouquet of flowers. The one thing it wasn't was daily existence. They would "live it up" when they got out of this fuckin' prison camp; this was just marking time. It had always been like that. And if the trip, the vacation, the retirement, the enjoyments of real life, the lousy job, bratty kids, or onerous mortgage got you down, there was the old reliable hereafter, the irrefutable promise of pie in the sky when you die. I found that idea offensive, that you had to die before you could get to live.

We heard the shout: Ausmarschieren! We had been milling around trying to keep warm, and the command from the guards to move out was almost welcome. We could sense that neither they nor their officers knew much more than that the Russian artillery was getting closer and that we had to go. We left at two o'clock in the afternoon in a straggling column, slogging through two-foot-deep snow and going cross-country because the roads were cut off by the advance forces of the Russians. Within half an hour, climbing the hills, slipping and sliding, wet and freezing, we were exhausted, and so even were the guards. But you couldn't rest for long because if you did you began to feel a beautiful, calm, peaceful lassitude and a desire to just stay utterly still without moving for the rest of your life, which wouldn't be long because it meant that you were rapidly freezing to death. We pushed and punched and forced our comrades back on their feet, but no one bothered with the guards. Some of them froze and died quietly as the column passed by.

The whole population of Germany was out on the roads, on the move, and flowing westward like a giant river converging, separating, dispersing into countless rivulets, and meeting again. But there was never again quite the same group and never the same direction; all the rules were off, and for months we would be carried along at random like debris on a flooded plain.

One night when it got dark, we had come to an open clearing in the forest and the guards told us to halt there for the rest of the night. Our group huddled together. All the prisoners were trying to shelter themselves from the relentless snow, but it turned wet and entered our bones as distilled misery.

"Why don't they just shoot us, and get it over with? Why are they bothering with us anyway?" Someone had asked the question we had often theorized about, but not with such urgency as now.

We found a way to explain this by deciding that preserving our lives, even under these conditions, was a sign that the Germans were sure they were losing the war. When it ended, their top mucky-mucks would need us as bargaining chips with which to negotiate escape for any and all the war crimes they had committed. On the contrary, if they really thought they could win, we would have been *kaputt* long ago.

No one could sleep. We felt like salmon lying on a bed of ice in a fish-store window. Then, it must have been near midnight, they marched in a small group of Russian prisoners. The Russians had always been segregated.

"Look at 'em. They look like animals. Maybe they live like animals." Artie made a face. "No wonder they do so good in the woods."

All the Russian prisoners' heads had been shaved. Their clothes were crumpled and old, and they had not eaten well. When the head is shaved and there is not enough to eat, the eyes grow large and deep in the sockets, the lips draw back from the teeth, the cheeks fall in, and one does begin to look like an animal, a comic monkey. I could see what Artie meant. I also thought I could see something else.

One of the Russians said in German, "We must make a fire."

"Are you serious?" I said. "In this snow?"

The Russians laughed and said, "Come, we will see."

Sam, Artie Blumberg, and I got up with some others and followed them to the edge of the clearing where they approached a tree. Two of them took out knives and quickly cut away fifteen-inch sections of bark, stripped the inner surface in thin shreds, and handed them to us.

"Quickly," they said, "put these under your arms, but not next to the skin. Even cold the skin is damp."

They cut small branches and then bigger ones and began to look for dead wood. Other prisoners, curious, came up and were put to work. When the Russians were finished, they went to the center of the clearing and made a pile of the biggest branches. Then they cleared a four-foot opening of snow and made a bed of kindling. We gave them our underarm bark strips and held our blankets to form a tent. They asked for matches and touched them to the bark, and we thrilled to see a flame. Working fast, they piled on the rest of the small dried branches. Around them, spaced close enough to heat and dry but not burn, they piled the bigger branches and the dead wood. By now all the prisoners in the clearing were heading toward the heat and light of the miraculous fire. The guards too came and held their hands out toward the flames.

I tried to imagine if the Russians knew how strange and subconsciously menacing they seemed to all of those now inching as close as they could to the fire. Most had been force-fed all their lives on relentless anti-Soviet rhetoric, and they might even regard this little event as a demonstration of the Russians' mythic rather than human qualities.

"Geez," said Artie Blumberg, as if to prove the point, "them Russkie fuckers is scary."

Before they disappeared next day in the westward-flowing maelstrom of refugees, deserters, retreating soldiers, dispirited guards, and bedraggled prisoners, those "scary Russkie fuckers," in a spirit of what would normally be called Christian charity, revealed another little item in their survival kit. First, you put small round stones in an ordinary tin can. As you march along the road, you will see tall grasses, many with seeds at the top. After the seeds are ground by the agitating of the stones in the can, they can be boiled in water to yield nutrition. We did it. Sometimes, we agreed, it didn't taste so bad; and sometimes it tasted like petrified dog dung.

"Better than starving," I said.

"Barely," said John Givens, "just barely."

If we didn't know where we were going, neither did the guards. We zigzagged aimlessly through East Prussia, Pomerania, and Mecklenburg, following a rough line along the Baltic Sea. It is not travel-poster country. The few trees bent submissively away from the relentless push of the northern wind, and no self-respecting bird would have made a home in one; nor do I remember ever hearing a bird sing in Germany. We marched all day on feet rubbed raw and red, and blistered from shoes made stiff as boards from wet snow.

For some of the POWs—sick, weakened from months of debilitating camp life, with old wounds kicking up—it was too much. They would fall behind. And when they fell behind, they disappeared. Guards, when asked about them, would shrug their shoulders and sometimes point meaningfully to their rifles.

We slogged along silently all day, stopping for a few minutes about once an hour for a short rest. We were silent because talk took energy, and there wasn't much to talk about anyway. Heads down, we watched our own feet move as though they belonged to someone else, and we followed them mechanically and disinterestedly. We circled around most of the villages and towns, but when we did go through one, the citizens would open their shutters and spit at us, defiantly screaming insults and *"Heil Hitler!"*

After the first few nights in the open, we slept mostly in barns. The guards made attempts to negotiate with farmers for food, for themselves as well as for us, without much success, even when they threatened violence and sometimes used it. Charles Darwin would have been bemused to see his evolutionary cycle shift, grinding gears into full reverse. Within weeks we were back to Cro-Magnon man, hairy, club-wielding, savage hunter-gatherers, suspicious, beady-eyed, and vicious. It got down to where even our own little group felt stresses.

"Sam Vitale," said John Givens, "you're a prick. You're holding out on us. You stashed some eggs in your pack. I saw you."

"They wasn't no eggs."

"They was eggs. I can tell eggs at one hundred yards."

Sam was infuriated. He dug into his pack, brought out two turnips, and threw them at John.

"Here, Wasp bastard, go fry these."

We were sitting on straw in a corner of a barn, protected from the wind but still tense with accumulated cold. I thought it was a good time to break out my last can of liver pâté. It was generally tasteless and universally detested, so it was no surprise that some sadists had seen to it that no Red Cross parcel was ever without it. Just now it didn't matter about taste; it was enough that it was food.

But it was frozen food, and it was all I could do to slice it. Automatically I put the first slice in my mouth and then fell back in indescribable agony. The roof of my mouth and my tongue were glued fast to the frozen pâté as though in a burning vise. Deep in my throat I screamed, but it came out in muffled sobs. My friends could see what had happened but could do nothing to help. I was sure that if I moved my mouth, half my tongue would fall off.

When my body heat set me free, the roof of my mouth and my tongue were already forming painful white blisters, so painful that for days I forgot completely about being hungry. As the world measures time, I removed the pâté in a few minutes, but for years later I woke many times in the dead of night to find my tongue pressed upward with such force that it hurt, and for me it is not yet over, even now.

Details of one day's life on the march faded quickly and were erased by the demanding imperatives of the never-ending struggle for survival. Impressions overlapped each other the way they do from the windows of a speeding train, blending and blurring the rich detail of each day's experience and leaving only quick, superficial snapshots.

Not much time was spent in thought. Maybe the American educational system is long on information and short on the thinking process. For instance, not many analyzed the merits of the curious bargain that developed in which the guards would let us out of the barn to forage around the area for food: so many minutes out for so many cigarettes. If you overstayed, you got shot—no excuse asked for, none given. The execution of the Yugoslav in Stalag Seventeen and much evidence since had convinced us that your true German would be much more comfortable breaking your neck than breaking a rule. But what about our side? I asked John Givens one night what he thought of the bargain, five cigarettes for five minutes, overtime a slug in the gut.

"What's wrong with it?" asked John.

"Doesn't it strike you that we're conspiring with the guard to cheapen life by equating its value to a few cigarettes for a few minutes of time?"

John looked at me honestly puzzled. Then he brightened. He didn't come from a banking background for nothing.

"The market makes the price," he explained. "They want the smokes, we want the time. I bet if smokes get scarcer they'll buy us more time. That's how everything works."

"Yeah," I said, "I bet it does."

He was right, of course, as I realized after a little reflection. Generals played that market all the time. (How many men will it "cost" to take that town? Seven hundred? Might play a little hell with our "reserves." Better check with Headquarters. Take it! they say, at all "costs." It would straighten our lines; neatness counts.) Much as I tried I could not get used to thinking of myself as an expendable asset, especially since I was now one in the enemy's investment portfolio.

We still had a small supply of cigarettes, and food was getting scarcer all the time, so a few nights later Sam Vitale, Artie Blumberg, and I made a deal with the guards for twenty minutes of forage time. Potatoes we knew we could get. All the farmers built a similar mound out from the house to bury them in. We were looking for more—a chicken, perhaps, eggs, or a goose. We slid a barn door open and went in.

It was a moonlit night. We could make out cows, and there were two horses side by side in a stall. Then Baaaa, Baaaa—unmistakably sheep. There weren't many, and they sounded nervous. They were in a pen behind a six-foot wall. We hoisted ourselves up for a look. There were maybe half a dozen, and two very small lambs.

"MEAT," breathed Sam. "Jeez. Walking lamb chops. *Bellissima Madonna!* I thank you personally." Sam was on his knees.

"Just a fuckin' minute," hissed Artie. "Them animals are alive. They ain't meat till they're in a butcher shop with a little sign sayin' how much a pound."

I had been looking around. Hanging on a wall, neatly arranged, were some tools. Among them was a shovel with a fairly long wooden handle.

"Be quiet," I said, and brought the shovel over. "We have to break off part of this handle. It's too long. Here, stick one end behind this door hinge. Artie, give me your coat to muffle the sound when it cracks. OK. Push."

We pushed together, and the handle cracked off leaving a piece about two feet long. Sam had caught on. "Perfect," he said.

Artie became suspicious. "What you assholes got in mind?"

"Tell him, Sam."

"Because you are a runty little city prick," said Sam, "it is your time at bat. You've been elected to go over this wall and bang a lamb on the head. Milt and I will help you get out."

"Fuck you in spades," said Artie.

"Listen, you little shit," I whispered. All our talk was in whispers. "We don't have much time. Grab him, Sam."

We each took a side and almost flung him over the wall, tossing the club in after him. The sheep began to be noisy.

"Hit a lamb. Quick," said Sam.

"OK, OK," said Artie, trying to position himself. He finally got one cornered, raised the club, and brought it down in more of a caress than a smash.

The lamb let out an indignant bleat.

"Hit 'im hard, goddammit. You want to get us all killed?" Sam was furious.

"I can't," said Artie. "He's looking at me."

"Artie, listen," I had an inspiration. "Close your eyes and swing down as hard as you can."

It had to be pure dumb luck, but Artie swung and the lamb fell over unconscious. We got them both back over the wall and Sam went to work with his all-purpose knife, which he had ground down from a German bayonet that had cost him three whole packs of Lucky Strikes from a guard back in the camp.

Sam worked feverishly and I tried to help. Artie wouldn't look. There was blood all over the place. Tearing and cutting, we managed to get one foreleg off at the shoulder. The other sheep were now bleating their heads off.

We sent Artie to the door as a lookout and continued to butcher.

"Lights!" hissed Artie in alarm. "There's lights goin' on in the farmhouse!"

"We've still got a couple of minutes," I said. "It's damn near zero. They've got to put some clothes on."

"Shit," said Artie, checking his watch. "We only got about three minutes left to get back to our own barn!"

We had the other foreleg off, pulled and torn more than carved.

"OK, let's go," said Sam. "We each got a leg."

"What about Artie?" I said.

"Right," said Sam, and with a few deft cuts sliced out the lamb's liver and tossed it to Artie. He held it for a few seconds and then, almost gagging, dropped it and ran after us back toward our barn. The two guards looked at their watches and shook warning fingers at us as we went in.

In the morning we lined up on the road to continue the march, and Sam and I were the butt of much earthy GI humor as we each stood there dangling a bloody leg of lamb. As much to avoid embarrassment as anything, I stuck mine inside my shirt.

"That's a good idea," nodded Sam, following suit. "It'll be our turn to laugh when we get to chow time."

Walking on the icy, snowy roads, or sometimes cross-country, was very tiring. It was the custom to stop once an hour for a ten-minute rest. Since we slept in barns, everyone had stocked up on kindling wood, ripped from doors or windows or picked up from random lumber, and when we stopped fires appeared at once.

At the first stop, Sam said, "OK, time for the blue-plate special of the day."

"Waiter," I announced, "I believe I'll have the roast leg of lamb." And I took the bloody, hairy stump and held the end into the blaze.

It smoked and charred, and after a while about an inch of it looked like it was cooked.

"Who wants to be first?" I held the unsightly, smelly stump out to my friends. They shrank back in disgust.

"I think I have fallen among vegetarians," I said with some bravado, and began to gnaw as they watched to see my expression.

To my own surprise, it tasted pretty good, a profound tribute to hunger. John Givens held out his hand and I passed him the leg. He chewed on it for a minute or two.

"Not bad," he said judiciously. "Needs mint."

When it got to Artie, all the done part had been eaten, and he had to wait till we stopped again an hour later.

Sam and I carried our prize for a couple of days until the lamb began to stink so bad that no one would eat it. There wasn't much meat left, just bone and hair. Still, I hated to part with it, as people do with any possession.

January became February and then March. And still we trudged, dragging our feet more slowly, wearied into numbness, uncurious anymore about where we were going, or why, or even what might happen to us. We did everything automatically, like zombies. Even the palliative of humor had died down, since it took too much energy.

Nevertheless, each day was replete with social pedagogy. We learned things as we marched through towns that had been leveled into unrecognizable piles of gray rubble, like finding a huge Singer Sewing Machine plant standing in pristine, untouched glory, not a bomb-hit within a quarter of a mile. Accident? Perhaps. Hard not to wonder though.

Or coming on the remains of what once was a proud town square, its surrounding shops, churches, and municipal buildings all now flattened and deserted. Our intended direction lay diagonally across the park, but as we started the guard noticed, still readable, a small sign printed with an unmistakable message—*Verboten!* The sergeant-guard halted the column.

"We cannot go this way," he said.

"Why not?"

Pointing to the sign, "It is forbidden."

What gorgeous, perfectly wonderful soldiers, these Germans.

"But there is no town here any more, no park, no square, no people. Who is there to forbid it?" we asked.

He was angry. Were we stupid or something? Didn't we understand that if people didn't obey orders there would be anarchy, confusion, chaos?

He made us march completely around the deserted square. I translated what the guard had said to the others.

"Jerks," they decided; dumb, rigid, sour Krauts.

John Givens saw it differently, and he was upset. "With blind discipline like that," he brooded, "how can they ever lose this fuckin' war?"

Whatever strength we had had to begin with, even the strongest of us, was by the third week in March nearly gone. My own weight, normally 175 to 180, couldn't have been much over 105 pounds. For the sick, and for those whose old wounds, aggravated by the relentless pressure of the forced marching, had opened and festered, it was torture. Even pushed roughly, threatened, and hit with rifle butts, they just couldn't keep up.

Eighty such hopeless stragglers were culled from the main column and formed into a unit that would perforce move more slowly. I was put in charge of the group. I was wearing a dirty, torn Eisenhower jacket. On the sleeves were the insignia and stripes of a master sergeant, the rank I had used in the OSS.

For weeks we had seldom seen German officers, except for those who rode by our column in camouflaged staff cars with flags flying from the front fenders. Lately though, a German captain who rode a ridiculously large, prancing, black horse would gallop madly toward us from somewhere up forward and scream at the guards to speed up the pace. His name, we learned, was Meinzer, and he punctuated his absurd commands with waves of his pistol, a huge long-barreled Luger that he pointed directly at the head of whomever he was addressing, which did have a way of focusing attention.

"*Jawohl! Heil Hitler!*" Stiff as a ramrod, the lead guard would give his salute and stand at frozen attention till the Captain disappeared on his flying steed. Then he would let loose with a stream of cursing, guttural commands to the other guards, who in their turn would rid themselves of the resentment they felt at the unfairness of upper-class, horseback-riding captains by taking it out on the hapless prisoners with vigorous smashes to the small of the back with the butt ends of their old Mauser rifles.

"*Schnell! Schnell!*" the lead guard, a sergeant, ordered.

I couldn't stand it; I had to try something. "*Nein!*" I yelled, holding up my hand, "*Langsammer!*" (Go slower!)

Before the lead guard could sort out a reaction, I pointed to his arm patch.

"*Du bist nur Feldwebel*" (you are only a sergeant), I said, with some hint of what I hoped came through as disdain.

"Ich bin ein OBERFELDWEBEL!" (I, on the other hand, am a MASTER sergeant!)

I relied on his being familiar with the U.S. insignia and on the condition of his reflexes. I was right on both. For a split second he stared balefully at my arm. Then his came up in a perfectly executed regulation salute.

I turned away and began to march forward at a speed throttled down as much as I dared to try. Without a word the sergeant fell into step behind me. We sauntered, looked about, and almost enjoyed the walk.

I had to silence some giggles from the KGFs (prisoners of war in German are *Kriegsgefangener*). The more humorless people are, the more they hate to be laughed at. Victories as good to the taste as this one are generally brief, though. This one was no exception—two days as sweet as ripe cherries.

On the third day, Captain Meinzer showed up again, not on a horse this time. He was riding in the cab of a Mercedes-Benz open lorry, and in the back were half a dozen GI prisoners. (Dimly, some attic in my head that stores odd thoughts noted that Krupps, Thyssen, Benz, Volkswagen, etc., seemed quite comfortable living with nazism. Capitalism and democracy are not synonymous.)

The captain and the sergeant guard held a brief chat and then approached me.

"You are under arrest. You will be turned over to the Gestapo." The captain had a gift for coming right to the point.

"Why?"

"You have resisted army commands. That is sabotage. Into the truck!"

Gestapo and sabotage were two very ominous words. The silence and grim faces of the other prisoners in the truck showed they knew this was bad. A tough-looking, blond, hundred-percent-Aryan young guard swung himself up into the truck with us, cradled his rifle affectionately across his knees, shouted to the driver, and we bounced off heading, as far as I could tell, west.

When I got a chance, I asked the others why they had been picked out.

"Who the hell knows. Arguing with the stupid guards."

"Attitude. They didn't like my attitude."

"Tried to hide in the last barn we slept in. Figured they wouldn't miss me."

The young Aryan ordered us to shut up.

Extreme punishment for such minor reasons might be a sign of mounting hysteria in the face of the growing certainty of a disastrous defeat. The thought was consoling and frightening at the same time. There might be a mock trial, but sooner or later the Gestapo would shoot us. There could be no other outcome once they took charge. It would be only a question of time, and a short time at that.

It was almost dark when we reached the outskirts of what seemed to be a good-sized town, and I caught sight of a roadside sign that said Salzwedel. The streets were rough and cobblestoned. We didn't turn off, so I figured we must be heading toward the center. We came to a central square, and in the middle was a large stone building with barred ground-floor windows. It was clearly a municipal building, a police headquarters, and a prison. It was very dark, and because of the blackout against bombing, no lights would come on, so we wouldn't know much about where we were until morning. A massive double door faced onto a narrow alley. Two guards opened it, and we were shoved into a large room already occupied by maybe a dozen others. There were no beds, only narrow wooden platforms piled with straw.

The other prisoners had been rounded up from other segments of the vast columns of marching prisoners. They didn't know much more than we did, but they did know things that were enormously important.

Salzwedel was a commercial and farming center. French, Dutch, and Belgian prisoner-slaves provided all the farms with labor. They roamed about, seemingly free, but were held there by the strongest chains of all. Their countries were occupied by the Nazis, and their families were known, listed, and watched. Immediate, brutal reprisal was visited on wives and children when prisoners did not behave.

Some had been in the Salzwedel area since the spring of 1940, since the ignoble betrayal of France by its right-wing ideologues, its Pierre Lavals and Philippe Pétains. The prisoners had built an underground information network, and some had acquired radios. They listened to the BBC, so they knew where the fighting was, where the fronts were. The Americans were less than two hundred miles away, they said, and advancing eastward toward Berlin, and toward Salzwedel.

The small, barred windows of our common cell were just above our heads, and on one side they faced the street. The French- and Dutch-speaking prisoners had learned at once of the presence of Allied KGFs, and along with information about the war, they passed food and wine through the bars. The resident prisoners offered us Bratwurst sandwiches on heavy dark bread, cheese, and a local wine. The wine was strong, with a bitter edge to it.

"Don't think I'm not grateful," I said to the GI who handed it to me, "but this wine must be Hitler's favorite. It's arrogant."

"Careful with it," said the GI. "It'll knock you on your ass."

Somewhere not too far away we heard screams, running feet, and shots. Then more shots. Sounded like rifle shots, we thought. Pistols too, probably. Helpless, as we were, they were alarming, fearful sounds. What the hell was going on?

"Been happening the last couple of nights," said a GI who had been there when we arrived. "The Frenchies think everything's breaking down—army fighting with the police, the Gestapo shooting whatever moves in the dark."

The big, dark room was heavy with nervous tension as the talk continued, punctuated by far-off screams that upset us and made us unconsciously keep our voices low.

"One thing's for sure," said a deep voice from somewhere toward the back. "When Germans start shootin' Germans, we sure as hell ain't long for this world."

The distilled, unassailable purity of logic in the statement ended the talk. As if we had taken a vote, we lapsed into a discouraged silence.

I got up and went toward the primitive john in the corner. I didn't have to ask where it was—I could smell it. Romantics think prisoners dream of sex; gourmands think they dream of food. Neither is right. They dream of reclining like Roman emperors on great white rolls of toilet paper.

Coming back, I passed the entry doors and noticed a thin sliver of light. I went closer and heard the gravelly sounds of German talk. A prisoner who had been there a few days told me that the doors were always locked during the day but at night the two guards leaned their chairs back and kept the doors slightly open so they could hear what we were doing inside. It gave me something to think about.

Next morning early we were all rousted out, piled into trucks, and driven to a road-building site. We were given picks and shovels and ordered to get to work leveling the flinty surface. There were half a dozen aging, steel-helmeted guards and a younger, ramrod-stiff, foppishly turned out lieutenant.

Anyone with half an eye could see that we had barely enough strength and energy to lift a pick let alone swing it, but the lieutenant had venom to vent and us to vent it on. He strutted up and down barking orders and pointing his baton like a British officer in Peshawar showing the Gurkhas a thing or two.

The guards followed suit without much enthusiasm.

"I saw this movie," muttered the GI next to me through his teeth. "It was about a chain gang in the South."

A rest was called and I approached the lieutenant. "Pardon me," I said in my best German, "but we are not in condition to do this work. We have no strength. We have been prisoners for too long. Besides, you must know that the war is almost over. The little we can do here is meaningless."

To my surprise the lieutenant was not angry at all, but he was contemptuously sarcastic.

"You are stupid to think the war is over. *Nein*, it just begins," he was actually sneering. "This stage, yes, it is over," he continued, "but very soon you will fight with us against the Russians. The war will go on and you will need us because we are the best fighters, the best soldiers in the world."

His eyes had glazed over and he was staring into his vision of the future. "*Ja,*" he continued, "the West must destroy the East."

The son of a bitch is a lunatic, I decided, a true believer. It had taken only a dozen years of fascism for war to become religion in Germany.

They dumped us back in the Salzwedel jail just before dark, and I broached an idea that I had been thinking about to a few others.

"As soon as the Gestapo has a free moment from shooting German civilians, we will be executed," I said, "agreed?"

"Agreed."

"Is there a good chance the Dutch and Frenchies will bring us more of that evil wine tonight?"

"Sure."

"Let's not drink it, a sacrifice that I admit I personally find easy to make. I suggest we offer it to the guards at the door. If they begin to drink it, we offer them more. If it doesn't make them sick, maybe it'll make them sleepy. Then we take turns and make a break, whoever wants to."

"How do we decide who goes first?"

"If you'll notice what's irritating your ass as you sit right now, we're well provided. We'll draw straws."

The word was spread, and there was no opposition. Actually, it was two Belgians who first showed up with a couple of bottles.

Debate turned on who would be least likely to arouse suspicion if he offered wine without asking the guard for anything in return. Bill Riley, a Boston lad and a seasoned trader, solved the problem.

"I'll do it. I'll tell them I want to swap for some local beer they can bring me tomorrow."

More wine came from a Frenchman, and then Bill went to the door. It was closed so he banged on it. A guard's head appeared and we could hear conversation. It was going on too long—maybe they smelled something. They wouldn't fall for it, I thought; it was too obvious.

Dammit, this looks like the end of the line. My hands were sweating.

Then a bottle was handed out. The door remained partly open, and Bill came back to us.

"What the hell took so goddamn long?" I framed the question that was in every mind.

Bill shrugged. "I was having a hard time making a good deal for the beer swap. Couldn't let them get away with that shit, now could I?"

We posted a spy at the door, and he reported that the wine was being drunk and the guards were doing more talking. We could hear an occasional laugh. It was time for another move.

"How about two bottles this time," someone suggested.

"Good move."

Everyone looked at Riley. "OK, OK, I won't screw around. Gimme the booze."

The two bottles were not only accepted, they were seized. More than an hour went by and it was nearing midnight. There had been silence for some time. We had to check.

"Let me," said Riley.

"Be careful. Don't fuck it up now."

Bill was insulted. "Let somebody else do it then."

"No, no, go ahead. Jeez. Everybody's a fuckin' primer donner."

The door was open about seven inches. Bill scouted the area. In a couple of minutes he was back.

"What's the scoop?" We were anxious, excited, and apprehensive too.

"Good. And bad," reported Riley judiciously. "Both Krauts asleep, that's good, right?"

Right.

"But they've got their damn chairs leaned up against the doors so if the doors move the least bit they'll sure as hell tip over and wake up, and that's bad, right?"

"Shit." Collectively.

"Told you it was bad," said Riley.

"We've got no choice," I said after a minute. "We've got to try. Get the straws."

"Right," said Riley, "but not for you. It was your idea, and you're entitled to first crack. After that we'll draw for next, if there is a next."

"You shouldn't go alone. Choose a partner," said someone.

I looked around. The choice was obvious, the red-headed, pint-sized kid from Philadelphia, Eddie Lang, the butt of jokes about how he had managed to sneak into the army by crawling under the tent in boot camp, probably.

"Come on, Runt," I said, "we're the point team."

It was the tenth of April and still very chilly, but I stripped down to my underwear, made a rolled-up bundle of my clothes, and stepped up to the narrowly open door.

As Riley had said, both guards had their chairs tilted up against the doors, rifles across their laps. The one on the left was snoring in short, horsey snorts.

I pressed up against the crevice, not thinking at that moment of the incredibly complicated master plan of the universe that had seen to it that I would lose 70 of my normal 175 pounds so that I would have a fighting chance of squeezing through this ridiculously narrow fissure at precisely this moment in Greenwich time.

Close, but it wasn't quite possible. I needed a couple more inches. The prisoners stared at me silently.

I shrugged. What the hell, I might as well try. Hardly breathing I got my head sideways in the door and began ever so carefully to push. The guard's chair moved perceptibly forward. I was almost halfway through. Only a couple of centimeters more. Another forward tip. I was positive the guard was about to pitch forward on his face. Instead he stirred, gave a couple of grunts, and slumped farther down in his chair. Good man, I reflected, knows enough to lower the center of gravity. I moved on through and they handed me my clothes. Eddie Lang came through like a greased eel.

The prisoners who had brought us food had also clued us in to a good deal of information about the area. Head for a barn, they said, hide at a farm. We will find you and help you.

We were in a narrow alley that opened on a square. I got my clothes on as fast as I could, and from the square we headed out of town going southwest. Far off we heard shooting, but where we were it was quiet. Staying in the shadow of the houses we moved quickly, and in twenty minutes we were in open country.

"Should we hide on one of these farms?" asked Eddie.

I didn't think so. Not yet.

"Let's get as far as we can before daylight," I suggested. "It's about 2 A.M., so we've got at least two more hours."

About 4 A.M. we holed up in a haymow. There were half a dozen cows underneath, so we knew someone would be in soon to start milking. In half an hour we heard two men come in. We made no move till we heard them speak French. Then we made ourselves known.

Back in Stalag Two-B, my friends Charles and André had worked on my French enough so that I was able now to communicate reasonably well, and I explained who we were and how we had got there. They introduced themselves as Paul and Jean, and they were very pleased that we had been helped to escape by local farm-prisoners like themselves, and by local wine.

"Stay here," they said. "Here you will be safe and we will bring you food."

"Our plan was to hide by day and continue moving west by night till we meet up with the advancing Americans," I said.

"It is not a bad plan," said Paul, "but it is also not a very good plan. Every road crawls with German troops. There is great confusion and fighting also between the Army and the Gestapo, as you saw from the jail. Besides, why is it necessary to go there when the Americans already are coming here?"

"*Oui*," added Jean. "We have hidden also a radio. Each night we hear there the BBC. They tell where is the front and in which direction the armies make an advance."

Paul broke in again. "The Nazi beast is very dangerous when it is wounded and dying. On this farm there is only one German, the owner, a widow. She is old and does not leave the house. But German soldiers may come, so you must remain hidden."

Eddie was chewing his nails in frustration. "What's all the chitchat? Gimme a rundown, for Chris'sake. Ain't we partners?"

"Relax, Eddie," I said, "we were only discussing what's on the menu for breakfast."

He looked so stunned that I broke off the joke and told him everything in detail.

Then it was the morning of April 11, 1945. When the sun came up, Paul brought us hard-boiled eggs, black bread, and coffee in a small milk-can. And later that day, Paul and Jean brought plates, cups, and the local German newspaper. The paper said this was no time for the great German people to lose heart. Hitler was preparing a giant counteroffensive that would sweep the Allies into the sea and crush their armies into dust. This would be accomplished, the paper hinted, by secret weapons that Hitler and the general staff had been perfecting, weapons that were so devastating that nothing could withstand their power.

"Do you think anybody will fall for that shit?" asked Eddie when I translated it.

"Sure they will. War has nothing to do with truth. If the situation was reversed, we'd believe it too. We lie about ourselves and we lie about the enemy because otherwise we couldn't fight."

We were cramped, we had nothing to do, and the day dragged endlessly. That evening Jean and Paul were animated. According to the official communiqué on the BBC, the Americans were advancing rapidly all along their sector and were less than a hundred miles from the Elbe River, which meant about seventy-five miles from Salzwedel. Paul said he had seen an unbroken convoy of trucks, tanks, artillery pieces, and soldiers moving on the main road, that meant they might be preparing to set up a defensive line; and if they did there could be serious fighting around us, and we must be careful and lie low.

"Wonder how many others made it out of the Salzwedel jail?" Eddie voiced that evening, as we lay in the straw, what we had both been thinking about ever since we had squeezed our way past the sleeping guards. We had avoided the subject because of an unspoken dread that not many could possibly have managed it.

"No use floggin' it," I grunted. "Let's hope it was a miracle and they all did."

But neither Eddie nor I ever saw or heard of any of them again.

About 8 P.M. on April 12, Paul came to the barn with food and very sad news.

"Your great President Roosevelt has died. It came on the BBC."

"Cheer up, Paul, it's nothing but a phony propaganda broadcast," I said. Then I told him what had happened in Italy and gave him a little lecture about being less gullible. I must have been very convincing because he apologized and said he would certainly not be taken in like that ever again.

By the early evening of April 13, the rumble of heavy artillery had begun in the distance, and Paul and Jean both could not contain their excitement. Their radio said that the American Eighty-fourth Division, the Railsplitters, would be in Salzwedel by morning and that in some sectors the Allies were already nearing the Elbe.

"They deserve a proper welcome. Don't you think so, Eddie? If we start now, maybe we can make it to Salzwedel before they do. It will be a nice surprise," I suggested.

"I'll go," said Eddie, "but don't expect me to make a speech."

Paul and Jean were shocked.

"*Vous êtes fou!*" (you're nuts), they said in unison. Here it was safe. Why walk into trouble? If the Hun didn't shoot us, *les Américains* would. Or it could be a Hitler youth with a gun, anxious to serve the Fatherland.

"Listen," I said, "everything you say makes sense, but I've had it with being a prisoner. Two and a half years is enough. We'll take our chances and we'll be careful. Besides, by the time we get there, the PX will probably be open already."

We embraced, they kissed us on both cheeks, and before daylight we were on our way.

CHAPTER 15

1 9 4 5

As the sun came up, we circled around and entered the outskirts of Salzwedel from the east. Far to the west, we could hear sporadic rifle fire and the rumble of tanks but no artillery and no sounds of major fighting.

In fact, it was eerily quiet. Eddie and I walked in the center of the street in the direction we knew the main square to be. As we did, shutters closed in the houses on both sides, and we could feel the stares of cold, unfriendly eyes as we passed, our boots sounding in our own ears like gunshots on the rough cobblestones. Finally we were close enough to see the town center. There was no movement, but the squeal and clank of the big Shermans was very loud. Eddie and I began, almost automatically, to trot forward, and we reached the town center simultaneously with the Eighty-fourth Railsplitter Division.

In the center of the square there was a large, circular fountain ornamented with classical Greek figurines, from which water was intended to flow but didn't. Two tanks swerved off, one to each side, and let several machine-gun-mounted jeeps come through. They reached the west side of the fountain just as we reached the east. Smiling and happy we ran forward, until every jeep's machine gun trained on us and we heard a no-nonsense command of HALT!

"We're American prisoners," I shouted spreading out my arms. "We escaped."

"What outfit were you with?" the guns remained leveled.

We answered.

"When were you captured? Who were your officers? Where was your camp? What is your address in the U.S.? Name a U.S. Senator from your state. Where is Ebbets Field?" The questions poured out, suspicious and cold. Eddie and I glanced at each other, worried. We hadn't counted on this.

When we grew really alarmed at how long it was lasting, it ended suddenly. Two packs of Lucky Strikes came flying at us, and they waved us to approach.

"Damn!" I said, "that was one helluva third degree."

"Sorry," said the first lieutenant in the lead jeep, "had to do it. For the last three weeks we've been running into Germans in American uniforms pretending to be escaped prisoners. Our guys have been booby-trapped, hand-grenaded, and machine-gunned. We don't need any more casualties."

I asked about FDR. Was it true he was dead?

Yes. Two days ago.

We told the lieutenant about the jail and pointed it out across the square. Nope, he hadn't heard of any prisoners escaping from there, but maybe we could find out more at division headquarters. We piled into his jeep and headed up a main street to HQ. It was a very large building bustling with activity, soldiers, officers, jeeps, trucks, and motorcycles. We were bumped up, grade by grade, till Johnson, a full colonel, said other American prisoners had been recovered but none that fit the description we were giving him. He said we were now officially RAMPs (Recovered Allied Military Personnel) and would soon be flown to France and then home.

As we spoke, Colonel Edwards came in and complained to Johnson that they were running short of interpreters. Edwards was in charge of setting up civilian administrations in occupied areas.

"I'd like to volunteer, Sir," I said. "I've been interpreting in the prison camp for years. Besides, you will be advancing into territory that we have slogged through foot by foot, and I know it like the back of my hand."

"Deal," said Edwards briskly, "but only till Army corps sends up replacements. Against regulations for RAMPs to be in combat. Report to Lieutenant Romano. He'll get you settled in."

A billet had been set up for recovered prisoners.

"So long, Eddie," I said to Lang. "See you in RAMP camp."

Lieutenant Romano was the same one who had brought us there in his jeep. "You can stay with me," he said, "I've got a real big apartment. Lots of room."

It was very big, very ugly, and ostentatious, with blond art-deco furniture and lamps with nude black figurines holding up the shades as they stood on tiptoe on slabs of onyx. Romano said he was going out and would be back with some stuff for me. He brought a new pair of shoes, a webbed belt, ammunition, and a 45-caliber army-issue automatic.

I strapped it on, and somewhere in my being a change took place, though I didn't really understand its full significance. I stopped feeling like a prisoner. It occurred to me that one day I might want to explore the implications of the gun phenomenon, but for the moment I was content to feel the pleasure of freedom. Romano told me to call him Vic. We talked a while and then, exhausted, I fell on one of the over-stuffed beds. But after years of straw and slats I couldn't stand it, so I stretched out on the bare floor, where I felt fine and slept like a baby.

An overnight miracle had occurred in Salzwedel. The city awoke free of Nazis—there was not one to be found. More amazing, if the population was to be believed, there had never been any. All those dis-ciples of the master race who had reviled, spit upon, and cursed us when we had passed by as despised polyglot prisoners were now de-scending on the victors with fawning smiles, bowing and scraping and lying in their teeth about how they had always hated Hitler and the war and everything he stood for, and had always wished for us to come and put an end to the Nazis, and did we have any chocolate please?

The sycophants who paraded through Colonel Edwards's office ap-plying to become city administrators and bureaucrats were especially detestable. They were well dressed and well fed and had obviously prospered as beneficiaries of the Nazi system. Something in their bear-ing convinced me that their obsequious veneer only barely hid their thorough contempt and antipathy for the hybrid, racially mongrelized vulgarians who were invading and desecrating their Vaterland.

Colonel Edwards's willingness to accept the thin, self-serving stories they had concocted about themselves drove me up the wall.

"Sir," I said to him, "these people are liars. We are putting the Nazis right back in control."

"I know that, Sergeant," Edwards used a tone with me that one might use with a not quite bright child, "but there is no alternative. I've got to get this town functioning again without delay, and there's no one else who can do it. Finding and training democratic elements would take months. We can't wait that long. We have a war to win."

I stood there thinking that if we win, Nazis stay in power, and if we lose, Nazis stay in power, so what does winning mean? I did not, however, express my new respect for the institution of bureaucracy and the immortality of bureaucrats.

Outside headquarters, the streets were filled with people—older men, women, girls, and young children sizing up the GIs, working on their sympathies, saying what they thought the GIs wanted to hear, smiling and laughing and pretending that this was one of the happiest days of their lives. For conquering armies it must have been like this from the beginning. Flowers were thrown at the feet of Caesars, Alexanders, Napoleons, and Genghis Khans. Even in beloved Barcelona. I had seen pictures of Franco's hated troops marching up the Diagonal at the close of the Spanish Civil War, all the while being kissed and hugged by citizens who lined the way and cheered for them, and even for the butcher, Franco.

Who were these people who appeared magically from nowhere to kiss the feet of yesterday's enemy? They were survivors, the anonymous, nonparticipants, the uninvolved, the masses. And they were wiser perhaps than appeared at first glance. After all, what real difference did the cast of characters at the top make to them? They still would have to find work to do, scratch for bread, pay rent, struggle for bare existence, and pay tribute to the powerful.

It was intellectually acceptable in theory, but not yet to me, on that day in Salzwedel. The day before was too fresh in my memory. I could still see those same faces twisted and contorted with hatred, and when I spoke to the other RAMPs they felt the same way. A GI arm around a fraulein's waist made us uncomfortable, and we turned away.

Colonel Edwards came out and told Lieutenant Romano that he needed more transport, but there were no cars to be had in town.

"Who said so?" I butted in.

"Everybody. There are no functioning autos in Salzwedel. Haven't been for years."

"Colonel, I'll make you a deal. If I get you a car, can I have one?"

Colonel Edwards smiled, "Sure, take a couple. Pass 'em out to your friends." He walked away chuckling.

"C'mon, Vic, get the jeep."

"Where we goin'?"

"I'm not sure, but I've got an idea. You've been around this town. Try to remember the fanciest street with the biggest houses, and let's start there."

It was a beautiful tree-lined street, and there was no doubt about the most imposing mansion in the middle of the block. It sneered at its neighbors.

"That's the one, Vic," I said. "Let's go."

A cold-eyed, well-dressed, middle-aged lady answered the door.

What did we want?

To talk to her husband.

Not home.

Vic turned to go.

I unholstered my automatic. "We're coming in."

She protested but fell back.

I made a little speech in my best German. I told her that I had been a prisoner for years in her unspeakable country and was far short of evening the score to avenge innocent deaths, and that I would be most happy to begin right here. Then I pointed the pistol at her head.

"Heinrich, Heinrich," she screamed, and Heinrich, heavy in the neck and with oversized rings on most of his fat fingers, came huffing in.

His opening gambit was righteous outrage at this crude invasion, but when I repeated in pretty fair German what I had said to his wife, emphasizing with jabs of the forty-five into his ample middle, he deflated like a leaky balloon.

"Cars," I said, "autos, where are they?"

"There are no cars. Not one. They do not exist."

"There are always cars. Where are they hidden?"

"No, no. No cars. I swear."

I turned to Vic. "I'm sorry," I said, "I'll just have to shoot these people. They're lying." I made sure to say it in German.

"Show them!" screamed Mrs. Heinrich. "Show them!"

Heinrich tried to salvage a trace of self-respect. "There are a few cars, but they are buried. They do not function. They are useless. Of course, if they worked, I would have told you about them at once."

"Of course," I said. "Let's go."

Vic grabbed my arm, "How the hell did you know?"

"I didn't know about the cars, but I've come to know a lot about Germany and the Germans."

Near the railroad station there was a long, dilapidated shed. Inside, junk was piled around haphazardly, and the place looked abandoned. Heinrich walked to one end and began to remove floorboards. They were covered with dirt and straw but they came away easily, revealing a heavy tarpaulin. Vic and I pulled at it, and there was the roof of a sedan clearly visible under it.

"We'll need help," said Vic, "mechanics, and if any of these will run, gas and oil."

We decided Vic should drop the Heinrichs off at their house, and then, without arousing anybody's curiosity, he should come back with a work detail. Vic did better than that. He brought a couple of squads from the auto park, towing equipment, gas, and oil.

Twelve automobiles had been buried under the shed. Most wouldn't run and were hardly worth repairing. But with two we struck gold.

One was a top-of-the-line 1940 Ford sedan, dark blue, that couldn't have had more than six thousand miles on it, and the other was a mile-long Mercedes touring car that was the twin of the one familiar as Hitler's own—the one he always stood up in, giving his stiff-armed salute to the booted Brownshirts for the benefit of the newsreels of the world.

The GIs got the Ford working beautifully, but it looked and sounded flimsy next to the Mercedes. The entire crew knew by this time about my deal with the colonel.

"Which one do you think I should keep?" I asked.

It was unanimous. "Keep the fuckin' Mercedes," they yelled as one, revealing the virulent antipathy to officers that runs through the veins of the enlisted men of every army in the world.

It was worked out carefully. Vic drove the Ford and I drove the Mercedes, parking it around the corner from headquarters. Then the two of us drove up in the Ford and paged Col. Edwards.

"Here's your car, Sir. How do you like it?"

The Colonel couldn't believe it. "You guys are terrific." Edwards walked around the Ford, checked it out, listened to the motor, and patted me on the back.

"Good work, Sarge," he said. "Dammed good work." And then as an afterthought, "I don't suppose you found anything for yourself?"

"Well, Sir, matter of fact I did. If you'll wait here a second I'll bring it around."

I raced around the corner and got behind the wheel.

"Enjoy your little ride," said one of the GIs. "The brass sure as hell won't let you keep this baby."

I wasn't so sure either, but I shifted the giant, outside gear lever into one of its many forward speeds and zoomed up in front of the colonel.

Word had spread rapidly among the troops, and GIs were perched all around, busily laying bets on the outcome.

"Holy shit," breathed Colonel Edwards.

I jumped out and saluted. "Sir," I said, "may I drive you somewhere?"

He started to laugh. "A deal's a deal." Then, more seriously, "I have a pretty good idea what the POWs have gone through. Enjoy the car. And thanks for the lesson in how to deal with the Germans."

I kept the car for two weeks as the Eighty-fourth advanced into territory that held such recent and painful memories. Just beyond Salzwedel a concentration camp was liberated, and as the living skeletons stumbled out, all my irrational, subjective responses were intensified into a general condemnation of the whole Germanic people. I knew it was wrong, that it was the reverse of the anti-Semitic coin, of the redneck's hatred of all blacks, but I couldn't help it.

What made it worse was translating for Colonel Edwards and listening to protestations of innocence, denial of guilt, and denial of knowledge. All the bland, complacent, smug, sly, beer-belly lies. So I wasn't too upset when the colonel said orders had come that all RAMPs must be sent immediately to France for repatriation to the States.

How about the Mercedes?

"Take it," said Edwards, "but I don't think you'll make it to Paris."

I didn't. At a checkpoint near Frankfurt, a young major assured me that I had been lucky to get that far and that the car was sure to be confiscated, being without papers and all, long before I got to Paris. I learned later that other POWs had driven to Paris with no problems. Very glib, that major; probably owns a fleet of foreign cars today.

It was a short flight from Frankfurt to Camp Lucky Strike in Le Havre. It was a transfer camp. Young men arrived from the States for military duty and shortly thereafter, as very old men, were repatriated. The camp was on a hill overlooking Le Havre. The Luftwaffe had completely obliterated what had stood there before, a sort of French Ellis Island with barracks and a high fence, a wistfully nostalgic place for me, like the memory of a half-forgotten favorite tune.

Recovered prisoners were arriving in big numbers, and there were glad reunions for some who hadn't seen each other for months. I went first to the Red Cross and fired off a message to Roberta. I knew she had been without word since the march had begun in January and that she must be beside herself with worry. I couldn't say much, just that I was alive and well and desperately impatient to see her.

We cleaned up and were reoutfitted, given $25 each, and fed. I had forgotten how much food Americans are used to eating and wasting. Some prisoners, too long hungry, gorged their shrunken stomachs and had convulsions, and at least one died. The irony was not lost on anyone.

It was a nondescript troop ship that we boarded two days later, but it looked like a fine luxury liner to me. Out at sea a strong wind blew constantly and though it wasn't stormy it was brisk and cold. On that first day out, I had plenty of time to think.

Camp Lucky Strike, on the hill above Le Havre, had filled my mind with another time, another war, another return from the killing ground of ideas that became bullets. As the ship's gentle rocking cradled me, I found myself reaching backward in time searching for an elusive thread of meaning. I groped for a logical connection between this war and this ship and an earlier war and another ship, and even before that, back to whatever it was that wove the pattern of my existence.

Near midnight, a siren blast aroused me, stiff and cold, into full consciousness of exactly where I was, on a troop ship coming home from World War II. A false submarine alarm had jolted me out of sleep.

Part of me wanted to continue the search for answers. Was my anti-Fascism just another way to justify war? I didn't think so. I knew I would do it all over again. But that was a kind of cop-out too. There must be a way to oppose war *and* fascism, both at the same time.

To be honest, being a soldier was far from dull. That's part of the problem, that basic, gut appeal. Perhaps we had to jazz up civilian life and put the troops on permanent latrine duty.

What nagged at me the most was that I wasn't quite sure what "winning" a war meant. If you looked without illusions at history, who won what?

My fellow veterans on the ship didn't give any of this a thought. If they didn't care about the forces that shaped their lives and sometimes determined their deaths, why should I? Because I wanted to understand my world. Just living in it wasn't enough. Cows did that.

The first day out, a ship-wide crap game had begun. Dice had appeared on every deck through the ubiquitous GI magic practiced by devout gamblers, who remained on their knees for so many hours praying to the gods of luck that when they finally went broke they were too stiff to stand up, and they fell over in a heap groaning and cursing. Even then they wouldn't leave but would become part of the gallery, staring with the intentness of hypnotized cobras as the piles of money grew larger and the number of players grew smaller.

It was fast company and I fully expected my twenty-five bucks to disappear at twice the speed of light, but I got lucky and began the slow move from the outskirts to the center of the action. Inexorably, like dust before a giant vacuum cleaner, all the money on that ship would be sucked up and into the bulging pockets of one instantly rich GI.

The process took days, and as in all gambling, even penny-ante poker, the money lost its meaning and could as well have been toothpicks.

On the day before we landed, seven players were left bleary-eyed and semitranced, and I was still in the game. My luck was phenomenal. I had thousands of dollars stuck in my pockets, in my shirt, everywhere. The fever had me so bad that I hardly noticed I had started to lose. The soiled, crumpled bills went out in a trickle, then a flood. Still I couldn't stop.

Near midnight the loudspeaker blared out.

May 1945—New York, New
York, it's a wonderful town!
I'm a bit emaciated, a bit
untidy, but happy to be back
and still able to grin about
it all.